CORE FOCUS

GRADE 7

TEST PRACTICE
for Common Core

Techla S. Connolly, CAGS, M.A.T.

and

Carrie Meyers, M.S.

BARRON'S

About the Authors

Techla S. Connolly has been teaching middle-school English Language Arts and Reading for fifteen years in Revere, Massachusetts. She has worked with colleagues to develop the 7th grade ELA curriculum and create common writing prompts in her district. Techla's current focus in her role as classroom teacher is to integrate exciting and engaging lessons based around the Common Core standards into her daily practice.

Carrie Meyers has taught math to students from kindergarten through college for more than eighteen years. Through most of her career, Carrie has excited and educated middle-level adolescents by integrating science and other real-life applications into her math classes. Carrie's current focus is to help teachers see the power that Science, Technology, Engineering, and Mathematics (STEM) education can have in their classroom by creating and providing Professional Development Institutes for teachers nationally, increasing teacher content knowledge as well as pedagogical methodology.

Acknowledgments

I would like to extend gratitude and appreciation to my colleagues at the SBA Middle School, particularly Joanne Wille   ᵗᵃⁿce and Christine Gray and Ann McLaughlin for their insight and encouragement. I'd   Lisa Connolly and Patrick McElligott for their patience and support.-

Carrie would like to e   pport her and all
her successes. She   d many questions
throughout the boo

All inquiries should be addressed to:
Barron's Educational Series, Inc.
250 Wireless Boulevard
Hauppauge, New York 11788
www.barronseduc.com

ISBN: 978-1-4380-0706-9

Library of Congress Control Number: 2015941098

Manufactured by: B11R11
Date of Manufacture: August 2015

PRINTED IN THE UNITED STATES OF AMERICA
9 8 7 6 5 4 3 2 1

CONTENTS

ENGLISH LANGUAGE ARTS

Reading: Literature

Reading: Informational Text

Writing

MATH

Geometry

Statistics and Probability

NOTE TO PARENTS AND EDUCATORS

About Barron's Core Focus Workbooks

Barron's recognizes the need to create products to help students navigate the Common Core State Standards being implemented in schools across America. To meet this need, we have created grade-specific workbooks that will help bring the Common Core standards to life and to ensure that students are prepared for these national assessments. It is our hope that students can work through these books independently or with the guidance of a parent or teacher.

Barron's Core Focus workbooks are meant to supplement the Common Core teaching that students are receiving in their classrooms. These workbooks, all created by dedicated educators, provide specific practice on the Common Core standards through a variety of exercises and question types, including multiple-choice, short-answer, and extended-response. The questions are organized to build on each other, increasing student understanding from one standard to the next, one step at a time, and they challenge students to apply the standards in different formats. Both the English Language Arts (ELA) and Math sections of the books end with a review test—this is a great way to sum up what the student has learned and reviewed from the exercises throughout.

What is Common Core?

> "The standards are designed to be robust and relevant to the real world, reflecting the knowledge and skills that our young people need for success in college and careers."

> (2012 Common Core State Standards Initiative)

Simply put, the Common Core is a series of standards that spells out exactly what students are expected to learn in English Language Arts and Mathematics throughout their years in school. These standards are fairly consistent across all grades and are designed so that students, teachers, and parents can understand what students should be learning and achieving at each grade level. Standards are organized to provide a clear understanding of the core concepts and procedures that students should master at each step of the way through school.

Unlike previous standards that were created by individual states, the Common Core is meant to be consistent throughout the country, providing all students with an equal and fair opportunity to learn English Language Arts (ELA) and Math. These standards are also designed to teach students how to apply this knowledge to their everyday lives and experiences.

By sharing the same standards, states can more accurately gauge and compare students' progress and the quality of education received. The ultimate goal of Common Core is to ensure that all students, no matter which state or part of the country they are from, will be equally ready and prepared for college and the workforce.

What Is a Standard?

A standard is a skill that should be learned by a student. Standards are organized by *domains*, which are larger groupings of related standards. For instance, in Grade 7 math, there are five domains: "Ratios and Proportional Relationships," "The Number System," "Expressions and Equations," "Geometry," and "Statistics and Probability."

Under the domain "Geometry," there are six individual standards which highlight a specific skill or understanding that a student should gain. One standard, **G.B.5**, directs students to "use facts about supplementary, complementary, vertical, and adjacent angles in a multi-step problem to write and solve simple equations for an unknown angle in a figure."

ENGLISH LANGUAGE ARTS

The English Language Arts standards are separated into different strands. The 6–8 standards are comprehensive and are divided into the following areas—Reading, Writing, Speaking and Listening, and Language. The Common Core has designated separate reading standards for both fiction and nonfiction texts. These standards are identified as Reading: Literature and Reading: Informational Text. Most importantly, the reading standards emphasize engaging all students in the reading process. To meet the standards, students are expected to read multiple forms of text types that, in turn, provide deeper literary experiences for all students. The Common Core also emphasizes the importance of text complexity. "Through extensive reading of stories, dramas, poems, and myths from diverse cultures and different time periods, students gain literary and cultural knowledge as well as familiarity with various text structures and elements." (2012 Common Core State Standards Initiative)

Each of the 6–8 strands is arranged within a College and Career Readiness Anchor Standard. The Anchor Standards are the overarching goals of a K–12 curriculum. These standards remain constant in all grades. Each grade level's strands are built as scaffolds in order to achieve "official" College and Career Readiness Anchor Standards by the end of grade 12. The College and Career Readiness Anchor Standards for Reading Literature and Informational Text focus on identifying key ideas and details, craft and structure, and the integration of knowledge and ideas. To meet the Common Core reading standards, students are expected to read, respond, and interact with an array of text types of varying complexities. The College and Career Readiness Anchor Standards for Writing focus on text types and purposes, production and distribution of writing, and research to build and present knowledge. To meet the Common Core writing standards, students are expected to write persuasive, narrative, and informational text. The College and Career Readiness Anchor Standards for Speaking and Listening focus on comprehension, collaboration, and presentation of knowledge and ideas. The speaking and listening standards focus heavily on students' ability to actively participate, engage, and present academic information in multiple settings. The College and Career Readiness Anchor Standards for Language focus on the conventions of standard English, vocabulary acquisition and use, and knowledge of language.

The Common Core standards are also designed to help students create digital literature and use technology to communicate ideas and knowledge. The English Language Arts standards are a vision of what it means to be literate in the twenty-first century. These standards foster imperative learning experiences for the twenty-first century learner. "The skills and knowledge captured in the ELA/literacy standards are designed to prepare students for life outside the classroom. They include critical-thinking skills and the ability to closely and attentively read texts in a way that will help them understand and enjoy complex works of literature." (2012 Common Core Initiative)

MATH

The Common Core mathematics standards were developed as a connected progression of learning throughout grades K–12. Ideally, this will enable teachers to close achievement gaps and give students the foundational skills necessary to continue in their learning. The Common Core provides teachers with an opportunity to build a deep and rich understanding of mathematical concepts. Instruction of Common Core mathematics standards encompasses the mathematical practices as well. These practices include skills that math students in every grade are expected to master. The mathematical practices bring rigor and rich learning opportunities to the classroom.

In grade 7, students extend their knowledge of ratios, proportions, and percents, and they will further their algebraic skills by writing, interpreting, and using expressions and equations. New to students will be the manipulation of all rational numbers through various operations, work with three-dimensional figures, and the introduction of probability concepts. Students will continue to develop an understanding of statistics by drawing inferences on two data distribution as well as begin laying the foundation for 8th grade linear equation concepts. The Common Core standards are related across grade levels as well as across the domains. For example, Geometry standards share a number of common relationships with the Operations and Algebra standards. This connectedness helps students prepare for the real world—remember, we don't use just one skill to balance our checkbook or determine the amount of paint for a room in our home. We have to be able to apply a variety of skills every day, and the goal of the Common Core math standards is to help prepare students for this fact. The Common Core also supports mathematical understanding of concepts that are developmentally appropriate for students. These standards allow students to build strong number sense in the early grades as they learn to count, order numbers, and compare numbers to help them think about numbers flexibly and understand the relationships between numbers as they move into the higher grades.

This workbook also focuses on the mathematical practices that help students develop a deeper mathematical thinking process. The practices include making sense of problems and persevering in solving them, reasoning abstractly and quantitatively, constructing viable arguments, and critiquing the reasoning of others. Students also will focus on modeling with mathematics, using appropriate tools, attending to precision, making use of structure, and looking for repeated reasoning.

HOW TO USE THIS BOOK

This test practice workbook is organized by standard—one step at a time—in the order that students will likely see the concepts in the classroom or other learning environment. Each applicable standard is organized in an easy-to-navigate spread(s) providing exposure to the Common Core in the simplest way possible.

In this workbook, students will be able to build skills in multiple formats by answering multiple-choice, short-answer, and extended-response questions. Answers and explanations are included at the end of each section so students, parents, and teachers can easily assess the student's response. These explanations are an important part of the learning process as they provide information on the understanding needed to answer each question, common misconceptions students have, and an explanation of how a student might best approach the question. These explanations will help students not only check the accuracy of their responses but also learn how they can improve their responses. Students using **Barron's Core Focus** workbooks will practice each of the specific content standards as they learn them, and also thoroughly review all the concepts in Math or English Language Arts through the cumulative assessments.

In addition to the practice spreads covering specific standards, each section ends with a comprehensive practice test allowing students to monitor their general progress in either English Language Arts or Math. Answers and explanations provide additional guidance and instruction.

> A complete listing of all the grade 7 English Language Arts and Math Common Core standards can be found at the end of this book in Appendices A and B.

FEATURES AND BENEFITS

Barron's Core Focus workbooks provide educators, parents, and students with an opportunity to enhance their knowledge and practice grade-level expectations within the Common Core English Language Arts and Math standards. Each workbook in this series provides questions that specifically correlate to each standard. Every answer explanation provides helpful insight into a student's understanding, identifying common misconceptions and then providing multiple strategies. Each workbook also provides a cumulative assessment for each content area in Math and English Language Arts. Throughout the workbooks, there are tip boxes that contain a variety of information and expose students to vocabulary, tips, and strategies.

- Parents can use this workbook to encourage learning at home. This workbook can be used as guided practice or extra exposure to concepts students may be struggling to master in school.

- Educators can use the workbooks in their classrooms to identify how to assess each standard. These workbooks give teachers insight into what students should be able to do independently in order to master the standard. The detailed answer explanations provide opportunities for teachers to recognize misconceptions students may have about specific standards and how to successfully approach questions applicable to each standard.

- Students can use these workbooks at home to build their knowledge of English Language Arts and Math content. They can practice the content they have learned, are learning, or are going to learn. The workbooks can help prepare students for what's to come and/or as remedial practice for concepts they find challenging. The explanations in the workbooks are extremely valuable to students as they work independently, increasing their awareness of concepts and improving their confidence as they work through each question.

The benefits that **Barron's Core Focus** workbooks will provide students, parents, and educators are endless as the Common Core is implemented in schools across America.

> **Common Core State Standards Initiative**
> *http://www.corestandards.org/*
>
> **PARCC**
> *http://www.parcconline.org/*
>
> **Smarter Balance Assessment Consortium**
> *www.smarterbalanced.org*

ENGLISH LANGUAGE ARTS

The English Language Arts Standards are separated into different strands. The grades 6 through 8 standards are comprehensive and divided into the following areas: Reading, Writing, Speaking and Listening, Foundational Skills, and Language. The Common Core has designated separate Reading Standards for both fiction and informational texts. These standards are identified as Reading: Literature and Reading: Informational Text. In this section students will practice skills covering a variety of standards. Each section covers a specific standard and provides the student with practice through multiple-choice, short-answer, and extended-response questions.

CITING TEXTUAL EVIDENCE

RL.7.1 Cite several pieces of textual evidence to support what the text says explicitly as well as inferences drawn from the text.

Directions: Read the excerpt below from chapter 1 of Lewis Carrol's *Alice's Adventures in Wonderland* and answer the questions that follow.

1   Alice was beginning to get very tired of sitting by her sister on the bank, and of having nothing to do: once or twice she had peeped into the book her sister was reading, but it had no pictures or conversations in it, "and what is the use of a book," thought Alice, "without pictures or conversation?"

2   So she was considering in her own mind (as well as she could, for the hot day made her feel very sleepy and stupid), whether the pleasure of making a daisy-chain would be worth the trouble of getting up and picking the daisies, when suddenly a white rabbit with pink eyes ran close by her.

> Inferences are what the author wants you to get out of a passage, even though it is not explicitly stated. To make inferences, read between the lines to figure out the author's intended meaning based on details and clues given in the reading.

3   There was nothing so *very* remarkable in that; nor did Alice think it so *very* much out of the way to hear the Rabbit say to itself, "Oh dear! Oh dear! I shall be late!" (when she thought it over afterwards, it occurred to her that she ought to have wondered at this, but at the time it all seemed quite natural); but when the Rabbit actually *took a watch out of its waistcoat-pocket*, and looked at it, and then hurried on, Alice started to her feet, for it flashed across her mind that she had never before seen a rabbit with either a waistcoat-pocket, or a watch to take out of it, and burning with curiosity, she ran across the field after it, and fortunately was just in time to see it pop down a large rabbit-hole under the hedge.

4   In another moment down went Alice after it, never once considering how in the world she was to get out again.

5   The rabbit-hole went straight on like a tunnel for some way, and then dipped suddenly down, so suddenly that Alice had not a moment to think about stopping herself before she found herself falling down a very deep well.

6   "Well!" thought Alice to herself, "after such a fall as this, I shall think nothing of tumbling down stairs! How brave they'll all think me at home! Why, I wouldn't say anything about it, even if I fell off the top of the house!" (Which was very likely true.)

7   Down, down, down. Would the fall *never* come to an end! "I wonder how many miles I've fallen by this time?" she said aloud. "I must be getting somewhere near the centre of the earth. Let me see: that would be four thousand miles down, I think—" (for, you see, Alice had learnt several things of this sort in her lessons in the schoolroom, and though this was not a *very* good opportunity for showing off her knowledge, as there was no one to listen to her, still it was good practice to say it over) "—yes, that's about the right distance—but then I wonder what Latitude or Longitude I've got to?" (Alice had no idea what Latitude was, or Longitude either, but thought they were nice grand words to say.)

8   Presently she began again. "I wonder if I shall fall right *through* the earth! How funny it'll seem to come out among the people that walk with their heads downward! The Antipathies, I think—" (she was rather glad there *was* no one listening, this time, as it didn't sound at all the right word) "—but I shall have to ask them what the name of the country is, you know. Please, Ma'am, is this New Zealand or Australia?" (and she tried to curtsey as she spoke—fancy *curtseying* as you're falling through the air! Do you think you could manage it?) "And what an ignorant little girl she'll think me for asking! No, it'll never do to ask: perhaps I shall see it written up somewhere."

9   Down, down, down. There was nothing else to do, so Alice soon began talking again. "Dinah'll miss me very much tonight, I should think!" (Dinah was the cat.) "I hope they'll remember her saucer of milk at tea-time. Dinah my dear! I wish you were down here with me! There are no mice in the air, I'm afraid, but you might catch a bat, and that's very like a mouse, you know. But do cats eat bats, I wonder?" And here Alice began to get rather sleepy, and went on saying to herself, in a dreamy sort of way, "Do cats eat bats? Do cats eat bats?" and sometimes, "Do bats eat cats?" for, you see, as she couldn't answer either question, it didn't much matter which way she put it. She felt that she was dozing off, and had just begun to dream that she was walking hand in hand with Dinah, and saying to her very earnestly, "Now, Dinah, tell me the truth: did you ever eat a bat?" when suddenly, thump! thump! down she came upon a heap of sticks and dry leaves, and the fall was over.

10   Alice was not a bit hurt, and she jumped up on to her feet in a moment: she looked up, but it was all dark overhead; before her was another long passage, and the White Rabbit was still in sight, hurrying down it. There was not a moment to be lost: away went Alice like the wind, and was just in time to hear it say, as it turned a corner, "Oh my ears and whiskers, how late it's getting!" She was close behind it when she turned the corner, but the Rabbit was no longer to be seen: she found herself in a long, low hall, which was lit up by a row of lamps hanging from the roof.

11   There were doors all round the hall, but they were all locked; and when Alice had been all the way down one side and up the other, trying every door, she walked sadly down the middle, wondering how she was ever to get out again.

12   Suddenly she came upon a little three-legged table, all made of solid glass; there was nothing on it except a tiny golden key, and Alice's first thought was that it might belong to one of the doors of the hall; but, alas! either the locks were too large, or the key was too small, but at any rate it would not open any of them. However, on the second time round, she came upon a low curtain she had not noticed before, and behind it was a little door about fifteen inches high: she tried the little golden key in the lock, and to her great delight it fitted!

1. Based on the first two paragraphs of the excerpt, what can you infer about Alice's feelings at the beginning of the story?
    (A) She likes to sleep.
    (B) She likes flowers.
    (C) She loves to read.
    (D) She is easily bored.

2. What can you infer about Alice's personality based on paragraphs 4–6 in the excerpt?
    (A) She is not very smart and easily confused.
    (B) She is curious and impulsive.
    (C) She is sensitive and cares greatly for animals.
    (D) She is scared and cautious.

3. Based on the details in the passage, which BEST describes the rabbit's attitude toward Alice?
    (A) He is selfish and does not want the girl to steal from him.
    (B) He is shy and doesn't want to be seen by the girl.
    (C) He is preoccupied and is unaware of the girl's presence.
    (D) He is rude and blatantly ignoring the girl.

4. What details from the text show that this is not any ordinary rabbit hole that Alice has entered?

_____

_____

_____

_____

_____

_____

_____

5. Which details from the passage show that Alice has an active imagination?

_____

_____

_____

_____

_____

_____

_____

(Answers are on page 91.)

FINDING THE THEME AND CENTRAL IDEAS

RL.7.2 Determine a theme or central idea of a text and analyze its development over the course of the text; provide an objective summary of the text.

Directions: Read *The Emperor's New Suit* by Hans Christian Andersen (1837) and answer the questions that follow.

Many, many years ago lived an emperor, who thought so much of new clothes that he spent all his money in order to obtain them; his only ambition was to be always well dressed. He did not care for his soldiers, and the theatre did not amuse him; the only thing, in fact, he thought anything of was to drive out and show a new suit of clothes. He had a coat for every hour of the day; and as one would say of a king "He is in his cabinet," so one could say of him, "The emperor is in his dressing-room."

> The central idea may be stated (written explicitly in the text) or unstated (not written word for word but implied in the work). The focus is on the most important **ideas** (not lessons) in the reading, not the small details.

One day two swindlers came to this city; they made people believe that they were weavers, and declared they could manufacture the finest cloth to be imagined. Their colours and patterns, they said, were not only exceptionally beautiful, but the clothes made of their material possessed the wonderful quality of being invisible to any man who was unfit for his office or unpardonably stupid.

"That must be wonderful cloth," thought the emperor. "If I were to be dressed in a suit made of this cloth I should be able to find out which men in my empire were unfit for their places, and I could distinguish the clever from the stupid. I must have this cloth woven for me without delay." And he gave a large sum of money to the swindlers, in advance, that they should set to work without any loss of time. They set up two looms, and pretended to be very hard at work, but they did nothing whatever on the looms. They asked for the finest silk and the most precious gold-cloth; all they got they did away with, and worked at the empty looms till late at night.

"I should very much like to know how they are getting on with the cloth," thought the emperor. But he felt rather uneasy when he remembered that he who was not fit for his office could not see it. Personally, he was of opinion that he had nothing to fear, yet he thought it advisable to send somebody else first to see how matters stood. Everybody in the town knew what a remarkable quality the stuff possessed, and all were anxious to see how bad or stupid their neighbours were.

"I shall send my honest old minister to the weavers," thought the emperor. "He can judge best how the stuff looks, for he is intelligent, and nobody understands his office better than he."

The good old minister went into the room where the swindlers sat before the empty looms. "Heaven preserve us!" he thought, and opened his eyes wide, "I cannot see anything at all," but he did not say so. Both swindlers requested him to come near, and asked him if he did not admire the exquisite pattern and the beautiful colours, pointing to the empty looms. The poor old minister tried his very best, but he could see nothing, for there was nothing to be seen. "Oh dear," he thought, "can I be so stupid? I should never have thought so, and nobody must know it! Is it possible that I am not fit for my office? No, no, I cannot say that I was unable to see the cloth."

"Now, have you got nothing to say?" said one of the swindlers, while he pretended to be busily weaving.

"Oh, it is very pretty, exceedingly beautiful," replied the old minister looking through his glasses. "What a beautiful pattern, what brilliant colours! I shall tell the emperor that I like the cloth very much."

"We are pleased to hear that," said the two weavers, and described to him the colours and explained the curious pattern. The old minister listened attentively, that he might relate to the emperor what they said; and so he did.

Now the swindlers asked for more money, silk and gold-cloth, which they required for weaving. They kept everything for themselves, and not a thread came near the loom, but they continued, as hitherto, to work at the empty looms.

Soon afterwards the emperor sent another honest courtier to the weavers to see how they were getting on, and if the cloth was nearly finished. Like the old minister, he looked and looked but could see nothing, as there was nothing to be seen.

"Is it not a beautiful piece of cloth?" asked the two swindlers, showing and explaining the magnificent pattern, which, however, did not exist.

> An objective summary concisely states the important information and events from the reading. A strong objective summary contains a beginning, middle, and end, contains only factual information from the reading, and offers **no opinions**.

"I am not stupid," said the man. "It is therefore my good appointment for which I am not fit. It is very strange, but I must not let anyone know it;" and he praised the cloth, which he did not see, and expressed his joy at the beautiful colours and the fine pattern. "It is very excellent," he said to the emperor.

Everybody in the whole town talked about the precious cloth. At last the emperor wished to see it himself, while it was still on the loom. With a number of courtiers, including the two who had already been there, he went to the two clever swindlers, who now worked as hard as they could, but without using any thread.

"Is it not magnificent?" said the two old statesmen who had been there before. "Your Majesty must admire the colours and the pattern." And then they pointed to the empty looms, for they imagined the others could see the cloth.

"What is this?" thought the emperor, "I do not see anything at all. That is terrible! Am I stupid? Am I unfit to be emperor? That would indeed be the most dreadful thing that could happen to me."

> The theme is the **message** or **lesson** learned from the story; the **universal truth that can be applied to the reader's life.**

"Really," he said, turning to the weavers, "your cloth has our most gracious approval;" and nodding contentedly he looked at the empty loom, for he did not like to say that he saw nothing. All his attendants, who were with him, looked and looked, and although they could not see anything more than the others, they said, like the emperor, "It is very beautiful." And all advised him to wear the new magnificent clothes at a great procession which was soon to take place. "It is magnificent, beautiful, excellent," one heard them say; everybody seemed to be delighted, and the emperor appointed the two swindlers "Imperial Court weavers."

The whole night previous to the day on which the procession was to take place, the swindlers pretended to work, and burned more than sixteen candles. People should see that they were busy to finish the emperor's new suit. They pretended to take the cloth from the loom, and worked about in the air with big scissors, and sewed with needles without thread, and said at last: "The emperor's new suit is ready now."

The emperor and all his barons then came to the hall; the swindlers held their arms up as if they held something in their hands and said: "These are the trousers!" "This is the coat!" and "Here is the cloak!" and so on. "They are all as light as a cobweb, and one must feel as if one had nothing at all upon the body; but that is just the beauty of them."

"Indeed!" said all the courtiers; but they could not see anything, for there was nothing to be seen.

"Does it please your Majesty now to graciously undress," said the swindlers, "that we may assist your Majesty in putting on the new suit before the large looking-glass?"

The emperor undressed, and the swindlers pretended to put the new suit upon him, one piece after another; and the emperor looked at himself in the glass from every side.

"How well they look! How well they fit!" said all. "What a beautiful pattern! What fine colours! That is a magnificent suit of clothes!"

The master of the ceremonies announced that the bearers of the canopy, which was to be carried in the procession, were ready.

"I am ready," said the emperor. "Does not my suit fit me marvellously?" Then he turned once more to the looking-glass, that people should think he admired his garments.

The chamberlains, who were to carry the train, stretched their hands to the ground as if they lifted up a train, and pretended to hold something in their hands; they did not like people to know that they could not see anything.

The emperor marched in the procession under the beautiful canopy, and all who saw him in the street and out of the windows exclaimed: "Indeed, the emperor's new suit is incomparable! What a long train he has! How well it fits him!" Nobody wished to let others know he saw nothing, for then he would have been unfit for his office or too stupid. Never emperor's clothes were more admired.

"But he has nothing on at all," said a little child at last. "Good heavens! Listen to the voice of an innocent child," said the father, and one whispered to the other what the child had said. "But he has nothing on at all," cried at last the whole people. That made a deep impression upon the emperor, for it seemed to him that they were right; but he thought to himself, "Now I must bear up to the end." And the chamberlains walked with still greater dignity, as if they carried the train which did not exist.

1. What is the theme of the story?
   - (A) One must not be easily persuaded by pride to believe what he/she knows to be false.
   - (B) Vanity should be appreciated.
   - (C) Keep your friends close but your enemies closer.
   - (D) It's more important to be kind than honest.

2. Which of the following details BEST helps to convey the theme of the story?
   - (A) "Many, many years ago lived an emperor, who thought so much of new clothes that he spent all his money in order to obtain them; his only ambition was to be always well dressed."
   - (B) "'Really,' he said, turning to the weavers, 'your cloth has our most gracious approval;' and nodding contentedly he looked at the empty loom, for he did not like to say that he saw nothing."
   - (C) "'But he has nothing on at all,' said a little child at last."
   - (D) "And he gave a large sum of money to the swindlers, in advance, that they should set to work without any loss of time."

3. Which of the following BEST represents the **central ideas** in the text?
    (Choose all that apply. There is more than one correct answer.)
    (A) The emperor waved a lot in the parade.
    (B) A child at the parade was the only one to say that the emperor was not wearing clothes.
    (C) Two swindlers came to town to sell the emperor beautiful, but invisible clothes.
    (D) Everyone in town was excited about the clothes.
    (E) The emperor and his staff pretended that they could see the suit.
    (F) The clothes turned out to be invisible but no one wanted to tell the emperor.
    (G) The beautiful suit had a lot of color and a long train.

4. On the lines provided, choose the most important main events from the story and write them in chronological order to create an objective summary of the text.

    _____

    _____

    _____

    _____

    _____

    _____

    _____

    _____

    _____

    _____

    _____

    _____

    _____

    _____

5. Which of the following should NOT be included in an objective summary of the story?
   - Ⓐ The weavers are evil and should be punished for tricking the emperor and the townspeople.
   - Ⓑ The emperor realizes that he is wearing no clothes but continues down the parade route.
   - Ⓒ One of the emperor's courtiers visits the swindlers but does not admit that he cannot see the clothing.
   - Ⓓ The townspeople compliment the emperor on his new suit during the parade.

   Explain your answer.

   _____

   _____

   _____

   _____

   _____

   _____

6. Which of the following is the BEST possible new title for this story?
   - Ⓐ The Story of the Cheating Weavers
   - Ⓑ The Little Boy Who Finally Told the Truth
   - Ⓒ The Disastrous Parade
   - Ⓓ The Lie and the Invisible Suit

   Explain your answer.

   _____

   _____

   _____

   _____

   _____

   _____

(Answers are on page 91.)

ANALYZING SETTING AND CHARACTER

RL.7.3 Analyze how particular elements of a story or drama interact (e.g., how setting shapes the character or plot).

Directions: Read the excerpt below from chapter 2 of L. Frank Baum's *The Wonderful Wizard of Oz* and answer the questions that follow.

Chapter 2
The Council with the Munchkins

She was awakened by a shock, so sudden and severe that if Dorothy had not been lying on the soft bed she might have been hurt. As it was, the jar made her catch her breath and wonder what had happened; and Toto put his cold little nose into her face and whined dismally. Dorothy sat up and noticed that the house was not moving; nor was it dark, for the bright sunshine came in at the window, flooding the little room. She sprang from her bed and with Toto at her heels ran and opened the door.

The little girl gave a cry of amazement and looked about her, her eyes growing bigger and bigger at the wonderful sights she saw.

The cyclone had set the house down very gently—for a cyclone—in the midst of a country of marvelous beauty. There were lovely patches of greensward all about, with stately trees bearing rich and luscious fruits. Banks of gorgeous flowers were on every hand, and birds with rare and brilliant plumage sang and fluttered in the trees and bushes. A little way off was a small brook, rushing and sparkling along between green banks, and murmuring in a voice very grateful to a little girl who had lived so long on the dry, gray prairies.

While she stood looking eagerly at the strange and beautiful sights, she noticed coming toward her a group of the queerest people she had ever seen. They were not as big as the grown folk she had always been used to; but neither were they very small. In fact, they seemed about as tall as Dorothy, who was a well-grown child for her age, although they were, so far as looks go, many years older.

Three were men and one a woman, and all were oddly dressed. They wore round hats that rose to a small point a foot above their heads, with little bells around the brims that tinkled sweetly as they moved. The hats of the men were blue; the little woman's hat was white, and she wore a white gown that hung in pleats from her shoulders. Over it were sprinkled little stars that glistened in the sun like diamonds. The men were dressed in blue, of the same shade as their hats, and wore well-polished boots with a deep roll of blue at the tops.

The men, Dorothy thought, were about as old as Uncle Henry, for two of them had beards. But the little woman was doubtless much older. Her face was covered with wrinkles, her hair was nearly white, and she walked rather stiffly.

When these people drew near the house where Dorothy was standing in the doorway, they paused and whispered among themselves, as if afraid to come farther. But the little old woman walked up to Dorothy, made a low bow and said, in a sweet voice:

"You are welcome, most noble Sorceress, to the land of the Munchkins. We are so grateful to you for having killed the Wicked Witch of the East, and for setting our people free from bondage."

Dorothy listened to this speech with wonder. What could the little woman possibly mean by calling her a sorceress, and saying she had killed the Wicked Witch of the East? Dorothy was an innocent, harmless little girl, who had been carried by a cyclone many miles from home; and she had never killed anything in all her life.

But the little woman evidently expected her to answer; so Dorothy said, with hesitation,

"You are very kind, but there must be some mistake. I have not killed anything."

"Your house did, anyway," replied the little old woman, with a laugh, "and that is the same thing. See!" she continued, pointing to the corner of the house. "There are her two feet, still sticking out from under a block of wood."

Dorothy looked, and gave a little cry of fright. There, indeed, just under the corner of the great beam the house rested on, two feet were sticking out, shod in silver shoes with pointed toes.

"Oh, dear! Oh, dear!" cried Dorothy, clasping her hands together in dismay. "The house must have fallen on her. Whatever shall we do?"

"There is nothing to be done," said the little woman calmly.

"But who was she?" asked Dorothy.

"She was the Wicked Witch of the East, as I said," answered the little woman. "She has held all the Munchkins in bondage for many years, making them slave for her night and day. Now they are all set free, and are grateful to you for the favor."

"Who are the Munchkins?" inquired Dorothy.

"They are the people who live in this land of the East where the Wicked Witch ruled."

"Are you a Munchkin?" asked Dorothy.

"No, but I am their friend, although I live in the land of the North. When they saw the Witch of the East was dead the Munchkins sent a swift messenger to me, and I came at once. I am the Witch of the North."

"Oh, gracious!" cried Dorothy. "Are you a real witch?"

"Yes, indeed," answered the little woman. "But I am a good witch, and the people love me. I am not as powerful as the Wicked Witch was who ruled here, or I should have set the people free myself."

"But I thought all witches were wicked," said the girl, who was half frightened at facing a real witch.

"Oh, no, that is a great mistake. There were only four witches in all the Land of Oz, and two of them, those who live in the North and the South, are good witches. I know this is true, for I am one of them myself, and cannot be mistaken. Those who dwelt in the East and the West were, indeed, wicked witches; but now that you have killed one of them, there is but one Wicked Witch in all the Land of Oz—the one who lives in the West."

"But," said Dorothy, after a moment's thought, "Aunt Em has told me that the witches were all dead—years and years ago."

"Who is Aunt Em?" inquired the little old woman.

"She is my aunt who lives in Kansas, where I came from."

The Witch of the North seemed to think for a time, with her head bowed and her eyes upon the ground. Then she looked up and said, "I do not know where Kansas is, for I have never heard that country mentioned before. But tell me, is it a civilized country?"

"Oh, yes," replied Dorothy.

"Then that accounts for it. In the civilized countries I believe there are no witches left, nor wizards, nor sorceresses, nor magicians. But, you see, the Land of Oz has never been civilized, for we are cut off from all the rest of the world. Therefore we still have witches and wizards amongst us."

"Who are the wizards?" asked Dorothy.

"Oz himself is the Great Wizard," answered the Witch, sinking her voice to a whisper. "He is more powerful than all the rest of us together. He lives in the City of Emeralds."

Dorothy was going to ask another question, but just then the Munchkins, who had been standing silently by, gave a loud shout and pointed to the corner of the house where the Wicked Witch had been lying.

"What is it?" asked the little old woman, and looked, and began to laugh. The feet of the dead Witch had disappeared entirely, and nothing was left but the silver shoes.

"She was so old," explained the Witch of the North, "that she dried up quickly in the sun. That is the end of her. But the silver shoes are yours, and you shall have them to wear." She reached down and picked up the shoes, and after shaking the dust out of them handed them to Dorothy.

"The Witch of the East was proud of those silver shoes," said one of the Munchkins, "and there is some charm connected with them; but what it is we never knew."

Dorothy carried the shoes into the house and placed them on the table. Then she came out again to the Munchkins and said:

"I am anxious to get back to my aunt and uncle, for I am sure they will worry about me. Can you help me find my way?"

The Munchkins and the Witch first looked at one another, and then at Dorothy, and then shook their heads.

"At the East, not far from here," said one, "there is a great desert, and none could live to cross it."

"It is the same at the South," said another, "for I have been there and seen it. The South is the country of the Quadlings."

"I am told," said the third man, "that it is the same at the West. And that country, where the Winkies live, is ruled by the Wicked Witch of the West, who would make you her slave if you passed her way."

"The North is my home," said the old lady, "and at its edge is the same great desert that surrounds this Land of Oz. I'm afraid, my dear, you will have to live with us."

Dorothy began to sob at this, for she felt lonely among all these strange people. Her tears seemed to grieve the kind-hearted Munchkins, for they immediately took out their handkerchiefs and began to weep also. As for the little old woman, she took off her cap and balanced the point on the end of her nose, while she counted "One, two, three" in a solemn voice. At once the cap changed to a slate, on which was written in big, white chalk marks: "LET DOROTHY GO TO THE CITY OF EMERALDS."

1. What feelings influence Dorothy's initial reaction to her setting when she awakes in the land of the Munchkins?
   - Ⓐ She is frightened so she begins to cry.
   - Ⓑ She is confused and becomes angry.
   - Ⓒ She is surprised and happy.
   - Ⓓ She is suspicious so she begins to yell.

2. Which of the following BEST describes the reason for Dorothy's feelings when she first wakes?
   - Ⓐ She is homesick for her pretty home in Kansas.
   - Ⓑ She does not like the look of the people who are approaching her.
   - Ⓒ The colors of the new setting hurt her eyes.
   - Ⓓ She is not used to such natural beauty and is appreciative of her surroundings.

3. Cite details from the text that demonstrate how the author portrays the magical setting of the Land of Munchkins.

   _____

   _____

   _____

   _____

   _____

   _____

   _____

   _____

   _____

   _____

4. Dorothy's character can BEST be described as
   Ⓐ careful and disbelieving
   Ⓑ innocent and curious
   Ⓒ shy and unfriendly
   Ⓓ sad and depressed

5. On the lines below, choose three details from the passage to justify your answer to question 4.

   1. _____

   _____

   _____

   2. _____

   _____

   _____

   3. _____

   _____

   _____

6. What is the most likely reason why Dorothy cries at the end of the passage?
   Ⓐ She is overwhelmed by the beauty of this new land.
   Ⓑ She is afraid of these new, odd people.
   Ⓒ She is upset by the possibility of not being able to return home.
   Ⓓ She is lonely without her dog, Toto.

(Answers are on page 92.)

WORD MEANING AND FIGURATIVE LANGUAGE

RL.7.4 Determine the meanings of words or phrases as they are used in a text, including figurative and connotative meanings; analyze the impact of rhymes and other repetitions of sounds (e.g., alliteration) on a specific verse or stanza of a poem or section of a story or drama.

Directions: Read the excerpt below from *A Christmas Carol* by Charles Dickens and answer the questions that follow.

Scrooge took his melancholy dinner in his usual melancholy tavern; and having read all the newspapers, and beguiled the rest of the evening with his banker's-book, went home to bed. He lived in chambers which had once belonged to his deceased partner. They were a gloomy suite of rooms, in a lowering pile of building up a yard, where it had so little business to be, that one could scarcely help fancying it must have run there when it was a young house, playing at hide-and-seek with other houses, and forgotten the way out again. It was old enough now, and dreary enough, for nobody lived in it but Scrooge, the other rooms being all let out as offices. The yard was so dark that even Scrooge, who knew its every stone, was fain to grope with his hands. The fog and frost so hung about the black old gateway of the house, that it seemed as if the Genius of the Weather sat in mournful meditation on the threshold.

> You can find the meaning of unknown words by using context clues. Look at how the author uses the word and what words surround it to help you figure out the meaning.

Now, it is a fact, that there was nothing at all particular about the knocker on the door, except that it was very large. It is also a fact, that Scrooge had seen it, night and morning, during his whole residence in that place; also that Scrooge had as little of what is called fancy about him as any man in the city of London, even including—which is a bold word—the corporation, aldermen, and livery. Let it also be borne in mind that Scrooge had not bestowed one thought on Marley, since his last mention of his seven years' dead partner that afternoon. And then let any man explain to me, if he can, how it happened that Scrooge, having his key in the lock of the door, saw in the knocker, without its undergoing any intermediate process of change— not a knocker, but Marley's face.

Marley's face. It was not in impenetrable shadow as the other objects in the yard were, but had a dismal light about it, like a bad lobster in a dark cellar. It was not angry or ferocious, but looked at Scrooge as Marley used to look: with ghostly spectacles turned up on its ghostly forehead. The hair was curiously stirred, as if by breath or hot air; and, though the eyes were wide open, they were perfectly motionless. That, and its livid colour, made it horrible; but its horror seemed to be in spite of the face and beyond its control, rather than a part or its own expression.

As Scrooge looked fixedly at this phenomenon, it was a knocker again.

To say that he was not startled, or that his blood was not conscious of a terrible sensation to which it had been a stranger from infancy, would be untrue. But he put his hand upon the key he had relinquished, turned it sturdily, walked in, and lighted his candle.

He did pause, with a moment's irresolution, before he shut the door; and he did look cautiously behind it first, as if he half-expected to be terrified with the sight of Marley's pigtail sticking out into the hall. But there was nothing on the back of the door, except the screws and nuts that held the knocker on, so he said "Pooh, pooh!" and closed it with a bang.

The sound resounded through the house like thunder. Every room above, and every cask in the wine-merchant's cellars below, appeared to have a separate peal of echoes of its own. Scrooge was not a man to be frightened by echoes. He fastened the door, and walked across the hall, and up the stairs; slowly too: trimming his candle as he went.

1. What is the meaning of the word *melancholy* as it is used in the first sentence of the excerpt?
   - Ⓐ Depressing
   - Ⓑ Boring
   - Ⓒ Comforting
   - Ⓓ Exciting

2. Which other words in the first paragraph help you to understand the meaning of the word melancholy? (Choose all that apply.)
   - Ⓐ Dreary
   - Ⓑ Business
   - Ⓒ Gloomy
   - Ⓓ Forgotten
   - Ⓔ Mournful
   - Ⓕ Home

3. Which BEST describes the author's intention of repeating the word melancholy in the first sentence of the excerpt?
   - Ⓐ It is the most important word in the whole paragraph.
   - Ⓑ To emphasize the gloomy tone of the paragraph.
   - Ⓒ To highlight the poor cooking skills of the restaurant Scrooge chooses.
   - Ⓓ To stress the M sound as important.

4. What type of figurative language is used in the last sentence of paragraph 1?

   Ⓐ Simile

   Ⓑ Metaphor

   Ⓒ Onomatopoeia

   Ⓓ Personification

Connotation is the feeling of a word. An author intentionally chooses words that have positive, negative, or neutral connotations to help convey meaning.

5. How does this use of figurative language contribute to the tone of the passage?

_____

_____

_____

_____

_____

_____

_____

_____

_____

_____

_____

_____

_____

_____

_____

6. What is the connotation of the word *dismal* as it is used in the third paragraph of the passage? "It was not in impenetrable shadow as the other objects in the yard were, but had a *dismal* light about it, like a bad lobster in a dark cellar."

Ⓐ Positive

Ⓑ Negative

Ⓒ Neutral

Ⓓ There is no connotation.

7. What is the significance of the following sentence? "To say that he was not startled, or that his blood was not conscious of a terrible sensation to which it had been a stranger from infancy, would be untrue."

_____

_____

_____

_____

_____

_____

_____

_____

_____

_____

_____

_____

_____

(Answers are on page 92.)

ANALYZING POETRY

RL.7.5 Analyze how a drama's or poem's form or structure (e.g., soliloquy, sonnet) contributes to its meaning.

Directions: Read the poem "Should Be..." by Ann McLaughlin and Shakespeare's "Sonnet XVIII" and answer the questions that follow.

Should Be...

Love can be the floating of a feather
Precious, light, fluttering
Tickling your nose as it floats by.

Love can be the crashing of a wave
Overwhelming, sudden, crushing
Knocking you over where you stand.

Love can be the smashing of a mirror
Crashing, bleeding, blank
You can no longer see yourself.

Love should be a warm winter coat
Cozy, supportive, protecting
The kind that lasts season after season.

> Poets use figurative language, repetition, and tone to convey meaning to the reader. Looking at the structure of a poem and individual words used by the poet can help you understand it better.

1. What is the central idea of the first stanza of the poem?
   Ⓐ Love can go unnoticed by others.
   Ⓑ Love can be violent and dangerous.
   Ⓒ Love can sometimes be pleasant but temporary.
   Ⓓ Love can be powerful and surprising.

2. What is the connotation of the word *fluttering* as it is used in the first stanza of the poem?
   Ⓐ Positive
   Ⓑ Negative
   Ⓒ Neutral
   Ⓓ There is no connotation.

3. How is the tone of the last stanza of the poem different from the first three? What specific words help develop this shift of tone in the last stanza?

   _____

   _____

Sonnet XVIII

Shall I compare thee to a summer's day?
Thou art more lovely and more temperate:
Rough winds do shake the darling buds of May,
And summer's lease hath all too short a date:
Sometime too hot the eye of heaven shines,
And often is his gold complexion dimm'd;
And every fair from fair sometime declines,
By chance or nature's changing course untrimm'd;
But thy eternal summer shall not fade
Nor lose possession of that fair thou owest;
Nor shall Death brag thou wander'st in his shade,
When in eternal lines to time thou growest:
    So long as men can breathe or eyes can see,
    So long lives this and this gives life to thee.

> Rhyme schemes are written out in letters; A is the first line, B is the second line, and so on. The lines that rhyme with each other are given the same letters.

4. What is the rhyme scheme of the poem?

_____

_____

5. How does the poem's structure contribute to the development of the poem?

_____

_____

6. What is Shakespeare saying about summer in lines 3, 4, 5, and 6 of his poem?
   - Ⓐ It is too hot and can make you uncomfortable.
   - Ⓑ The weather is not perfect or lasting.
   - Ⓒ The season is windy and begins too early.
   - Ⓓ Summer is the best season.

7. What is the intention of Shakespeare comparing his love to a summer's day?
   - Ⓐ To show that he loves both his lady and the season of summer equally.
   - Ⓑ To demonstrate that his love is going to fade just like summer.
   - Ⓒ To convey that she could never be as good as summer.
   - Ⓓ To show that she is more beautiful than summer and his love will last.

(Answers are on page 93.)

CHARACTERS' POINT OF VIEW

> **RL.7.6** Analyze how an author develops and contrasts the points of view of different characters or narrators in a text.

Directions: Read the two excerpts from *Flipped* by Wendelin Van Draanen and answer the questions that follow.

Excerpt #1
Bryce "Diving Under"

All I've ever wanted was for Julie Baker to leave me alone. For her to back off—you know, just give me some *space*.

It all started the summer before second grade when our moving van pulled into her neighborhood. And since we're done with the *eighth* grade, that, my friend, makes more than a half a decade of strategic avoidance and social discomfort.

She didn't just barge into my life. She barged and shoved and wedged her way into my life. Did we invite her to get into our moving van and start climbing all over boxes? No! But that's what she did, taking over and showing off like only Julie Baker can.

My dad tried to stop her. "Hey!" he says as she's catapulting herself on board. "What are you doing? You're getting mud everywhere!" So true, too. Her shoes were, like, caked with the stuff.

She didn't hop out though. Instead, she planted her rear end on the floor and started pushing a big box with her feet. "Don't you want some help?" She glanced my way. "It sure looks like you *need* it."

I didn't like the implication. And even though my dad had been tossing me the same sort of look all week, I could tell he didn't like this girl either. "Hey! Don't do that," he warned her. "There are some really valuable things in that box."

"Oh. Well, how about this one?" She scoots over to a box labeled LENOX and looks my way again. "We should push it together!"

"No, no, no!" my dad says, then pulls her up by the arm. "Why don't you run along home? Your mother's probably wondering where you are."

This was the beginning of my soon-to-become-acute awareness that the girl cannot take a hint. Of any kind. Does she zip on home like a kid should when they've been invited to leave? No. She says, "Oh, my mom knows where I am. She said it was fine." Then she points across the street and says, "We just live right over there."

My father looks to where she is pointing and mutters, "Oh, boy." Then he looks at me and winks as he says, "Bryce, isn't it time to go inside and help your mother?"

1. From what point of view is this excerpt told?
   - Ⓐ First person
   - Ⓑ Third person limited
   - Ⓒ Second person
   - Ⓓ Third person omniscient

2. What is Bryce's attitude toward Julie Baker in the story? What evidence from the story led to this conclusion?

   _____

   _____

   _____

   _____

   _____

   _____

   _____

   _____

   _____

3. What effect do the rhetorical questions in the passage have in demonstrating Bryce's feelings about Julie?

   _____

   _____

   _____

   _____

   _____

   _____

   _____

   _____

   _____

Excerpt #2
"Flipped"

The first day I met Bryce Loski, I flipped. Honestly, one look at him and I became a lunatic. It's his eyes. Something in his eyes. They're blue, and framed in the blackness of his lashes, they're dazzling. Absolutely breathtaking.

It's been over six years now, and I learned long ago to hide my feelings, but oh, those first days. Those first years! I thought I would die from wanting to be with him.

***

I was too excited not to charge across the street, but I did try to be civilized once I got into the moving van. I stood outside looking in for a record-breaking length of time, which was hard because there he was! About halfway back! My new sure-to-be best friend, Bryce Loski.

Bryce wasn't doing much of anything. He was more hanging back, watching his father move boxes into the lift gate. I remember feeling sorry for Mr. Loski because he looked worn out, moving boxes all by himself. I also remember that he and Bryce were wearing matching turquoise polo shirts, which was really cute. Really *nice*.

When I couldn't stand it any longer, I called, "Hi!" into the van, which made Bryce jump, and then quick as a cricket, he started pushing a box like he'd been working all along.

I could tell by the way Bryce was acting so guilty that he was supposed to be moving boxes, but he was sick of it. He'd probably been moving things for days! It was easy to see that he needed a rest. He needed some juice! Something.

It was also easy to see that Mr. Loski wasn't about to let him quit. He was going to keep on moving boxes around until he collapsed, and by then Bryce might be dead. Dead before he'd have the chance to move in!

The tragedy of it catapulted me into the moving van. I had to help! I had to save him!

4. What is Julie's attitude toward Bryce Loski in the excerpt? What evidence from the excerpt led you to this conclusion?

_____

_____

_____

_____

_____

5. What effect do the author's use of exclamation points have on demonstrating Julie's opinion of Bryce in the excerpt?

_____

_____

_____

_____

_____

6. The first excerpt is written from Bryce's point of view and the second is written from Julie's point of view. How would the passages be different if written from the father's point of view? Choose a section of the text and rewrite it from the father's point of view on the lines below.

_____

_____

_____

_____

_____

(Answers are on page 93.)

CITING EVIDENCE IN INFORMATIONAL TEXT

RI.7.1 Cite several pieces of textual evidence to support what the text says explicitly as well as inferences drawn from the text.

Directions: Read the excerpt below from *Steve Jobs: The Man Who Thought Different* by Karen Blumenthal and answer the questions that follow.

1   Though Steve Jobs had battled cancer for years, somehow his death felt unexpected.

2   Within hours after the news came out, there was an outpouring of grief from around the world that was unprecedented for a business executive. In front of Apple's headquarters at One Infinite Loop in Cupertino, in front of Apple stores from San Francisco to New York to China, people came to pay their respects. They left apples, whole and bitten. They brought their iPhones and their iPads, with messages of sadness and appreciation.

3   It was as if a world-famous movie star or rock star had died. U2's Bono called Jobs "the hardware software Elvis." His face was on the cover of magazines from *People* to *The Economist*, and many publications rushed out special issues commemorating his life, which flew off the shelves.

5   In her eulogy, which was reprinted in the *New York Times*, Mona Simpson shared her brother's loyalty, his love of beauty, his incredible tenacity, and his hard work. Before he lost consciousness for the last time, she wrote, "He'd look at his sister Patty, then for a long time at his children, then at his life's partner, Laurene, and then over their shoulders past them.

5   "Steve's final words were:

6   'OH WOW. OH WOW. OH WOW.'"

> You can use details and clues in a passage to make inferences.

7   Still in his prime years as a businessman, he had left much unfinished. He had been deeply involved in plans for Apple's new headquarters, going through design after design, and insisting that it include the apricot orchards that dotted the valley when he was a boy. He had hoped Apple would figure out a better way to provide television to the masses. And realizing that many kids are no longer assigned lockers, he hoped to find a way to make textbooks more available electronically, perhaps selling iPads with textbooks already loaded.

8   He left the company mid-roar. The Apple he ran was fifteen times bigger than the one he took over in 1997. In the fiscal year that ended just before he died, Apple recorded sales of $108 billion, reflecting even faster growth than the year before. Nearly 24 cents of every $1 of sales was pure profit. Though his computers and smart phones were among the most expensive on the market, Apple had sold more than 72 million phones, more than 42 million iPods, 32 million iPads, and almost 17 million computers in one year.

9   He had become phenomenally wealthy, worth an estimated $7 billion, according to *Forbes* magazine, with the largest piece from his Disney stock, followed by his Apple holdings.

10   Only a few business icons in history changed a single industry, but Jobs remade several. He wasn't the creator of the personal computer, but he was the voice and face of the revolution. He didn't make the wonderful, computer-animated Pixar movies, but he made them happen. He put digital music and the Internet in our pockets in an elegant way, and he made our lives easier by insisting that every gadget Apple made— and thus, the gadgets that many others made in response—be simple and fun to use.

11   At a memorial service for Apple employees, Tim Cook, Apple's new CEO, said that one of the lessons Jobs taught him was that "simple can be harder than complex. You have to work hard to get your thinking clear enough to make it simple. But it's worth it in the end, because once you get there, you can move mountains."

1. What can you infer from Steve Jobs' last words?
   - Ⓐ   He is excited about all that Apple has accomplished.
   - Ⓑ   He is surprised that so many people came to see him in the hospital.
   - Ⓒ   He is proud of his family and the life he has built.
   - Ⓓ   He is overwhelmed by all of the work he has left unfinished.

2. What evidence is there that Steve Jobs has improved the Apple brand?

   _____

3. What evidence is there in the excerpt that supports the following statement: Steve Jobs' products made our lives easier.

   _____

4. Based on the text, why do you think that so many people admired Steve Jobs?
   - Ⓐ   He created products that gave millions access to convenient technology.
   - Ⓑ   He was a great businessman.
   - Ⓒ   He was very wealthy and generous.
   - Ⓓ   He became as famous as a movie star or rock star.

5. Provide two pieces of textual evidence from the excerpt that show that Steve Jobs still had big ideas for Apple even at the end of his life.

   _____

6. What can you infer about the future of Apple based on your evidence?

   _____

(Answers are on page 94.)

FINDING CENTRAL IDEAS

RI.7.2 Determine two or more central ideas in a text and analyze their development over the course of the text; provide an objective summary of the text.

Directions: Read the excerpt below from chapter 5 of *I Am Malala* by Malala Yousafzai with Patricia McCormack and answer the questions that follow.

> The central idea is sometimes implied, and not always written explicitly in the text. The focus is on the most important **ideas** (not lessons) in the reading, not the small details.

1   I didn't think much of this difference until later, after the mufti's visit to our house. One day I was playing with neighborhood children in the alley, and when we were choosing up sides for a game of cricket, one of the boys said he didn't want me on his team.

2   "Our school is better than yours," he said, as if that explained things.

3   I didn't agree one bit. "My school is the better one," I said.

4   "Your school is bad," he insisted. "It's not on the straight path of Islam."

5   I didn't know what to make of this, but I knew he was wrong. My school was a heaven.

6   Because inside the Khushal School, we flew on wings of knowledge. In a country where women aren't allowed out in public without a man, we girls traveled far and wide inside the pages of our books. In a land where many women can't read the prices in the markets, we did multiplication. In a place where, as soon as we were teenagers, we'd have to cover our heads and hide ourselves from the boys who'd been our childhood playmates, we ran as free as the wind.

7   We didn't know where our education would take us. All we wanted was a chance to learn in peace. And that is what we did. The crazy world could carry on outside the walls of the Khushal School. Inside, we could be who we were.

8   Our only concerns, once we dropped our schoolbags in the classroom, were the same as any child's at school: Who would get the highest grade on the day's test, and who would sit with whom at recess?

9   It was a point of pride for me that almost every year in primary school, I won the trophy for first place at the end of the term. I was considered one of the top girls—and the principal's daughter—and some girls thought maybe there was a connection between the two. But it was a point of pride for my father that he gave me no special treatment. And the proof was obvious to everyone when a new girl came to school when I was about nine.

10   Her name was Malka-a-Noor, and she was bright and determined, but I did not think she was nearly as clever as me. So on the last day of school that year, when the awards were announced, I was stunned. She had gotten first place and I was second.

11   I smiled politely as she received her trophy, but the minute I got home I burst into tears. When my father saw me, he comforted me, but not in the way I wanted. "It's a good thing to come in second," he said. "Because you learn that if you can win, you can lose. And you should learn to be a good loser, not just a good winner."

12   I was too young—and too stubborn—to appreciate his words. (And, truth be told, I still prefer to be first.) But after that term, I worked extra hard so I would never have to learn that particular lesson again!

13   Another of my regular worries was whether Moniba was angry with me. She was my best friend, bookish like me, almost like my twin. We sat together whenever we could—on the bus, at recess, in the classroom—and she made me laugh as no one else could. But we had a habit of fighting, and always over the same thing: when another girl came between us.

> To find the theme, think about what you believe that the author is trying to teach you or what he/she wants you to get out of the reading.

14   "Are you my friend or hers?" Moniba would say if I sat with another girl at recess.

15   "Moniba," I'd say, "you were the one ignoring me!"

16   The worst part is when Moniba would refuse to talk to me. Then I would get angry at her for being so angry at me! Sometimes these spats would last for days. Eventually I would miss her too much and I would take responsibility for the fight. (I seemed to always take the blame!) Then she would make a funny face, and we'd fall apart laughing and forget our differences. Until the next time a girl came between us.

17   How could a place where I learned so much and laughed so much be bad?

1. Based only on the details in the passage, what does Malala value most?
   (There is more than one correct answer.)
   - Ⓐ Education
   - Ⓑ Family
   - Ⓒ Competition
   - Ⓓ Friendship
   - Ⓔ Recreation
   - Ⓕ Feminism

2. What evidence in the passage led you to make the choices above?

   _____

   _____

   _____

   _____

   _____

3. According to the excerpt, why does Malala think her school is like heaven?
   (List at least three reasons.)

   _____

   _____

   _____

   _____

   _____

4. Which of the following BEST demonstrates the central idea of paragraph 6?
   - Ⓐ Not all girls were entitled to the right of an education.
   - Ⓑ It is a description of a typical day in Malala's school.
   - Ⓒ Malala is willing to fight for the right to go to school.
   - Ⓓ The restrictions of women in the outside world did not limit Malala's educational experience in her school.

5. According to the excerpt, why were Malala and Moniba friends, even though they often argued?

_____

_____

_____

_____

_____

6. Which of the following BEST describes the author's main purpose in paragraphs 9–12?

An objective summary contains only factual information from the reading and offers **no opinions**.

Ⓐ To demonstrate that Malala gets upset when she does not win.

Ⓑ To show that Malala is jealous of the new girl in school.

Ⓒ To explain that Malala realizes that she needs to work hard to succeed.

Ⓓ To show the close relationship that Malala has with her father.

7. Use the lines below to write an objective summary of the excerpt that focuses on the central ideas and important details.

_____

_____

_____

_____

_____

(Answers are on page 94.)

CONNECTING EVENTS, IDEAS, AND INDIVIDUALS

RI.7.3 Analyze the interactions between individuals, events, and ideas in a text (e.g., how ideas influence individuals or events, or how individuals influence ideas or events).

Directions: Read the excerpt below from chapter 1 of *Warriors Don't Cry* by Melba Pattillo Beals and answer the questions that follow.

1   Inside Central, everyone who wasn't talking about getting us out of school seemed to be talking about the upcoming production of *The Mikado*. I listened intently for every little crumb of information I could get. I felt a vicarious delight just being near the excitement. From what I could learn, the production was nearly professional, with many props and fancy equipment I'd never even heard of. How I longed to be included or at least permitted to attend. I thought I had resigned myself to being left out, but it was haunting me again.

2   The segregationist's campaign against us seemed to get even worse during that week. Sign-carrying, card-dispensing, tripping, kicking crusaders revved up their efforts to reduce our numbers to zero. Meanwhile, Mrs. Huckaby, the woman I considered to be somewhat near fair and rational about the whole situation, had lapsed back into her attitude of trying to convince me there was nothing going on. It seemed as though whenever I reported anything to her, she would work herself up into a lather: I was seeing things; was I being too sensitive; did I have specific details?

3   When she stopped behaving in a reasonable way, she took away the only point of reference that I had. I desperately tried to understand how such an intelligent woman could be reasonable and understanding one moment, then seem so cold, distant, and dispassionate the next. I supposed she must be under an enormous weight and doing her best. I tried to see the overall picture—to remember that over the long haul, she had been a tiny pinpoint of light in the otherwise very dark experience of dealing with Central High's administration. But once again I had to accept the fact that I shouldn't be wasting my time or energy hoping anyone would listen to my reports. I was on my own.

1. Which of the following BEST describes the changes in Mrs. Huckaby's reaction to the narrator's complaints?
    - (A) She is under a lot of stress at her job.
    - (B) She is feeling a lot of pressure from the segregationists.
    - (C) She was growing weary of the narrator's constant complaining.
    - (D) She is unhappy with the school's administration.

2. How does the narrator's attitude change from the beginning of the passage until the end?

_____

_____

_____

_____

_____

3. What details does the author give to help the reader understand the shift in the narrator's mood?

_____

_____

_____

_____

_____

4. Which evidence BEST describes the narrator's attitude towards Mrs. Huckaby?
   Ⓐ "It seemed as though whenever I reported anything to her, she would work herself up into a lather: I was seeing things; was I being too sensitive; did I have specific details?"
   Ⓑ "But once again I had to accept the fact that I shouldn't be wasting my time or energy hoping anyone would listen to my reports."
   Ⓒ "Meanwhile, Mrs. Huckaby, the woman I considered to be somewhat near fair and rational about the whole situation, had lapsed back into her attitude of trying to convince me there was nothing going on."
   Ⓓ "I supposed she must be under an enormous weight and doing her best."

5. The narrator states, "I thought I had resigned myself to being left out, but it was haunting me again." How does this quote show how she is treated in the school?

_____

_____

_____

_____

_____

(Answers are on page 95.)

35

WORD MEANING AND FIGURATIVE LANGUAGE IN INFORMATIONAL TEXT

RI.7.4 Determine the meanings of words and phrases as they are used in a text, including figurative, connotative, and technical meanings; analyze the impact of a specific word choice on meaning and tone.

Directions: Read the excerpt below from *Navy Seal Dogs: My Tale of Training Canines for Combat* by Mike Ritland and answer the questions that follow.

1   The dog lay in the shade of a palm tree, his head up and his ears at attention. He was scanning the desert scrubland, vigilant, the muscles beneath the heavy fur of his flanks taut and ready. Even from behind him, I could see his tongue lolling out of the side of his mouth, flopping like a pink fish.

2   "Chopper," the man beside me said.

3   The dog turned to look at us, his expression keenly alert, his dark eyes intent.

4   "*Heerre*"

5   The dog sprang to his feet and made his way across the dusty yard. Under other circumstances, I might have tensed up at the sight of a 75-pound package of fierce determination approaching. However, I could see a very tiny softening of the muscles around the eyes as he neared and recognition dawned on them. He knew who I was.

6   He also knew not to approach me first, even though the two of us had spent the first few months of his life in the United States together. As commanded, he came up to Brett, his former SEAL team handler. He sat down alongside the man he served with on dozens of dangerous missions for six years. Now they were living on a small ranch outside Ranchita, California. Brett and Chopper had ceased being on active military duty only three months earlier, but they both would have chafed at being called "retirees."

7   Chopper sat, still very much at attention, until Brett told him it was okay. Then Chopper looked at me, and I gave his head a few rubs with the flat of my hand. I ran my hand down his shoulder and along his rib cage. He was still in fighting form, but I noticed that he relaxed a bit and leaned into me. I smiled at this sign of affection and appreciation for the attention I was giving him.

8   I noticed that the fur around Chopper's muzzle and eyes had lightened a bit since I'd last seen him. It was no longer the deep ebony that had glowed like a spit-polished dress boot. The slight unevenness to the side of one of his large ears was still there, though. Some scuffle as a pup in his kennel outside of Tilburg in the Netherlands had left him with an identifying mark. In my mind it was never a flaw. Rather, it was a mark of distinction.

1. What is the meaning of the word *vigilant* as it is used in the first paragraph of the excerpt?

    Ⓐ Alert

    Ⓑ Angry

    Ⓒ Strong

    Ⓓ Uncomfortable

2. Which other words in the first paragraph help you to understand the meaning of the word *vigilant*? (Choose all that apply.)

    Ⓐ Ready

    Ⓑ Muscles

    Ⓒ Taut

    Ⓓ Attention

    Ⓔ Scanning

    Ⓕ Flopping

    > You can find the meaning of unknown words by using context clues.

3. What part of speech is the word *keenly* as it is used in paragraph 3?

    Ⓐ Noun

    Ⓑ Verb

    Ⓒ Adjective

    Ⓓ Adverb

4. What is the effect of the phrase *a 75-pound package of fierce determination* as it is used in paragraph 5?

    Ⓐ It helps to convey the main idea of the paragraph.

    Ⓑ To emphasize the dog's size and aggressiveness.

    Ⓒ To highlight that the dog is strong and hardworking.

    Ⓓ To stress that the author is generally uncomfortable around dogs.

5. How does the phrase, "It was no longer the deep ebony that had glowed like a spit-polished dress boot," in paragraph 8 contribute to the passage?

    _____

    _____

    _____

6. What is the BEST synonym for the word *scuffle* as it is used in the last paragraph of the passage?

    Ⓐ Shuffle

    Ⓑ Hurry

    Ⓒ Fight

    Ⓓ Punishment

(Answers are on page 95.)

TEXT STRUCTURE

RI.7.5 Analyze the structure an author uses to organize a text, including how the major sections contribute to the whole and to the development of the ideas.

Directions: Read the excerpt below from an article posted on the website *http://energy.gov/ articles/history-electric-car* and answer the questions that follow.

Gas shortages spark interest in electric vehicles

Over the next 30 years or so, electric vehicles entered a sort of dark ages with little advancement in the technology. Cheap, abundant gasoline and continued improvement in the internal combustion engine hampered demand for alternative fuel vehicles.

Fast forward to the late 1960s and early 1970s. Soaring oil prices and gasoline shortages—peaking with the 1973 Arab Oil Embargo—created a growing interest in lowering the U.S.'s dependence on foreign oil and finding homegrown sources of fuel. Congress took note and passed the Electric and Hybrid Vehicle Research, Development, and Demonstration Act of 1976, authorizing the Energy Department to support research and development in electric and hybrid vehicles.

Around this same time, many big and small automakers began exploring options for alternative fuel vehicles, including electric cars. For example, General Motors developed a prototype for an urban electric car that it displayed at the Environmental Protection Agency's First Symposium on Low Pollution Power Systems Development in 1973, and the American Motor Company produced electric delivery jeeps that the United States Postal Service used in a 1975 test program. Even NASA helped raise the profile of the electric vehicle when its electric Lunar rover became the first manned vehicle to drive on the moon in 1971.

Yet, the vehicles developed and produced in the 1970s still suffered from drawbacks compared to gasoline-powered cars. Electric vehicles during this time had limited performance—usually topping at speeds of 45 miles per hour—and their typical range was limited to 40 miles before needing to be recharged.

Environmental concern drives electric vehicles forward

Fast forward again—this time to the 1990s. In the 20 years since the long gas lines of the 1970s, interest in electric vehicles had mostly died down. But new federal and state regulations begin to change things. The passage of the 1990 Clean Air Act Amendment and the 1992 Energy Policy Act—plus new transportation emissions regulations issued by the California Air Resources Board—helped create a renewed interest in electric vehicles in the U.S.

During this time, automakers began modifying some of their popular vehicle models into electric vehicles. This meant that electric vehicles now achieved speeds and performance much closer to gasoline-powered vehicles, and many of them had a range of 60 miles.

One of the most well-known electric cars during this time was GM's EV1, a car that was heavily featured in the 2006 documentary *Who Killed the Electric Car?* Instead of modifying an existing vehicle, GM designed and developed the EV1 from the ground up. With a range of 80 miles and the ability to accelerate from 0 to 50 miles per hour in just seven seconds, the EV1 quickly gained a cult following. But because of high production costs, the EV1 was never commercially viable, and GM discontinued it in 2001.

With a booming economy, a growing middle class and low gas prices in the late 1990s, many consumers didn't worry about fuel-efficient vehicles. Even though there wasn't much public attention to electric vehicles at this time, behind the scenes, scientists and engineers—supported by the Energy Department—were working to improve electric vehicle technology, including batteries.

A new beginning for electric cars

While all the starts and stops of the electric vehicle industry in the second half of the 20th century helped show the world the promise of the technology, the true revival of the electric vehicle didn't happen until around the start of the 21st century. Depending on whom you ask, it was one of two events that sparked the interest we see today in electric vehicles.

The first turning point many have suggested was the introduction of the Toyota Prius. Released in Japan in 1997, the Prius became the world's first mass-produced hybrid electric vehicle. In 2000, the Prius was released worldwide, and it became an instant success with celebrities, helping to raise the profile of the car. To make the Prius a reality, Toyota used a nickel metal hydride battery—a technology that was supported by the Energy Department's research. Since then, rising gasoline prices and growing concern about carbon pollution have helped make the Prius the best-selling hybrid worldwide during the past decade.

(Historical footnote: Before the Prius could be introduced in the U.S., Honda released the Insight hybrid in 1999, making it the first hybrid sold in the U.S. since the early 1900s.)

The other event that helped reshape electric vehicles was the announcement in 2006 that a small Silicon Valley startup, Tesla Motors, would start producing a luxury electric sports car that could go more than 200 miles on a single charge. In 2010, Tesla received a $465 million loan from the Department of Energy's Loan Programs Office—a loan that Tesla repaid a full nine years early—to establish a manufacturing facility in California. In the short time since then, Tesla has won wide acclaim for its cars and has become the largest auto industry employer in California.

Tesla's announcement and subsequent success spurred many big automakers to accelerate work on their own electric vehicles. In late 2010, the Chevy Volt and the Nissan LEAF were released in the U.S. market. The first commercially available plug-in hybrid, the Volt has a gasoline engine that supplements its electric drive once the battery is depleted, allowing consumers to drive on electric for most trips and gasoline to extend the vehicle's range. In comparison, the LEAF is an all-electric vehicle (often called a battery-electric vehicle, an electric vehicle or just an EV for short), meaning it is only powered by an electric motor.

Over the next few years, other automakers began rolling out electric vehicles in the U.S.; yet, consumers were still faced with one of the early problems of the electric vehicle—where to charge their vehicles on the go. Through the Recovery Act, the Energy Department invested more than $115 million to help build a nationwide charging infrastructure, installing more than 18,000 residential, commercial and public chargers across the country. Automakers and other private businesses also installed their own chargers at key locations in the U.S., bringing today's total of public electric vehicle chargers to more than 8,000 different locations with more than 20,000 charging outlets.

At the same time, new battery technology—supported by the Energy Department's Vehicle Technologies Office—began hitting the market, helping to improve a plug-in electric vehicle's range. In addition to the battery technology in nearly all of the first generation hybrids, the Department's research also helped develop the lithium-ion battery technology used in the Volt. More recently, the Department's investment in battery research and development has helped cut electric vehicle battery costs by 50 percent in the last four years, while simultaneously improving the vehicle batteries' performance (meaning their power, energy and durability). This in turn has helped lower the costs of electric vehicles, making them more affordable for consumers.

Consumers now have more choices than ever when it comes to buying an electric vehicle. Today, there are 23 plug-in electric and 36 hybrid models available in a variety of sizes—from the two-passenger Smart ED to the midsized Ford C-Max Energi to the BMW i3 luxury SUV. As gasoline prices continue to rise and the prices on electric vehicles continue to drop, electric vehicles are gaining in popularity—with more than 234,000 plug-in electric vehicles and 3.3 million hybrids on the road in the U.S. today.

The future of electric cars

It's hard to tell where the future will take electric vehicles, but it's clear they hold a lot of potential for creating a more sustainable future. If we transitioned all the light-duty vehicles in the U.S. to hybrids or plug-in electric vehicles using our current technology mix, we could reduce our dependence on foreign oil by 30–60 percent, while lowering the carbon pollution from the transportation sector by as much as 20 percent.

To help reach these emissions savings, in 2012 President Obama launched the EV Everywhere Grand Challenge—an Energy Department initiative that brings together America's best and brightest scientists, engineers and businesses to make plug-in electric vehicles as affordable as today's gasoline-powered vehicles by 2022. On the battery front, the Department's Joint Center for Energy Storage Research at Argonne National Laboratory is working to overcome the biggest scientific and technical barriers that prevent large-scale improvements of batteries.

And the Department's Advanced Research Projects Agency-Energy (ARPA-E) is advancing game-changing technologies that could alter how we think of electric vehicles. From investing in new types of batteries that could go further on a single charge to cost-effective alternatives to materials critical to electric motors, ARPA-E's projects could transform electric vehicles.

In the end, only time will tell what road electric vehicles will take in the future.

1. Under which heading would you find information about electric cars that are currently on the market?
   - (A) *Gas shortages spark interest in electric vehicles*
   - (B) *Environmental concern drives electric vehicles forward*
   - (C) *A new beginning for electric cars*
   - (D) *The future of electric cars*

2. Why does the author choose to title the sections in this way? What effect does this have on the reader's understanding of the motivations behind the development of electric cars?

   _____

   _____

   _____

3. Which of the following alternate headings would be appropriate for the third section of the text?
   - (A) The Development of Electric Cars Begins
   - (B) Celebrities Weigh in on the Electric Car Debate
   - (C) Prius vs. Tesla
   - (D) Affordable Options for Electric Cars

   > Authors use headings to help organize information. Pay attention to the way the sections are organized and the headings that are used to organize the ideas.

4. Explain your answer with textual evidence from the third section of the text.

   _____

   _____

   _____

5. How does the last sentence of the text contribute to the overall meaning?
   - (A) It shows that the success of electric cars is uncertain, just as their development has been.
   - (B) It explains that there is little support for the future of electric cars from the current government administration.
   - (C) It demonstrates that the author still has many questions about electric cars.
   - (D) It concisely sums up all of the information in the excerpt.

(Answers are on page 96.)

DETERMINING THE AUTHOR'S POINT OF VIEW

RI.7.6 Determine an author's point of view or purpose in a text and analyze how the author distinguishes his or her position from that of others.

Directions: Read the article from the website (https://www.fdic.gov/consumers/consumer/news/cnspr08/managing.html) and answer the questions that follow.

For Teens:
How to Ace Your First Test Managing Real Money in the Real World

1   As a teen, you're beginning to make some grown-up decisions about how to save and spend your money. That's why learning the right ways to manage money...right from the start...is important. Here are suggestions.

2   **Save some money before you're tempted to spend it.** When you get cash for your birthday or from a job, automatically put a portion of it—at least 10 percent, but possibly more—into a savings or investment account. This strategy is what financial advisors call "paying yourself first." Making this a habit can gradually turn small sums of money into big amounts that can help pay for *really* important purchases in the future.

Also put your spare change to use. When you empty your pockets at the end of the day, consider putting some of that loose change into a jar or any other container, and then about once a month put that money into a savings account at the bank.

3   "Spare change can add up quickly," said Luke W. Reynolds, Chief of the FDIC's Community Affairs Outreach Section. "But don't let that money sit around your house month after month, earning no interest and at risk of being lost or stolen." If you need some help sorting and counting your change, he said, find out if your bank has a coin machine you can use for free. If not, the bank may give you coin wrappers. Some supermarkets and other non-banking companies have self-service machines that quickly turn coins into cash, but expect to pay a significant fee for the service, often close to 10 cents for every dollar counted, plus you still have to take the cash to the bank to deposit it into your savings account.

4   **Keep track of your spending**. A good way to take control of your money is to decide on maximum amounts you aim to spend each week or each month for certain expenses, such as entertainment and snack food. This task is commonly known as "budgeting" your money or developing a "spending plan." And to help manage your money, it's worth keeping a list

of your expenses for about a month, so you have a better idea of where your dollars and cents are going.

5   "If you find you're spending more than you intended, you may need to reduce your spending or increase your income," Reynolds added. "It's all about setting goals for yourself and then making the right choices with your money to help you achieve those goals."

6   **Consider a part-time or summer job**. Whether it's babysitting, lawn mowing, or a job in a "real" business, working outside of your home can provide you with income, new skills, and references that can be useful after high school or college. Before accepting any job, ask your parents for their permission and advice.

7   **Think before you buy**. Many teens make quick and costly decisions to buy the latest clothes or electronics without considering whether they are getting a good value.

8   "A $200 pair of shoes hawked by a celebrity gets you to the same destination at the same speed as a $50 pair," said Reynolds. "Before you buy something, especially a big purchase, ask yourself if you really need or just want the item, if you've done enough research and comparison-shopping, and if you can truly afford the purchase without having to cut back on spending for something else."

9   **Be careful with cards**. Under most state laws, you must be at least 18 years old to obtain your own credit card and be held responsible for repaying the debt. If you're under 18, though, you may be able to qualify for a credit card as long as a parent or other adult agrees to repay your debts if you fail to do so.

10   An alternative to a credit card is a debit card, which automatically deducts purchases from your savings or checking account. Credit cards and debit cards offer convenience, but they also come with costs and risks that must be taken seriously.

11   **Protect yourself from crooks who target teens**. Even if you're too young to have a checking account or credit card, a criminal who learns your name, address, and Social Security number may be able to obtain a new credit card using *your* name to make purchases.

12   One of the most important things you can do to protect against identity theft is to be very suspicious of requests for your name, Social Security number, passwords, or bank or credit card information that come to you in an e-mail or an Internet advertisement, no matter how legitimate they may seem.

13   "Teens are very comfortable using e-mail and the Internet, but they need to be aware that criminals can be hiding at the other end of the computer screen," said Michael Benardo, manager of the FDIC's financial crimes section. These types of fraudulent requests can also come by phone, text message, or in the mail.

14   **Be smart about college.** If you're planning to go to college, learn about your options for saving or borrowing money for what could be a major expense—from tuition to books, fees, and housing. Also consider the costs when you search for a school. Otherwise, when you graduate, your college debts could be high and may limit your options when it comes to a career path or where you can afford to live.

1. Based on the author's attitude in the excerpt, which of the following statements would he most likely agree with?

   (A) The best thing to do with your coins is to deposit them in a self-counting coin machine at a supermarket or other non-banking companies.

   (B) Credit and debit cards are easy and risk-free for teens to have access to quick cash.

   (C) You should save some of the money that you are gifted or have earned for big purchases you want to make down the road.

   (D) It is okay to give away your password over the Internet if you think that the source is reliable.

2. Provide textual evidence to support your answer to question 1 and explain.

   _____

   _____

   _____

   _____

   _____

3. What effect does the author's choice of placing the phrase, "paying yourself first" in quotation marks have in demonstrating his point of view?

   _____

   _____

   _____

   _____

   _____

4. Which of the following people would most likely disagree with the advice in the article?

    Ⓐ Your parents

    Ⓑ The owner of a retail store

    Ⓒ A financial advisor

    Ⓓ The loan officer at a college

5. Based on your answer to question 4, rewrite a section of the text from that person's point of view on the lines below.

_____

_____

_____

_____

_____

_____

_____

_____

_____

_____

_____

_____

_____

_____

_____

_____

_____

(Answers are on page 96.)

TRACING AND
EVALUATING ARGUMENTS

RI.7.8 Trace and evaluate the argument and specific claims in a text, assessing whether the reasoning is sound and the evidence is relevant and sufficient to support the claims.

Directions: Read the excerpt from *Inside of a Dog: What Dogs See, Smell and Know* by Alexandra Horowitz and answer the questions that follow.

1   Animals exist in time, they use time; but so they experience time? Surely, they do. At some level there is no difference between existing in time and experiencing time: time must be perceived to be used. What people mean, I suspect, in asking whether animals experience time is, Do animals have the same feelings about time that we do? Can dogs sense the passage of a day? And, critically, are dogs bored all day, at home alone?

2   Dogs have plenty of experience of the Day, if no word *day* to call it. We are the first source of their knowledge of days: we organize the dog's day in parallel with ours, providing landmarks and surrounding them with ritual. For instance, we provide all sorts of cues for when the dog's mealtime is. We head for the kitchen or pantry. It may be our mealtime, too, so we begin to load the refrigerator, wafting food smells about, and making a racket with pots and plates. If we glance at the dog and coo a little, any remaining ambiguity is erased. And dogs are naturally habitual, sensitive to activities that recur. They form preferences—places to eat, to sleep, to safely pee—and notice preferences of yours.

3   But in addition to all those visible and olfactory cues, does the dog naturally know that it is dinnertime? I know owners who insist they can set the clock by their dog. When he moves to the door, it's precisely the time to go out; when he moves to the kitchen, sure enough, it's time to be fed. Imagine removing all the cues the dog has about the time of day: all of your movements, any environmental sounds, even light and dark. The dog still knows when it's time to eat.

4   The first explanation is that dogs wear an actual clock—though internally. It is in the so-called *pacemaker* of their brain, which regulates the activities of other cells of the body through the day. For a few decades neuroscientists have known that circadian rhythms, the sleep and alertness cycles that we experience every day, are controlled by a part of the brain in the hypothalamus called the SCN (suprachiasmatic nucleus). Not only humans have a SCN: so do rats, pigeons, dogs—every animal, including insects, with a complex nervous system. These neurons and others in the hypothalamus work together to coordinate daily wakefulness, hunger, and sleep.* Deprived entirely of cycles of light and dark, we would still go through circadian cycles; without sun it takes just over twenty-four hours to complete a biological day.

*With age, dogs sleep more but enter paradoxical—REM—sleep less than in youth. Scientists have theories but no final explanation for why dogs dream—and they dream vividly, if their eye fluttering, claw curling, tail twitching, and yelping in sleep is any indication. As in humans, one theory names dreams the accidental result of paradoxical sleep, which itself is a time of bodily restoration; alternatively, dreams might function as a time to practice, in the safety as one's imagination, future social interactions and physical fears or to review interactions and feats past.

1. Look at the first paragraph of the excerpt. What is the main claim the author is making?
   - (A) Animals have the same feelings about time as we do.
   - (B) Dogs and other animals do, in fact, experience time.
   - (C) There is no difference between existing in time and experiencing time.
   - (D) Dogs can sense the passage of a day.

2. What technique does the author use to make her claim?

   _____

3. According to paragraph 2, what evidence is there that humans have an effect on a dog's knowledge of days?

   _____

4. Which evidence BEST supports the author's main claim?
   - (A) Owners can set their clock by their dog.
   - (B) Dogs are naturally habitual and notice activities that recur.
   - (C) Dogs sleep more when they are older but experience less REM sleep.
   - (D) Dogs have a SCN that coordinates wakefulness, hunger, and sleep.

5. What techniques does the author use in her reasoning to persuade her readers to agree with her conclusions?

   _____

6. Which of the following could the author have added to strengthen her argument?
   - (A) Quotes from scientific experts about the topic.
   - (B) Pictures of dogs going through their daily routine.
   - (C) A personal story about her own dog following her cues.
   - (D) A chart about a dog's activities in the course of a typical day.

7. Do you think that the author effectively supports her claim in the excerpt? Explain your answer.

   _____

(Answers are on page 96.)

COMPARING AND CONTRASTING AUTHOR PRESENTATIONS

> **RI.7.9** Analyze how two or more authors writing about the same topic shape their presentations of key information by emphasizing different evidence or advancing different interpretations of facts.

Text 1

Directions: Read the excerpt from *In My Hands: Memories of a Holocaust Rescuer* by Irene Gut Opdyke with Jennifer Armstrong and answer the questions that follow.

1   On a morning in late May, Helen arrived with the wagon. I had already secured permission from Schulz to take the day off, and the Morrises had committed themselves to hiding by the roadside overnight. I did not ask how they would escape the Arbeitslager; if they could do it, they would. I would be on the road with the wagon. The *dorożka* had been rented from the farm with vodka and cigarettes I stole from the supply room. Abrupt, telegraphic flashes of surprise sparked in my mind as I climbed up onto the driving seat: trading in stolen goods, smuggling runaway Jews. It was almost unbelievable that I was the one doing these things.

2   I left Ternopol, going north toward the village of Janówka, begging the warm sun and the steady clop-clop of the horse's hooves to settle my nerves. I keep my gaze on the beast's bony rump moving in front of me, watching as the horse twitched at flies, tipping my ear to the whispery whisk of the long tail hairs which were flecked with bits of straw.

3   A kilometer or so outside Ternopol, the road narrowed as it went through a stand of birch trees. I heard a whistle, and then someone called my name. I pulled back on the reins, halting the *dorożka.* Ahead of me the road stretched empty until it rounded the corner of a potato field. A look over my shoulder showed the way was clear behind me. There was nothing to see but the dust from the wheels drifting sideways in the sunlight. I nodded, and the four Morrises slipped through the trees, clambering quickly into the bed of the *dorożka* and hiding themselves under the load of hay and bags of potatoes without speaking.

4   I clucked to the horse and we were off again. I had been stopped for less than a minute, and when I emerged from the copse of birch trees, no one could have known that the *dorożka* now had four new occupants. I breathed deeply, willing myself to stay relaxed and calm. After a while, the spire of a church came into view, and we

were soon rolling through the tiny village of Janówka. Chickens and geese scurried out of the road, scolding us as we passed. At the church, an old priest was bent over, tending a rosebush. He looked up at me and smiled kindly.

5   I could not say why, but his smile gave me new courage. I turned my face back to the road, and it seemed that in no time, the dark edge of the forest came into view, like a curtain being pulled across a window. The road was silent but for the hiss of the rubber tires over the dirt and the clopping of the horse's hooves. I suspected that I was being watched; we all knew by now that Puszcza Janówka now held more than foxes and wild boar. It was filled with fugitives and partisans, the war's outlaws. The Germans did not dare go in there in small patrols.

6   The road became narrow, and the shadows of the pines made pockets of cold air that we traveled through. I heard a far-off birdcall, and then another, and all the while, the horse was twitching his ears one way and then another, as though trying to locate something or someone nearby. At last, I reined the horse in and turned on the bench seat.

7   "This seems as good a place as any," I said.

8   The hay in the *dorożka* bed stirred, and one by one, the Morrises sat up, spitting out bits of dried grass and seeds and pulling hay from their hair. Herschl stood and helped his wife to her feet. Hermann was doing the same, and all four looked around them with a mixture of curiosity and trepidation.

9   "Our new home," Herschl said gamely.

10   They hopped down, as I did. Each in solemn turn shook my hand, while I clutched the reins so tightly with my other hand that the leathers left marks across my palm. "I'll bring supplies when I can," I said, roughly clearing my throat.

11   They stepped in among the trees, their footsteps muffled by the thick layer of pine needles. I stood, watching them walk deeper and deeper into the forest. They stood out brightly in a patch of sunlight, and the next moment they were gone.

12   I went to the horse's head, leaning my cheek against his muzzle and mingling my breath with his; I was the one who needed calming, not the horse. After a moment, I took the bridle and led the horse around, the wagon wheels bumping up onto the mossy shoulder of the road.

13   The following Sunday, I took two more of my friends from the laundry room, Abram Klinger and David Rosen, to the same spot. I held back the tears that threatened to come as they climbed down. I felt like a bad mother who had taken her children to the forest and left them there. For several minutes I watched them thread their way among the tree trunks, and then the darkness of the *puszcza* swallowed them.

1. In paragraph 1, the narrator states, "It was almost unbelievable that I was the one doing these things." What does the narrator have a hard time coming to grips with?
    - Ⓐ That she stole from the supply room.
    - Ⓑ That she had to smuggle goods and Jews.
    - Ⓒ That she had to borrow and drive a wagon on her own.
    - Ⓓ That she did not ask how her friends were going to escape the Arbeitslager.

2. What does the answer to the question above reveal about her point of view?

    _____

    _____

3. In paragraph 3, what precautions does the narrator take to make sure she and her friends are not caught? Why is it important that these details are included?

    _____

    _____

4. In the last paragraph the author states, "I felt like a bad mother who had taken her children to the forest and left them there." What does this reveal about her attitude toward helping her friends escape?

    _____

    _____

5. On the lines below, rewrite a section of the text from Herschl's point of view.

    _____

    _____

    _____

    _____

    _____

    _____

Text 2

Directions: Read the excerpt from *The Diary of a Young Girl* by Anne Frank and answer the questions that follow.

Wednesday, 8 July, 1942

Dear Kitty,

1   Years seem to have passed between Sunday and now. So much has happened, it is just as if the whole world had turned upside down. But I am still alive, Kitty, and that is the main thing, Daddy says.

2   Yes, I'm still alive, indeed, but don't ask where or how. You wouldn't understand a word, so I will begin by telling you what happened Sunday afternoon.

3   At three o'clock (Harry had just gone, but was coming back later) someone rang the front doorbell. I was lying lazily reading a book on the veranda in the sunshine, so I didn't hear it. A bit later, Margot appeared at the kitchen door looking very excited, "The S.S. have sent a call-up notice for Daddy," she whispered. "Mummy has gone to see Mr. Van Daan already." (Van Daan is a friend who works with Daddy in business.) It was a great shock to me, a call-up; everyone knows what that means. I picture concentration camps and lonely cells—should we allow him to be doomed like this? "Of course he won't go," declared Margot, while we waited together. "Mummy has gone to the Van Daans to discuss whether we should move into our hiding place tomorrow. The Van Daans are going with us, so we shall be seven in all." Silence. We couldn't talk anymore, thinking about Daddy, who, little knowing what was going on, was visiting some old people in the Joodse Invalide; waiting for Mummy, the heat and suspense, all made us very overawed and silent.

4   Suddenly the bell rang again. "That is Harry," I said. "Don't open the door." Margot held me back, but it was not necessary as we heard Mummy and Mr. Van Daan downstairs, talking to Harry, then they came in and closed the door behind them. Each time the bell went, Margot or I had to creep softly down to see if it was Daddy, not opening the door to anyone else.

5   Margot and I were sent out of the room. Van Daan wanted to talk to Mummy alone. When we were alone together in our bedroom, Margot told me that the call-up was not for Daddy, but for her. I was more frightened than ever and began to cry. Margot is sixteen; would they really take girls of that age away alone? But thank goodness she won't go, Mummy said so herself; that must be what Daddy meant when he talked about us going into hiding.

6   Into hiding—where would we go, in a town or the country, in a house or a cottage, when, how, where…?

7   These were questions I was not allowed to ask, but I couldn't get them out of my mind. Margot and I began to pack some of our most vital belongings into a school satchel. The first thing I put in was this diary, then hair curlers, handkerchiefs, schoolbooks, a comb, old letters; I put in the craziest things with the idea that we were going into hiding. But I'm not sorry, memories mean more to me than dresses.

8   At five o'clock Daddy finally arrived, and we phoned Mr. Koophuis to ask if he could come around in the evening. Van Daan went and fetched Miep. Miep has been in the business with Daddy since 1933 and has become a close friend, likewise her brand-new husband, Henk. Miep came and took some shoes, dresses, coats, underwear, and stockings away in her bag, promising to return in the evening. Then silence fell on the house; not one of us felt like eating anything, it was still hot and everything was very strange. We let our large upstairs room to a certain Mr. Goudsmit, a divorced man in his thirties, who appeared to have nothing to do on this particular evening; we simply could not get rid of him without being rude; he hung about until ten o'clock. At eleven o'clock Miep and Henk Van Santen arrived. Once again, shoes, stockings, books, and underclothes disappeared into Miep's bag and Henk's deep pockets, and at eleven-thirty, they too disappeared. I was dog-tired and although I knew it would be my last night in my old bed, I fell asleep immediately and didn't wake up until Mummy called me at five-thirty the next morning. Luckily it was not so hot as Sunday; warm rain fell steadily all day. We put on heaps of clothes as if we were going to the North Pole, the sole reason being to take clothes with us. No Jew in our situation would have dreamed of going with a suitcase full of clothing. I had on two vests, three pairs of pants, a dress, on top of that a skirt, jacket, summer coat, two pairs of stockings, lace-up shoes, wooly cap, scarf, and still more; I was nearly stifled before we started, but no one inquired about that.

9   Margot filled her satchel with schoolbooks, fetched her bicycle, and rode off behind Miep into the unknown, as far as I was concerned. You see, I still didn't know where our secret hiding place was to be. At seven-thirty the door closed behind us. Moortje, my little cat, was the only creature to whom I said farewell. She would have a good home with the neighbors. This was all written in a letter addressed to Mr. Goudsmit.

10   There was one pound of meat in the kitchen for the cat, breakfast things lying on the table, stripped beds, all giving the impression that we had left helter-skelter. But we didn't care about impressions, we only wanted to get away, only escape and arrive safely, nothing else. Continued tomorrow.

Yours, Anne

6. In the excerpt, Anne and her family are rescued by their friends. How does Anne's point of view differ from that of the rescuer, Irene Gut Opdyke, in the first passage? Which details does Anne focus on that reveal her feelings about having to make a quick escape?

    _____

    _____

    _____

7. According to paragraph 4, what precautions do the Frank family take to make sure that they are safe? Why is it important that these details are included?

    _____

    _____

    _____

8. Rewrite a section of the excerpt from Miep's point of view on the lines provided.

    _____

    _____

    _____

    _____

    _____

    _____

    _____

    _____

    _____

    _____

    _____

    _____

(Answers are on page 97.)

ARGUMENT WRITING

W.7.1 Write arguments to support claims with clear reasons and relevant evidence.

Directions: When responding to the following prompts, use the rubric as a guide (see page 98). Responses will likely be longer than the spaces provided. Please use additional paper as needed to meet the requirements.

> A strong argument acknowledges opposing claims and then refutes them by providing evidence that supports the claim that you want to emphasize.

1. Because the school committee has announced that it is considering requiring all students to wear uniforms for the upcoming school year, it has invited students to speak about the issue at a meeting. Write a speech to your school committee that argues whether or not you support the proposed uniform policy. Be sure that your position is clearly stated, that you offer logical evidence and sound reasoning, and convince your audience to agree with your argument.

_____

_____

_____

_____

_____

_____

2. You would like to get a pet, but your parents are concerned and worried about the responsibilities of pet ownership. Write a letter to your parents convincing them that you can handle the responsibilities and that you should be allowed to get a pet.

_____

_____

_____

_____

_____

_____

Directions: Read the following information about the flu shot from FLU.gov and respond to the prompt.

Vaccination and Vaccine Safety

Everyone 6 months of age and older should get the flu vaccine. Seasonal flu vaccines have a very good safety track record.

How effective is the flu vaccine?

The flu vaccine is the best protection against the flu this season. If you get the flu vaccine, you are 60% less likely to need treatment for the flu by a healthcare provider. Getting the vaccine has been shown to offer substantial other benefits including reducing illness, antibiotic use, time lost from work, hospitalizations, and deaths.

How should I get the vaccine?

There are two different types of flu vaccines, trivalent and quadrivalent.

Trivalent vaccines protect against 3 strains of the flu, A/H3N2, A/H1N1, and influenza B. Trivalent vaccines are available in:

- Traditional flu shots, approved for anyone 6 months and older
- Intradermal shots, which use a shorter needle, approved for anyone 18–64
- High dose shots approved for people over 65
- Cell based shots created using viruses grown in animal cells and approved for anyone over 18
- Recombinant shots created using DNA technology, approved for people 18–49 with severe egg allergies

Quadrivalent vaccines protect against 4 strains of the flu, A/H3N2, A/H1N1, and 2 strains of influenza B. Quadrivalent vaccines are available in:

- Traditional flu shots, approved for anyone 6 months and older
- Nasal spray, approved for healthy people from 2–49, except pregnant women

How long is my flu vaccination good for?

The flu vaccine will protect you for one flu season.

When should I get the vaccine?

Get the vaccine as soon as it is available in your area. Flu season **usually peaks in January or February**, but it can occur as late as May. Early immunization is the most effective, but it is **not too late** to get the vaccine in December, January, or beyond.

Does the flu vaccine work right away?

It takes about two weeks after vaccination for antibodies to develop in the body and provide protection against influenza virus infection. In the meantime, you are still at risk for getting the flu. That's why it's better to get vaccinated early in the fall, before the flu season really gets under way.

Is the vaccine safe?

Seasonal flu vaccines have a very good safety track record. Although there are possible side effects to vaccination, the Centers for Disease Control and Prevention and the Food and Drug Administration closely monitor the safety of seasonal flu vaccines.

Are there side effects?

Mild side effects usually begin soon after you get the vaccine and last one to two days. Possible mild side effects of the flu shot include:

- Soreness, redness, and swelling at the injection site
- Fainting, mainly in adolescents
- Headaches
- Fever
- Nausea

Possible mild side effects of the nasal spray include:

- Runny nose
- Wheezing
- Headache
- Vomiting
- Muscle aches
- Fever

Serious side effects usually begin within a few minutes to a few hours after receiving the shot. Possible serious side effects of vaccination include:

- Difficulty breathing
- Hoarseness
- Swelling around the eyes or lips
- Hives
- Paleness
- Weakness
- Racing heart
- Dizziness
- Behavior changes
- High fever

If you experience any of these reactions, seek medical attention immediately.

Can I get the flu from the vaccine?

No, you cannot get the flu from the flu shot or the nasal spray. The flu shot contains inactivated (killed) flu viruses that cannot cause illness. The nasal spray contains weakened live viruses. The weakened viruses only cause infection in the cooler temperatures found in the nose. The viruses cannot infect the lungs or other areas in the body where warmer temperatures exist.

Will I need to pay for the vaccine?

Most health insurance plans cover the cost of vaccines, but you should check with your insurance company before visiting your healthcare provider. Under the Affordable Care Act, many insurers are required to cover certain preventive services, like the flu vaccine, at no cost to you. If you do not have insurance or if it does not cover vaccines, help is available.

Is there anyone who should not get the vaccine?

Talk to your healthcare provider about vaccination if you have:
- A severe allergy to chicken eggs
- A history of severe reaction to a flu vaccination
- A moderate-to-severe illness with a fever (you should wait until you are better to get the vaccine)
- A history of Guillain–Barré Syndrome (a severe paralytic illness, also called GBS)

3. After reading the excerpt about the benefits and side effects of the flu shot, do you think that everyone should get one? Write an argument in favor or against getting the flu shot. Be sure to support your answer with evidence, acknowledge and dismiss opposing claims, and offer logical reasoning to support your claims.

_____

_____

_____

_____

_____

_____

_____

_____

4. Read the following statement: *Cell phones and personal tablets have no educational value and should not be allowed to be used in school for any purpose.* Write an argument that disagrees with this statement. Be sure to support your answer with evidence, acknowledge and dismiss opposing claims, and offer logical reasoning to support your claims.

_____

_____

_____

_____

_____

_____

_____

5. Your teacher is looking to add a new book to the reading list this semester. Think of a book that is enjoyable and worthwhile for study and write a proposal to your teacher that convinces him or her that this is a good choice for your class.

_____

_____

_____

_____

_____

_____

_____

_____

6. Many Americans frequently order fast food or take out from local restaurants rather than cooking their own meals at home. Write an essay that argues either the benefits or the disadvantages of this practice. Be sure that your claims are strong and acknowledge a counterclaim.

_____

_____

_____

_____

_____

_____

_____

(Rubric on page 98.)

INFORMATIONAL WRITING

> **W.7.2** Write informative/explanatory texts to examine a topic and convey ideas, concepts, and information through the selection, organization, and analysis of relevant content.

Directions: When responding to the following prompts, use the rubric (see page 99) as a guide. The responses will likely be longer than the spaces provided. Please use additional paper as needed to meet the requirements.

1. Think about how to solve a word problem in Math. Explain the step-by-step process of how to solve a word problem to an elementary-school student. Imagine that this student has not learned to do this math problem yet. Organize your ideas logically and use appropriate transition words so that the process is clear.

_____

_____

_____

_____

_____

_____

2. Examine the three branches in the United States Government and how they function. (*http://www.usa.gov/Agencies/federal.shtml* is a good resource.) Use your knowledge to write a short essay to inform international students who have just entered your school how the U.S. government works. Be sure to select the most important information, organize your ideas logically, and include headings or appropriate transition words to clearly convey your main points.

_____

_____

_____

_____

_____

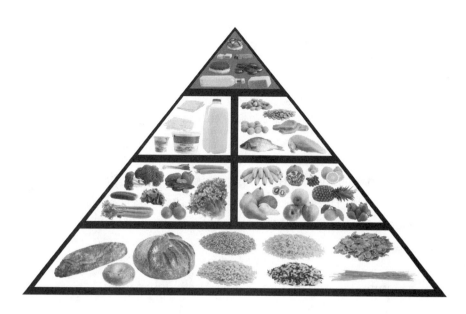

3. Examine the preceding health and diet diagram. Write an essay to explain how a balanced diet works and why it is important to your peers.

_____

_____

_____

_____

4. Write an essay that explains both positive and negative impacts of cell phones on today's society. Be sure to include the benefits as well as the disadvantages of having instant communication with others. Include headings to organize your information for the reader.

_____

_____

_____

_____

5. Write an essay that explains one of your family traditions. What is the purpose of this tradition? How did it start? Who is involved? How does it work?

_____

_____

_____

_____

(Rubric on page 99.)

NARRATIVE WRITING

W.7.3 Write narratives to develop real or imagined experiences or events using effective technique, relevant descriptive details, and well-structured event sequences.

Directions: When responding to the following prompts, use the rubric on page 100 as a guide. The responses will likely be longer than the spaces provided. Please use additional paper as needed to meet the requirements.

> A strong narrative has well-developed characters, a strong point of view, and a logical beginning, middle, and end.

1. Think back to a memorable day that you shared with your family or friends. This could be a vacation, a holiday, a party, or any special day. Describe your day and what made it special.

_____

_____

_____

_____

2. The first time you try something difficult can be scary and uncomfortable. Write a narrative about a time that you encountered a difficult task (learning to ride a bike, getting an especially hard school assignment, building something, facing a fear, and so on) and describe how you were able to overcome the difficulty.

_____

_____

_____

_____

3. Imagine that you were sent into space and have just discovered a new planet. Write a narrative that explains your adventure. Be sure to include details about your experience, including but not limited to the following: the way the planet looks, how this new environment feels, and who you might meet along the way.

_____

_____

_____

_____

4. Examine the preceding image of the shipwreck. Write a narrative explaining how you believe this event occurred.

_____

_____

_____

_____

5. Write a story that demonstrates the following theme: Although change can be scary, it can lead to new and exciting adventures.

_____

_____

_____

_____

6. Write an original story, based on either real or imaginary experiences, about a time when someone realizes that being "different" is not a bad thing; in fact, what makes people unique or special is a wonderful thing.

_____

_____

_____

_____

(Rubric on page 100.)

CONSIDERING TASK, PURPOSE, AND AUDIENCE

W.7.4 Produce clear and coherent writing in which the development, organization, and style are appropriate to task, purpose, and audience.

1. You would like to plan an educational field trip to a local museum for your class. Write an e-mail to your principal that outlines the trip and explains the reasons why it would be beneficial for students to visit the museum. Be sure to consider your purpose and audience when writing your e-mail.

   _____

   _____

   _____

   _____

   _____

   _____

2. You would like to get an after-school job as a tutor at a local community center. Write a letter to the director of the center that explains why you would be a good candidate for the job. Be sure to consider your purpose and audience when writing your letter.

   _____

   _____

   _____

   _____

   _____

   _____

   It is important to consider both your task and audience when writing. Think about who is reading or listening to your work and consider your tone, the level of formality, and the audience's prior knowledge of your topic when writing.

3. You have been asked to address your fellow students at an upcoming school assembly. Choose an issue in your school and write a speech about why it is important, as well as explain to students how they can make positive changes in the school regarding the issue. You may write about bullying, recycling, academic concerns, or any other issue that you consider relevant.

_____

_____

_____

_____

_____

_____

4. Write a review for a recent book that you have read or a movie that you have seen for the school newspaper. The school newspaper is read by students, teachers, parents, and local community members.

_____

_____

_____

_____

_____

_____

5. You have been asked to write an ongoing blog describing a typical day in a middle-school student's life. This blog is geared towards elementary students who will be entering middle school in the coming years. Some students are as young as nine years old, some have limited English skills, and many are nervous about entering middle school. Write an example of what a daily blog entry may say.

_____

_____

_____

_____

_____

_____

(Answers are on page 101.)

GRAMMAR AND USAGE

L.7.1 Demonstrate command of the conventions of standard English grammar and usage when writing or speaking.

Directions: Read the following set of sentences and answer the questions that follow.

> *Simple sentences* contain a subject and verb and express a complete thought. (This is also called an independent clause.)

1. Nathan is tired this morning, so his mother made him an extra-large cup of tea.

   This is an example of which type of sentence?
   - Ⓐ Simple
   - Ⓑ Compound
   - Ⓒ Complex
   - Ⓓ Fragment

2. Sheila goes to the mall to shop every Saturday.

   This is an example of which type of sentence?
   - Ⓐ Simple
   - Ⓑ Compound
   - Ⓒ Complex
   - Ⓓ Fragment

> *Compound sentences* contain two independent clauses joined by a coordinator.

3. When she arrived at the airport, Sarah realized that she would miss her flight because she forgot her passport.

   This is an example of which type of sentence?
   - Ⓐ Simple
   - Ⓑ Compound
   - Ⓒ Complex
   - Ⓓ Fragment

> A *complex sentence* has an independent clause joined by one or more dependent clauses.

4. Lisa washed her hands thoroughly after working in the garden.

    This is an example of which type of sentence?

    Ⓐ Simple

    Ⓑ Compound

    Ⓒ Complex

    Ⓓ Fragment

5. My friend Michelle wanted to go to the movies. I wanted to go to the movies. My friend wanted to see the new comedy. I wanted to see a horror movie.

    On the following lines, combine the four preceding clauses to form one sentence.

    _____

    _____

    _____

    _____

    _____

    _____

6. Amanda spent four hours reading her favorite book so she was unprepared for her Spanish test.

    Try rewriting the sentence above inserting the phrase, *instead of doing her homework*.

    _____

    _____

    _____

    _____

    _____

    _____

7. The family vacation was a disaster, not having packed warm clothes or boots.

The preceding sentence has a dangling modifier. Fix the sentence on the lines provided so that it makes sense. (You may have to omit or add words or change the order of the sentence.)

_____

_____

_____

_____

_____

_____

> A *modifier* changes, limits, or adds more information to a sentence. A *dangling modifier* occurs when the sentence is unclear about what is being modified.

8. Upon arriving at the museum, a painting caught my attention.

The preceding sentence has a dangling modifier. Fix the sentence on the lines provided so that it makes sense. (You may have to omit or add words or change the order of the sentence.)

_____

_____

_____

_____

_____

9. Weighing four hundred pounds, the farmer proudly showed off his prize pumpkin at the fair.

   The preceding sentence has a dangling modifier. Fix the sentence on the lines provided so that it makes sense. (You may have to omit or add words or change the order of the sentence.)

   _____

   _____

   _____

   _____

   _____

   _____

10. Though only fourteen years old, the university offered José a scholarship.

   The preceding sentence has a dangling modifier. Fix the sentence on the lines provided so that it makes sense. (You may have to omit or add words or change the order of the sentence.)

   _____

   _____

   _____

   _____

   _____

   _____

(Answers are on page 101.)

CAPITALIZATION, PUNCTUATION, AND SPELLING

L.7.2 Demonstrate command of the conventions of standard English capitalization, punctuation, and spelling when writing.

Directions: Each sentence is missing commas. Read each sentence. Then, rewrite the sentence on the lines provided, adding commas to separate the coordinate adjectives.

1. Slippery icy road conditions can make driving during a snowstorm dangerous.

   _____

   _____

   _____

2. The blond-haired blue-eyed girl was wearing a striped wool sweater.

   _____

   _____

   _____

3. After Juan's teacher told his parents that he was a smart hard-working student, they took him out for a delicious chocolate-flavored ice cream cone.

   _____

   _____

   _____

> Coordinate adjectives are two or more adjectives that come before and describe the same noun and are equal in relation to the noun.

Directions: Each of the sentences contains one or more spelling mistakes. Read each sentence. Then, rewrite the sentence on the line provided, correcting the misspelled words.

> Homophones are words that have the same sound but different spellings and meanings.

4. I don't like to waist time so I do my homework within won hour of getting home from school.

_____

_____

_____

5. There was a dear in Billy's back yard and it had the cutest white tale.

_____

_____

_____

6. When my little sister hurt her arm she was in a lot of pane so we took her to the doctor. He said that it was a brake and put her arm in a cast so it would heel properly.

_____

_____

_____

(Answers are on page 102.)

USING PRECISE LANGUAGE

L.7.3 Use knowledge of language and its conventions when writing, speaking, reading, or listening.

Directions: Each of the short paragraphs in the following section contains unnecessary words, phrases, or sentences. Read each paragraph. Then, rewrite the paragraph to eliminate the unnecessary language.

> When editing the paragraphs in this section, try to eliminate ideas that are repeated or are not necessary to express the overall meaning of the paragraph.

1. Even though many of the girls on the school council had little in common with each other, they were able to cooperate together to plan the school dance. They worked well with one another. Each and every one of them had a specific job to do and all of them did their part to make the event a success.

   _____

   _____

   _____

   _____

   _____

2. It is my personal opinion that school lunch periods should last a longer period of time. For example, if lunch starts at twelve noon, instead of ending twenty minutes later at 12:20, it should last forty-five minutes and end at 12:45. It is a true fact that many children do not have time to eat and digest their lunch in such a short time period. In the future to come, I hope that educational leaders will come to a consensus of opinion and the end result will be longer lunch times for students.

   _____

   _____

   _____

   _____

   _____

3. We had a History test in History class today. During the course of the test, we couldn't talk and had to remain silent. I was worried that I possibly might get something wrong but I wrote down all of the answers until my paper was filled to capacity. When we were completely finished answering the questions, there was an added bonus question at the end.

    _____

    _____

    _____

    _____

    _____

4. I have a problematic dilemma to solve. My dance recital is on the very same day as my flute concert. The recital and concert are on the same day so this is a big problem. I do not want to disappoint my choreographer who taught me dance or my music teacher who taught me the flute music. I know I have to make a definite decision soon in the near future but I wish I could postpone my decision until later.

    _____

    _____

    _____

    _____

    _____

5. I love and adore my new house. I want to live here forever and ever. Moving was an unexpected surprise but I finally have my own room that I don't have to share. I can decorate it exactly the same way I always wanted to. The living room is so big that we could add an additional couch if we wanted to. Never before did I have a yard and now mine is big enough to play games with my friends. I am really, truly happy here.

    _____

    _____

    _____

    _____

    _____

(Answers are on page 102.)

DEFINING UNKNOWN WORDS

L.7.4 Determine or clarify the meaning of unknown and multiple-meaning words and phrases, choosing flexibility from a range of strategies.

Directions: Read the following excerpt from Jane Austen's *Emma* and answer the questions that follow.

> Determining the part of speech of a word can help you to understand its meaning.

Emma Woodhouse, handsome, clever, and rich, with a comfortable home and happy disposition, seemed to unite some of the best blessings of existence; and had lived nearly twenty-one years in the world with very little to distress or vex her.

She was the youngest of the two daughters of a most affectionate, indulgent father; and had, in consequence of her sister's marriage, been mistress of his house from a very early period. Her mother had died too long ago for her to have more than an indistinct remembrance of her caresses; and her place had been supplied by an excellent woman as governess, who had fallen little short of a mother in affection.

Sixteen years had Miss Taylor been in Mr. Woodhouse's family, less as a governess than a friend, very fond of both daughters, but particularly of Emma. Between *them* it was more the intimacy of sisters. Even before Miss Taylor had ceased to hold the nominal office of governess, the mildness of her temper had hardly allowed her to impose any restraint; and the shadow of authority being now long passed away, they had been living together as friend and friend very mutually attached, and Emma doing just what she liked; highly esteeming Miss Taylor's judgment, but directed chiefly by her own.

The real evils, indeed, of Emma's situation were the power of having rather too much her own way, and a disposition to think a little too well of herself; these were the disadvantages which threatened alloy to her many enjoyments. The danger, however, was at present so unperceived, that they did not by any means rank as misfortunes with her.

1. What part of speech is the word *vex* as it is used in the first paragraph of the excerpt?
   - (A) Noun
   - (B) Verb
   - (C) Adjective
   - (D) Adverb

2. What is the meaning of the word *vex* as it is used in the first paragraph of the excerpt?

   Ⓐ Please

   Ⓑ Assist

   Ⓒ Trouble

   Ⓓ Justify

3. What other words in the sentence offered context clues to help determine the answer for question 2?

   _____

4. What part of speech is the word *governess* as it is used in the second paragraph of the excerpt?

   Ⓐ Noun

   Ⓑ Verb

   Ⓒ Adjective

   Ⓓ Adverb

5. What is the meaning of the word *governess* as it is used in the second paragraph of the excerpt?

   Ⓐ The wife of a Governor

   Ⓑ Best friend

   Ⓒ Sister

   Ⓓ A woman who is employed to take charge of a child's upbringing

6. Which of the definitions in the box below is not the proper definition of the word *chiefly* as it is used in the third paragraph?

chiefly
[**cheef**-lee] /ˈtʃif li/
adverb
1. **primarily; essentially:**
2. **mainly; mostly:**
adjective
3. **of, pertaining to, or like a chief:**

   Ⓐ Primarily; essentially

   Ⓑ Mainly; mostly

   Ⓒ Of, pertaining to, or like a chief

   Ⓓ All of the above

(Answers are on page 104.)

ENGLISH LANGUAGE ARTS PRACTICE TEST

My Name: _____

Today's Date: _____

Directions: Read the excerpt from Jack London's *The Call of the Wild*. Then, answer questions 1–11 about the passage.

> It is important to understand that the main characters in the passage are dogs, not humans.

1   Buck did not cry out. He did not check himself, but drove in upon Spitz, shoulder to shoulder, so hard that he missed the throat. They rolled over and over in the powdery snow. Spitz gained his feet almost as though he had not been overthrown, slashing Buck down the shoulder and leaping clear. Twice his teeth clipped together, like the steel jaws of a trap, as he backed away for better footing, with lean and lifting lips that writhed and snarled.

2   In a flash Buck knew it. The time had come. It was to the death. As they circled about, snarling, ears laid back, keenly watchful for the advantage, the scene came to Buck with a sense of familiarity. He seemed to remember it all—the white woods, and earth, and moonlight, and the thrill of battle. Over the whiteness and silence brooded a ghostly calm. There was not the faintest whisper of air—nothing moved, not a leaf quivered, the visible breaths of the dogs rising slowly and lingering in the frosty air. They had made short work of the snowshoe rabbit, these dogs that were ill-tamed wolves; and they were now drawn up in an expectant circle. They, too, were silent, their eyes only gleaming and their breaths drifting slowly upward. To Buck it was nothing new or strange, this scene of old time. It was as though it had always been, the wonted way of things.

3   Spitz was a practiced fighter. From Spitzbergen through the Arctic, and across Canada and the Barrens, he had held his own with all manner of dogs and achieved mastery over them. Bitter rage was his, but never blind rage. In passion to rend and destroy, he never forgot that his enemy was in like passion to rend and destroy. He never rushed till he was prepared to receive a rush; never attacked till he had first defended that attack.

4   In vain Buck strove to sink his teeth in the neck of the big white dog. Wherever his fangs struck for the softer flesh, they were countered by the fangs of Spitz. Fang clashed fang, and lips were cut and bleeding, but Buck could not penetrate his enemy's guard. Then he warmed up and enveloped Spitz in a whirlwind of rushes. Time and time again he tried for the snow-white throat, where life bubbled near to the surface, and each time and every time Spitz slashed him and got away. Then Buck took to rushing, as though for

the throat, when, suddenly drawing back his head and curving in from the side, he would drive his shoulder at the shoulder of Spitz, as a ram by which to overthrow him. But instead, Buck's shoulder was slashed down each time as Spitz leaped lightly away.

5   Spitz was untouched, while Buck was streaming with blood and panting hard. The fight was growing desperate. And all the while the silent and wolfish circle waited to finish off whichever dog went down. As Buck grew winded, Spitz took to rushing, and he kept him staggering for footing. Once Buck went over, and the whole circle of sixty dogs started up; but he recovered himself, almost in mid air, and the circle sank down again and waited.

6   But Buck possessed a quality that made for greatness—imagination. He fought by instinct, but he could fight by head as well he rushed, as though attempting the old shoulder trick, but at the last instant swept low to the snow and in. His teeth closed on Spitz's left fore leg. There was a crunch of breaking bone, and the white dog faced him on three legs. Thrice he tried to knock him over, then repeated the trick and broke the right fore leg. Despite the pain and helplessness, Spitz struggled madly to keep up. He saw the silent circle, with gleaming eyes, lolling tongues, and silvery breaths drifting upward, closing in upon him as he had seen similar circles close in upon beaten antagonists in the past. Only this time he was the one who was beaten.

7   There was no hope for him. Buck was inexorable. Mercy was a thing reserved for gentler climes. He maneuvered for the final rush. The circle had tightened till he could feel the breaths of the huskies on his flanks. He could see them, beyond Spitz and to either side, half-crouching for the spring, their eyes fixed upon him. A pause seemed to fall. Every animal was motionless as though turned to stone. Only Spitz quivered and bristled as he staggered back and forth, snarling with horrible menace, as though to frighten off impending death. Then Buck sprang in and out; but while he was in, shoulder had at last squarely met shoulder. The dark circle became a dot on the moon flooded snow as Spitz disappeared from view. Buck stood and looked on, the successful champion, the dominant primordial beast who had made his kill and found it good.

1. Based on the last two paragraphs of the excerpt, how does Buck's intelligence help him to defeat his enemy?
    (A) He tricked him by breaking his front legs and knocking him down.
    (B) He kept running away to tire Spitz out then bit him in the neck.
    (C) He snuck in from the outer circle to attack him.
    (D) He knew he needed to get the upper hand quickly and knocked him down first.

2. What can you infer about Buck's future in the excerpt?
    (A) The other dogs will all want to fight him now.
    (B) He will become a leader of the other dogs because they will respect and fear him.
    (C) Buck will be bullied by the other dogs.
    (D) Buck will live a calm and easy life.

3. What is the theme of the story?

  (A) One must be strong of both body and mind to survive in the wild.

  (B) Listen to your heart.

  (C) Keep your friends close but your enemies closer.

  (D) Good things come to those who wait patiently.

4 How does the setting contribute to the action in this excerpt?

  (A) The dogs had to constantly keep moving in order to stay warm so they would wrestle to get their blood pumping.

  (B) The dogs are required to travel in packs in order to feel safe from the enemies of surrounding villages.

  (C) The hot weather made the dogs impatient and irritable so they were all fighting with each other.

  (D) The harsh climate and geography of the Arctic require strength and cunning to survive, prompting Buck to desire mastery over his enemy.

5. What is the effect of the author's use of imagery in this sentence from paragraph 2?

  "There was not the faintest whisper of air—nothing moved, not a leaf quivered, the visible breaths of the dogs rising slowly and lingering in the frosty air."

  _____

  _____

6. What is the meaning of the word *inexorable* as it is used in paragraph 7?

  (A) Exhausted

  (B) Relentless

  (C) Merciful

  (D) Unaffected

7. Which evidence from the paragraph BEST supports your answer to question 6?

  (A) "Every animal was motionless as though turned to stone."

  (B) "He could see them, beyond Spitz and to either side, half-crouching for the spring, their eyes fixed upon him."

  (C) "Only Spitz quivered and bristled as he staggered back and forth, snarling with horrible menace, as though to frighten off impending death."

  (D) "Mercy was a thing reserved for gentler climes. He maneuvered for the final rush."

8. Re-read paragraphs 5 and 6 and consider how each of the dogs, Spitz and Buck, sees his chances of winning the fight. (Note: Use a separate sheet of paper to write your response.)

  _____

  _____

9. What is the evidence that BEST describes the turning point in the passage?

(A) "Spitz was untouched, while Buck was streaming with blood and panting hard."

(B) "Once Buck went over, and the whole circle of sixty dogs started up; but he recovered himself, almost in mid air, and the circle sank down again and waited."

(C) "But Buck possessed a quality that made for greatness—imagination. He fought by instinct, but he could fight by head as well he rushed, as though attempting the old shoulder trick, but at the last instant swept low to the snow and in."

(D) "As Buck grew winded, Spitz took to rushing, and he kept him staggering for footing."

10. On the lines provided, write an objective summary of the passage.

_____

_____

_____

_____

_____

_____

_____

_____

11. Imagine you are one of the dogs in the circle watching the fight between Buck and Spitz. Write a narrative describing what you see, how you feel, and what you are thinking during the struggle.

_____

_____

_____

_____

_____

_____

_____

_____

_____

_____

Nothing Gold Can Stay
Robert Frost

Nature's first green is gold,
Her hardest hue to hold.
Her early leaf's a flower;
But only so an hour.
Then leaf subsides to leaf.
So Eden sank to grief,
So dawn goes down to day.
Nothing gold can stay.

12. What is the rhyme scheme of the poem?

_____

13. What is the theme of the poem?
   Ⓐ Nature should be appreciated.
   Ⓑ Nothing can stay pure forever.
   Ⓒ Darkness comes after light.
   Ⓓ Time goes by very quickly.

14. Using context clues, what is the most likely meaning of the word *hue* in the second line of the poem?
   Ⓐ Smell
   Ⓑ Time
   Ⓒ Feeling
   Ⓓ Color

15. Choose one type of figurative language that the poet uses in his work (simile, personification, imagery, allusion, or alliteration) and explain how this use of language contributes to the overall meaning or tone of the poem.

_____

_____

_____

_____

_____

_____

1   In the colonies, the word "slavery" had a power of suggestion all its own. By 1774, it seemed to the leaders of the revolutionary movement that there was "a settled, fixed plan for *enslaving* the colonies, or bringing them under arbitrary government." John Dickenson had written, "*Those who are taxed* without their consent... are *slaves*." And Josiah Quincy exclaimed, "I speak it with grief—I speak it with anguish—Britons are our oppressors... *we are slaves.*" George Washington similarly expressed his conviction that the English government was "endeavoring by every piece of art and despotism to fix the shackles of slavery upon us," and so on. In a manner of speaking, the patriots spoke with a single metaphorical voice.

2   It was however, a delicate matter for the colonists to accuse the British of trying to enslave them, because abject slavery was such a prominent feature of colonial life. This was noted with irony, of course, in England, where Dr. Samuel Johnson, for example, asked, "How is it that the loudest yelps of liberty come from the drivers of slaves?" And Horace Walpole remarked, "I should think the souls of Africans would sit heavy on the swords of Americans." On this point too, John Wesley, the founder of Methodism, was a prolific pamphleteer for the imperial point of view. "The Negroes in America are slaves," he wrote, "the whites enjoy liberty. Is not then all this outcry about Liberty and Slavery mere rant, and playing upon words?"

3   The issue was hotly discussed. James Otis, holding that "by the law of nature" all men were "free born," wrote, "Does it follow that 'tis right to enslave a man because he is black? Will short curled hair like wool instead of Christian hair... help the argument? Can any logical inference in favor of slavery be drawn from a flat nose, a long or short face? Nothing better [than this] can be said in favor of a trade that is the most shocking violation of the law of nature, has a direct tendency to diminish the idea of the inestimable value of liberty, and makes every dealer in it a tyrant."

4   In Massachusetts, recent legislative efforts to abolish the slave trade had been blocked by the governor, but at the Harvard commencement of 1773, students had debated the issue, and many southerners were adamantly opposed to the practice and would have shed it had a majority been prepared to go along. It would be Jefferson's own tendentious argument, in the first draft of the Declaration of Independence, that the practice had been forced on the colonies by the British and perniciously bred into their economic life. The First Continental Congress, however, pledged itself to oppose the slave trade generally; Rhode Island, noting that "those who are desirous of enjoying all the advantages of liberty themselves should be willing to extend personal liberty to others," ruled that slaves imported into the colony would thereafter be freed. Connecticut followed suit; Delaware prohibited the importation of slaves; and Pennsylvania taxed the trade so heavily as almost to extinguish it there. Abigail Adams spoke for many when she wrote on September 24, 1774, "I wish most sincerely there was not a slave in the province. It always appeared a most iniquitous scheme to me—to fight ourselves

for what we are daily robbing and plundering from those who have as good a right to freedom as we have."

5   Conversely, the rhetoric of slavery had done much to arouse anti-British feeling, especially in the South, where white colonists had but to behold the degraded conditions of their own blacks to imagine themselves in a related plight. "English oppression" through taxes and trade regulations, of course, could not possibly have rendered them so abject, but the *idea* of it did much to influence their apprehensions.

16. What evidence is there to support the following statement, "The American colonists felt as though they were being treated like slaves by British rule," in paragraph 1?

_____

_____

_____

17. Which BEST describes the central idea of paragraph 2?
   Ⓐ   There is a lot of slavery in the American colonies.
   Ⓑ   Everyone deserves freedom so the slaves should be freed.
   Ⓒ   The colonists are just whining and ranting because they feel like the British are treating them unfairly.
   Ⓓ   It was a sensitive subject for the colonists to say they were enslaved when many owned slaves.

18. According to paragraph 4, which states made efforts to oppose the slave trade?

_____

_____

19. What is the purpose of the author's decision to include the quote from Abigail Adams in paragraph 4?
   Ⓐ   To demonstrate that she believes that everyone has a right to freedom, even slaves.
   Ⓑ   To explain why she is not a slave owner.
   Ⓒ   To show that slaves are getting robbed of their possessions.
   Ⓓ   To clarify the reasons why the patriots are fighting for their freedom from the British.

20. According to paragraph 5, what effect did the use of the word *slavery* have on anti-British feelings in the South?

_____

_____

21. What is the BEST synonym for the word *plight* as it is used in paragraph 5?

   (A) Explanation
   (B) Pledge
   (C) Dilemma
   (D) Promise

22. How might this author's point of view about the patriot's fight for liberty in America differ from that in a textbook describing the American Revolution?

   _____

   _____

23. Why does the author choose to write certain words in italics?

   (A) To define the meaning of the word slavery.
   (B) To emphasize that people believed they were enslaved by the British.
   (C) To clarify his main points about slaves.
   (D) To repeat important ideas.

24. Make an inference. How did the patriot's use of the word *slavery* help to drive the causes of the American Revolution? Write your answer on the lines below.

   _____

   _____

25. Citing textual evidence from the excerpt, write an argument essay discussing whether or not American colonists were truly enslaved by the British.

   _____

   _____

   _____

   _____

   _____

   _____

   _____

   _____

   _____

Directions: Read the excerpt from Emma Lazarus's "The New Colossus" and answer questions 26–30.

Not like the brazen giant of Greek fame,
With conquering limbs astride from land to land;
Here at our sea-washed, sunset gates shall stand
A mighty woman with a torch, whose flame
Is the imprisoned lightning, and her name
Mother of Exiles. From her beacon-hand
Glows world-wide welcome; her mild eyes command
The air-bridged harbor that twin cities frame.
"Keep, ancient lands, your storied pomp!" cries she
With silent lips. "Give me your tired, your poor,
Your huddled masses yearning to breathe free,
The wretched refuse of your teeming shore.
Send these, the homeless, tempest-tost to me,
I lift my lamp beside the golden door!"

26. What famous American structure is the poet describing in her poem?
   (A) The White House
   (B) The U.S.S. Constitution
   (C) The Statue of Liberty
   (D) The Lincoln Memorial

27. Which details in the poem support your answer to question 26?

   _____

   _____

   _____

28. What effect does the poet's use of personification have on the tone of the poem?

   _____

   _____

   _____

29. How does the poet portray her "Mother of Exiles"?
   (A) She feels that she represents hope.
   (B) She thinks that she is intimidating.
   (C) She believes that she is brave.
   (D) She considers her strong.

30. Your History teacher has given you an assignment to write a poem about a historical landmark to be read aloud in class. Choose a landmark and write a short poem that addresses the following: what the landmark looks like, where it is located, and what historical event the landmark represents.

_____

_____

_____

_____

_____

_____

_____

_____

Directions: Read the excerpt from Jack London's short story *To Build a Fire* and answer questions 31–38.

1   He was angry, and cursed his luck aloud. He had hoped to get into camp with the boys at six o'clock, and this would delay him an hour, for he would have to build a fire and dry out his foot-gear. This was imperative at that low temperature—he knew that much; and he turned aside to the bank, which he climbed. On top, tangled in the underbrush about the trunks of several small spruce trees, was a high-water deposit of dry firewood—sticks and twigs, principally, but also larger portions of seasoned branches and fine, dry, last-year's grasses. He threw down several large pieces on top of the snow. This served for a foundation and prevented the young flame from drowning itself in the snow it otherwise would melt. The flame he got by touching a match to a small shred of birch-bark that he took from his pocket. This burned even more readily than paper. Placing it on the foundation, he fed the young flame with wisps of dry grass and with the tiniest dry twigs.

2   He worked slowly and carefully, keenly aware of his danger. Gradually, as the flame grew stronger, he increased the size of the twigs with which he fed it. He squatted in the snow, pulling the twigs out from their entanglement in the brush and feeding directly to the flame. He knew there must be no failure. When it is seventy-five below zero, a man must not fail in his first attempt to build a fire—that is, if his feet are wet. If his feet are dry, and he fails, he can run along the trail for half a mile and restore his circulation. But the circulation of wet and freezing feet cannot be restored by running when it is seventy-five below. No matter how fast he runs, the wet feet will freeze the harder.

3   All this the man knew. The old-timer on Sulphur Creek had told him about it the previous fall, and now he was appreciating the advice. Already all sensation had gone out of his feet. To build the fire he had been forced to remove his mittens, and the fingers had quickly gone numb. His pace of four miles an hour had kept his heart pumping blood to the surface of his body and to all the extremities. But the instant he stopped, the action of the pump eased down. The cold of space smote the unprotected tip of the planet, and he, being on that unprotected tip, received the full force of the blow. The blood of his body recoiled before it. The blood was alive, like the dog, and like the dog it wanted to hide away and cover itself up from the fearful cold. So long as he walked four miles an hour, he pumped that blood, willy-nilly, to the surface; but now it ebbed away and sank down into the recesses of his body. The extremities were the first to feel its absence. His wet feet froze the faster, and his exposed fingers numbed the faster, though they had not yet begun to freeze. Nose and cheeks were already freezing, while the skin of all his body chilled as it lost its blood.

4   But *he was safe*. Toes and nose and cheeks would be only touched by the frost, for the fire was beginning to burn with strength. He was feeding it with twigs the size of his finger. In another minute he would be able to feed it with branches the size of his wrist, and then he could remove his wet foot-gear, and, while it dried, he could keep his naked feet warm by the fire, rubbing them at first, of course, with snow. The fire was a success. *He was safe.* He remembered the advice of the old-timer on Sulphur Creek, and smiled. The old-timer had been very serious in laying down the law that no man must travel alone in the Klondike after fifty below. Well, here he was; he had had the accident; he was alone; and he had saved himself. Those old-timers were rather womanish, some of them, he thought. All a man had to do was to keep his head, and he was all right. Any man who was a man could travel alone. But it was surprising, the rapidity with which his cheeks and nose were freezing. And he had not thought his fingers could go lifeless in so short a time. Lifeless they were, for he could scarcely make them move together to grip a twig, and they seemed remote from his body and from him. When he touched a twig, he had to look and see whether or not he had hold of it. The wires were pretty well down between him and his finger-ends.

5   All of which counted for little. There was the fire, snapping and crackling and promising life with every dancing flame. He started to untie his moccasins. They were coated with ice; the thick German socks were like sheaths of iron halfway to the knees; and the moccasin strings were like rods of steel all twisted and knotted as by some conflagration. For a moment he tugged with his numb fingers, then, realizing the folly of it, he drew his sheath-knife.

6   But before he could cut the strings, it happened. It was his own fault or, rather, his mistake. He should not have built the fire under the spruce tree. He should have built it in the open. But it had been easier to pull the twigs from the brush and drop them directly on the fire. Now the tree under which he had done this carried a weight of snow on its boughs. No wind had blown for weeks, and each bough was fully freighted. Each time he had pulled a twig he had communicated a slight agitation to the tree—an imperceptible agitation, so far as he was concerned, but an agitation sufficient to bring about the disaster. High up in the tree one bough capsized its load of snow. This fell on the boughs beneath, capsizing them. This process continued, spreading out and involving the whole tree. It grew like an avalanche, and it descended without warning upon the man and the fire, and the fire was blotted out! Where it had burned was a mantle of fresh and disordered snow.

31. Make an inference. Based on the first paragraph of the excerpt, what may have previously happened that would cause the character to have to build a fire?

_____

_____

32. What is the meaning of the word *ebbed* as it is used in paragraph 3?
   Ⓐ Flowed
   Ⓑ Appeared
   Ⓒ Clogged
   Ⓓ Built

33. Which word could be BEST used to describe the setting of the story?
   Ⓐ Spacious
   Ⓑ Beautiful
   Ⓒ Inviting
   Ⓓ Dangerous

34. In paragraph 4, the narrator repeats the phrase, "he was safe." What evidence is there in the rest of the paragraph that contradicts this statement?

_____

_____

35. According to paragraph 6, what was the main character's big mistake?
   Ⓐ He built his fire too high.
   Ⓑ He should not have untied his moccasins.
   Ⓒ He should not have traveled alone.
   Ⓓ He should not have built his fire underneath the spruce tree.

36. What effect does the sentence, "There was the fire, snapping and crackling and promising life with every dancing flame," have on the tone of paragraph 5?

_____

_____

37. Which evidence from the passage BEST describes the man's need to build a fire?

    Ⓐ "He worked slowly and carefully, keenly aware of his danger."

    Ⓑ "His wet feet froze the faster, and his exposed fingers numbed the faster, though they had not yet begun to freeze."

    Ⓒ "They were coated with ice; the thick German socks were like sheaths of iron halfway to the knees; and the moccasin strings were like rods of steel all twisted and knotted as by some conflagration."

    Ⓓ "The old-timer had been very serious in laying down the law that no man must travel alone in the Klondike after fifty below."

38. In the excerpt, the narrator describes how the main character builds a fire. Think about something that you know how to do well (fishing, knitting, riding a bike, conducting a science experiment) and explain how to complete this task.

    _____

    _____

    _____

    _____

    _____

    _____

    _____

    _____

Directions: The sentence below is missing commas. Read the sentence. Then, rewrite the sentence on the lines provided, adding commas to separate the coordinate adjectives.

39. In order to get from the island to the shore, the family must take a long tedious boat ride through wild treacherous seas.

    _____

    _____

40. Upon arriving at the carnival, a clown scared the little girl.

    The sentence above has a dangling modifier. Fix the sentence on the lines below so that it makes sense. (You may have to omit/add words or change the order of the sentence.)

    _____

    _____

Directions: The paragraph below contains unnecessary words, phrases, or sentences. Read each sentence carefully. Then, rewrite the paragraph to eliminate the unnecessary language.

41. Rosie and Rebecca are identical twins and look alike. The twins used to do everything together but now that they are older they each want to be their own individual people. Their mother used to dress them alike in matching clothes but now they have unique personal senses of style. They used to have similar likes and enjoyed the same things. However, now they prefer different activities that are dissimilar to one another.

_____

_____

_____

42. The following is an example of which type of sentence?

Norman takes his children to the park every Wednesday afternoon.
   Ⓐ Simple
   Ⓑ Compound
   Ⓒ Complex
   Ⓓ Fragment

Directions: Read the paragraph below. Identify the meaning of the vocabulary word and then identify the context clues that helped you figure out your answer on the line provided.

The ceremony was a solemn and despondent affair. There was an air of sadness amongst the mourners who lined the sidewalk waiting to pay their respects. The little girl did not quite understand what was happening but taking her cue from the adults that surrounded her, she began to cry, sobbing loudly into her mother's coat sleeve.

43. What is the meaning of the word *despondent* in the first sentence?
   Ⓐ Quiet
   Ⓑ Celebratory
   Ⓒ Gloomy
   Ⓓ Angry

44. List three other words in the passage that helped you determine the meaning of despondent.

_____

Directions: Read the sentences below. First, identify the implication of the mythological allusion. Then, explain your answer on the lines provided below.

45. Which character attribute is alluded to in the following sentence?

    The boy's Zeus-like abilities helped him succeed in his task.
    - Ⓐ Strength
    - Ⓑ Honesty
    - Ⓒ Beauty
    - Ⓓ Wealth

46. Explain the mythological reference that helped you determine this aspect of the boy's character.

    _____

    _____

47. What is the meaning of the phrase "cry wolf" in the following sentence?

    The girl's mother dismissed her daughter's pleas for help, as she had a tendency to "cry wolf."
    - Ⓐ Violently cry in frustration and anger.
    - Ⓑ Pretend there is a problem when there is not in order to get attention.
    - Ⓒ Disguise one's self in order to avoid being blamed for a mistake.
    - Ⓓ Lie to get people to like you.

48. Explain the literary reference that helped you determine the meaning of the phrase.

    _____

    _____

49. My sister Nicole went to the softball practice. I had dance class at 4:15. My mother had to drive us both. We had to rush.

    On the lines provided, combine the clauses to form one sentence.

    _____

    _____

50. My little cousin tried to bake a cake for my grandmother's birthday bye himself but he used one cup of flower instead of too so it did not taste good.

    On the lines provided, rewrite the sentence, correcting the spelling mistakes.

    _____

    _____

(Answers are on page 104.)

ENGLISH LANGUAGE ARTS ANSWERS EXPLAINED

Reading: Literature

Citing Textual Evidence (RL.7.1), page 2

1. **D. She is easily bored.** In these paragraphs, it is implied that Alice is looking for something to do and that neither reading nor picking flowers is very appealing to her. The following information cited from the text, "Alice was beginning to get very tired of sitting by her sister on the bank, and of having nothing to do," supports the answer.

2. **B. She is curious and impulsive.** Although this is not explicitly stated in the passage, it can be inferred from the sentence, "In another moment down went Alice after it, never once considering how in the world she was to get out again," that by not thinking about the consequences of her action of jumping in after the rabbit into the hole, she makes quick and impulsive decisions. Also, because she quickly followed the rabbit into the hole, she must be interested in him and curious about where he is going.

3. **C. He is preoccupied and is unaware of the girl's presence.** Although this is not explicitly stated in the passage, details in the passage show he was in a hurry and was not paying attention to the young ladies.

4. **Possible answers:** Alice falls down the hole for a very long time ("Down, down, down. Would the fall *never* come to an end!"), the fall seemed to take her down for many miles ("I must be getting somewhere near the centre of the earth. Let me see: that would be four thousand miles down, I think—"), there were lamps in the hallway ("…she found herself in a long, low hall, which was lit up by a row of lamps hanging from the roof"), there are doors all around ("There were doors all round the hall, but they were all locked;"), the rabbit talked ("…and was just in time to hear it say, as it turned a corner, 'Oh my ears and whiskers, how late it's getting!'").

5. **Possible answers:** Alice was not very surprised to see a talking rabbit ("There was nothing so *very* remarkable in that; nor did Alice think it so *very* much out of the way to hear the Rabbit say to itself, 'Oh dear! Oh dear! I shall be late!'"), she pictures herself falling from the top of a house and she imagines how her family at home will think that she is brave ("'How brave they'll all think me at home! Why, I wouldn't say anything about it, even if I fell off the top of the house!'"), she envisions that she has fallen through the earth ('I wonder if I shall fall right *through* the earth! How funny it'll seem to come out among the people that walk with their heads downward!'), she imagines conversations with strangers ('Please, Ma'am, is this New Zealand or Australia?'), she has a pretend conversation with Dinah about cats eating bats and bats eating cats ('Dinah my dear! I wish you were down here with me! There are no mice in the air, I'm afraid, but you might catch a bat, and that's very like a mouse, you know. But do cats eat bats, I wonder?').

Finding the Theme and Central Ideas (RL.7.2), page 6

1. **A. One must not be easily persuaded by pride to believe what he/she knows to be false.** In this excerpt, Hans Christian Anderson's protagonist, the Emperor, learns that he must not let his vanity, or his love of looking good, make him believe the lies that he hears from the swindlers. He knows that he cannot see the so-called fine clothes that the swindlers pretend to be making but he acts as if he can so that he does not look bad.

2. **B. "'Really,' he said, turning to the weavers, 'your cloth has our most gracious approval;' and nodding contentedly he looked at the empty loom, for he did not like to say that he saw nothing."** The story's theme is that you should not let pride persuade you to believe

things that are not true and this sentence shows that the emperor did just that and ended up paying the price for it later on.

3. **B., C., E., and F.** These are the biggest, most important ideas in the text. Answer A is incorrect because there is no mention of the emperor actually waving at the crowd. Answers D and G are true but are minor details in the text.

4. **Answers**: 1. Two swindlers came to town to sell the emperor beautiful, but invisible clothes. 2. The emperor and his staff pretended that they could see the suit. 3. The clothes turned out to be invisible but no one wanted to tell the emperor. 4. A child at the parade was the only one to say that the emperor was not wearing clothes.

5. **A. The weavers are evil and should be punished for tricking the emperor and the townspeople** should not be included in an objective summary because it is an opinion. Answers B, C, and D are all main ideas in the reading and should be included.

6. **D. The Lie and the Invisible Suit** This answer is correct because it focuses on the emperor and his people's lies to protect their own pride.

Analyzing Setting and Character (RL.7.3), page 12

1. **C. She is surprised and happy.** "The little girl gave a cry of amazement and looked about her, her eyes growing bigger and bigger at the wonderful sights she saw." Students may be distracted by answer A because the word *cry* is in the above sentence. Answer B is incorrect because although Dorothy is confused and shocked, she is not angry.

2. **D. She is not used to such natural beauty and is appreciative of her surroundings.** The sentence, "A little way off was a small brook, rushing and sparkling along between green banks, and murmuring in a voice very grateful to a little girl who had lived so long on the dry, gray prairies," helps give a clue to the answer. Students should understand that this contrast in setting demonstrates that Dorothy is astounded by the beauty around her because it is so different than where she lives.

3. **Possible answers:** "Therefore we still have witches and wizards amongst us," or "The feet

of the dead Witch had disappeared entirely, and nothing was left but the silver shoes," or "'The Witch of the East was proud of those silver shoes,' said one of the Munchkins, 'and there is some charm connected with them; but what it is we never knew.'"

4. **B. Innocent and curious.** Dorothy is innocent and believes what the good witch tells her without too much convincing.

5. **Possible answers:** "Dorothy was an innocent, harmless little girl, who had been carried by a cyclone many miles from home; and she had never killed anything in all her life," or "Dorothy listened to this speech with wonder," or "Dorothy was going to ask another question, but just then the Munchkins, who had been standing silently by, gave a loud shout and pointed to the corner of the house where the Wicked Witch had been lying."

6. **C. She is upset by the possibility of not being able to return home.** It is important to understand that is only when the good witch tells Dorothy that she will have to live with them that she gets upset. Answer A is wrong because Dorothy does appreciate the beauty of the new setting. Answer B is incorrect because she calls the people strange but she is not afraid of them. The author does mention that she is lonely but since Toto is with her, D is incorrect.

Word Meaning and Figurative Language (RL.7.4), page 18

1. **A. Depressing.** Based on the tone of the rest of the passage, students should use context clues to help them decide the meaning.

2. **A., C., and E.** The words *dreary*, *gloomy*, and *mournful* are synonyms of melancholy and add to the depressing tone of the paragraph.

3. **B. To emphasize the gloomy tone of the paragraph.** It is important to understand that the overall tone of the paragraph is sad and that is why the author repeats this word.

4. **D. Personification.** "The fog and frost so hung about the black old gateway of the house, that it seemed as if the Genius of the Weather sat in mournful meditation on the threshold" is an example of personification because it gives

humanlike qualities to unliving things. Weather cannot sit or be in mournful meditation because it is not alive. A *simile* compares two things using *like* or *as* and *metaphors* make comparisons without *like* or *as*. *Onomatopoeia* is a word that imitates a sound.

5. **Answer should be something like:** It contributes to the depressing and gloomy tone of the passage. By using personification to describe the weather, it makes the weather seem mournful, which contributes to the overall tone.

6. B. **Negative.** The simile *like a bad lobster in a dark cellar* shows that the connotation is negative. The meanings of the words horrible and horror later in this paragraph show that dismal is not meant to be positive.

7. **Answer:** Scrooge was scared and this is a feeling that he is not familiar with. The word *startled* means *frightened* and the phrase, "a terrible sensation to which it had been a stranger from infancy" shows that he is not easily scared so this feeling is unfamiliar to him.

Analyzing Poetry (RL.7.5), page 22

1. C. **Love can sometimes be pleasant but temporary.** It is important to understand that love is described as pleasant from the words *floating* and *light*. Also, the phrase "as it floats by" shows that this love does not always last. Answer A is incorrect because the word *your* implies that the reader is involved. Answers B and D are incorrect because the question asks specifically about the first stanza of the poem.

2. A. *Fluttering* has a positive connotation because it suggests a gentle flying and is usually associated with harmless creatures.

3. **Possible answers:** There is a positive connotation or feeling in the last stanza of the poem. The words *warm*, *cozy*, *supportive*, and *protecting* help the reader to understand that love should be kind and comfortable. Also, the speaker uses the words *should be* in the last stanza rather than *can be* as used in the first three stanzas.

4. **Answer:** A, B, A, B, C, D, C, D, E, F, E, F, G, G. This is the traditional rhyme scheme of an English or Shakespearian sonnet. There are

fourteen lines in this type of poem. The first line rhymes with the third, the second with the fourth, etc. and the last two lines rhyme with each other.

5. **Answer:** The first eight lines of the poem discuss the problems with summer and how the season fades away. Lines 9–12 focus on how the object of the speaker's affection has a lasting beauty. The last two lines of the poem show how the speaker believes that his love will always be beautiful in his eyes.

6. B. **The weather is not perfect or lasting.** The sonnet describes the summer as imperfect and fleeting. The speaker does talk about wind and that summer can be too hot. Overall, however, Shakespeare uses these descriptors to convey that the season is not always perfect and fades away. Answers A, C, and D are incorrect.

7. D. **To show that she is more beautiful than summer and his love will last.** The comparison that Shakespeare makes here is to point out the imperfections of summer and show that his love for his lady is more perfect than a summer's day and will not end the way that the season does.

Characters' Point of View (RL.7.6), page 24

1. A. **First Person.** The excerpt is told from the character Bryce's point of view. The author uses the words *I, me,* and *we* to help demonstrate the first-person point of view.

2. **Possible answers:** Bryce does not like Julie Baker and finds her to be a nuisance. Some evidence to support this is, "All I've ever wanted was for Julie Baker to leave me alone. For her to back off—you know, just give me some *space*," "…half a decade of strategic avoidance and social discomfort," and "This was the beginning of my soon-to-become-acute awareness that the girl cannot take a hint. Of any kind."

3. The author uses rhetorical questioning to point out that Julie does not act in the appropriate way to the social cues that Bryce and his father provide for her.

4. **Possible answers:** Julie really likes Bryce and most likely has a crush on him. Some evidence to support this is, "The first day I met Bryce Loski,

I flipped. Honestly, one look at him and I became a lunatic. It's his eyes. Something in his eyes. They're blue, and framed in the blackness of his lashes, they're dazzling. Absolutely breathtaking," or "It's been over six years now, and I learned long ago to hide my feelings, but oh, those first days. Those first years! I thought I would die from wanting to be with him," and "I also remember that he and Bryce were wearing matching turquoise polo shirts, which was really cute. Really *nice*."

5. The exclamation points show that Julie is enthusiastic and excited about meeting Bryce.

6. **Answers will vary.** The rewrite should also convey an annoyance of Julie Baker but since the new narrator is an adult, the tone should be more mature and logical.

READING: INFORMATIONAL TEXT

Citing Evidence in Informational Text (RI.7.1), page 28

1. C. **"He is proud of his family and the life he has built."** In the excerpt, Jobs looks around at his family members and beyond them and states, "OH WOW. OH WOW. OH WOW."

   This implies that he is happy to be surrounded by his family and when he looks beyond them it can be inferred that he is proud of the life he has built as well. The evidence that best supports the answer is: *"He'd look at his sister Patty, then for a long time at his children, then at his life's partner, Laurene, and then over their shoulders past them." "Steve's final words were: 'OH WOW. OH WOW. OH WOW.'"*

2. **Possible answers:** "In the fiscal year that ended just before he died, Apple recorded sales of $108 billion, reflecting even faster growth than the year before. Nearly 24 cents of every $1 of sales was pure profit. Though his computers and smart phones were among the most expensive on the market, Apple had sold more than 72 million phones, more than 42 million iPods, 32 million iPads, and almost 17 million computers in one year."

3. **Possible answer:** "He put digital music and the Internet in our pockets in an elegant way, and he made our lives easier by insisting that every gadget Apple made—and thus, the gadgets that many others made in response—be simple and fun to use."

4. A. **"He created products that gave millions access to convenient technology."** Although Jobs was a good businessman, wealthy, and famous, answer A is the best choice because the excerpt focuses on his accomplishments with Apple products and *how* people react to his work. Quotes that support this answer are **"U2's Bono called Jobs 'the hardware software Elvis'"** and "In front of Apple's headquarters at One Infinite Loop in Cupertino, in front of Apple stores from San Francisco to New York to China, people came to pay their respects. They left apples, whole and bitten. They brought their iPhones and their iPads, with messages of sadness and appreciation."

5. **Possible answers:** He was helping to design Apple's new headquarters. ("He had been deeply involved in plans for Apple's new headquarters, going through design after design, and insisting that it include the apricot orchards that dotted the valley when he was a boy.") He was working on Apple TV. ("He had hoped Apple would figure out a better way to provide television to the masses.") He was working on improving access to digital textbooks. ("And realizing that many kids are no longer assigned lockers, he hoped to find a way to make textbooks more available electronically, perhaps selling iPads with textbooks already loaded.")

6. **Possible answers:** They will continue to create new products inspired by Steve Jobs' ideas. Steve Jobs' legacy will continue to live on in future products.

Finding Central Ideas (RI.7.2), page 30

1. A. **"Education"** and D. **"Friendship"** are the best answers. The excerpt focuses on Malala's love for her school, her drive to do well in school, and her friendship with Moniba.

2. **See answers above.**

3. **Possible answers:** "Because inside the Khushal School, we flew on wings of knowledge," "In a

country where women aren't allowed out in public without a man, we girls traveled far and wide inside the pages of our books," "In a land where many women can't read the prices in the markets, we did multiplication," "In a place where, as soon as we were teenagers, we'd have to cover our heads and hide ourselves from the boys who'd been our childhood playmates, we ran as free as the wind," "All we wanted was a chance to learn in peace. And that is what we did," and "Inside, we could be who we were."

4. **D. "The restrictions of women in the outside world did not limit Malala's educational experience in her school."** Paragraph 6 focuses on how although women had to follow certain rules and had few rights in her society, she was free to learn in school.

5. **Possible answers:** "She was my best friend, bookish like me, almost like my twin," "We sat together whenever we could—on the bus, at recess, in the classroom—and she made me laugh as no one else could," and "Then she would make a funny face, and we'd fall apart laughing and forget our differences."

6. **C. "To explain that Malala realizes that she needs to work hard to succeed."** After getting upset about coming in second place at school and after talking with her father, Malala realizes that she needs to work hard in order to succeed.

7. **Answers will vary.** Students should include details about Malala's school and her friendship with Moniba. In addition, the summary should be written in a logical order and the summary should not contain any opinions.

Connecting Events, Ideas, and Individuals (RI.7.3), page 34

1. B. **"She is feeling a lot of pressure from the segregationists."** This is the best answer because in the first sentence of the paragraph, it describes how the segregationists' campaign is getting stronger. The excerpt also states later that the narrator knows that Mrs. Huckaby must be under a lot of pressure.

2. **Possible answers:** In the beginning of the passage, the narrator is excited about the upcoming school production and seems happy. However,

as the passage continues, she becomes more frustrated about school. She wants to be included in the school play at the beginning of the passage but by the end of the excerpt, she realizes that she is on her own.

3. **Possible answers:** The author includes details about the segregationists' campaign: "Sign-carrying, card-dispensing, tripping, kicking crusaders revved up their efforts to reduce our numbers to zero," and shows Mrs. Huckaby's dismissive attitude toward the narrator that is responsible for the narrator's shift in attitude.

4. D. **"I supposed she must be under an enormous weight and doing her best."** Answers A, B, and C are all evidence from the text regarding Mrs. Huckaby but talk about events that occurred rather than the narrator's attitude toward her.

5. **Possible answers:** This shows that the author has not been included before and is feeling left out. She thought that she had made peace with the fact that she has been left out but is upset that it is happening again.

Word Meaning and Figurative Language in Informational Text (RI.7.4), page 36

1. A. "**Alert.**" Based on the words in the rest of the paragraph that show that the dog was attentive, students should use context clues to help them decide the meaning.

2. A., D., **and** E. The words **"ready," "attention,"** and **"scanning"** show that the dog is alert and aware of his surroundings.

3. D. **"Adverb."** In the excerpt, the word keenly is used to describe alert which is an adjective that describes the dog's expression. Words that describe adjectives are adverbs.

4. B. **"To emphasize the dog's size and aggressiveness."**

5. **Possible answers:** The comparison of the dog's fur color to a "spit-polished dress boot" helps give a visual reference for the reader to understand the color black but it also relates to the overall passage because the dog has been trained for a branch of the military—the navy SEALs.

6. C. **"Fight."** The dog received a mark or injury from this scuffle so students should understand that he got this injury in a fight. Since "shuffle" and "hurry" are also definitions of the word scuffle, students may be distracted by answers A and B.

Text Structure (RI.7.5), page 38

1. C. **"A new beginning for electric cars"** The information for the cars currently on the market is located under the third heading. Students can find this answer by going back to the text.

2. **Possible answers:** The author uses the headings to describe the timeline and process of development of electric cars. The first two sections of the text describe how rising gas prices and environmental concerns contributed to the development of electric cars. The third talks more about the development and the last section discusses the future of electric cars.

3. A. **"The Development of Electric Cars Begins"** is the best answer.

4. The author discusses the first electric cars and how they have developed over time.

5. A. **"It shows that the success of electric cars is uncertain, just as their development has been"** is the best answer because it links the slow development of successful electric cars to the uncertain future success of the vehicles.

Determining the Author's Point of View (RI.7.6), page 42

1. C. **"You should save some of the money that you are gifted or have earned for big purchases you want to make down the road."** Although the author does mention that using coin machines is a way to count change, the author also warns us that there is a fee associated with the service. In addition, the author states that credit and debit cards are convenient, but that these cards do come with costs and risks. The author also warns the reader that giving away passwords, especially over the Internet can be very dangerous.

2. **See answers in number 1.**

3. **Possible answer:** This shows that the author feels very strongly about putting money into a savings account.

4. B. **"The owner of a retail store"** is the best answer because owners of stores would want you to spend money in their establishment. Students should take care to notice the word *disagree* in the question and not choose people that are likely to agree with the article's advice. Parents generally want their children to be smart about money decisions, a financial advisor would give similar advice to what is written in the article, and a loan officer at a college is likely to respect smart money choices made by candidates looking to seek financial assistance. Therefore, these answers can be dismissed.

5. **Answers will vary.** The rewrite should encourage teens to want to spend money at retail establishments because the owner of the store has an opposite point of view than the original author of the piece.

Tracing and Evaluating Arguments (RI.7.8), page 46

1. B. **"Dogs and other animals do, in fact, experience time."** The author does question whether or not dogs have the same feelings about time as humans do and asks if dogs can experience a day in the first paragraph so answers A and D may be distracting to students. The overall claim that the author is making and working to prove throughout the excerpt, however, is that dogs do experience time.

2. **Answer:** In the opening paragraph the author poses the question of whether or not dogs experience the passage of time and then answers affirmatively. **"Animals exist in time, they use time; but so they experience time? Surely, they do."** The author does not write the claim as a pointed statement but it is important to recognize that when she answers her own question, she is actually making a claim.

3. **Possible answers:** "We organize the dog's day in parallel with ours, providing landmarks and

surrounding them with ritual," "For instance, we provide all sorts of cues for when the dog's mealtime is," "We head for the kitchen or pantry," "It may be our mealtime, too, so we begin to load the refrigerator, wafting food smells about, and making a racket with pots and plates," and "If we glance at the dog and coo a little, any remaining ambiguity is erased."

4. D. **"Dogs have a SCN that coordinates wakefulness, hunger, and sleep."** This evidence is the strongest because it is more scientific than the other answers. Although answer C is factual, it does not specifically address the author's claim. Answer A reflects an opinion so it is not strong evidence. Answer B is true but offers no proof to back up the author's claim.

5. **Possible answers:** The author uses real life examples of how dogs act to make her points. Some examples are "When he moves to the door, it's precisely the time to go out," "When he moves to the kitchen, sure enough, it's time to be fed," and "The dog still knows when it's time to eat."

6. A. **"Included quotes from scientific experts about the topic."** This is the best answer because it would offer solid evidence from an expert about how dogs' brains and bodies work allowing them to experience time.

7. **If students answer Yes**; they should provide specific information from the excerpt to back up their answer. **If students answer No;** they should give specific reasons why and cite what is missing from the excerpt that would prove the claim.

Comparing and Contrasting Author Presentations (RI.7.9), page 48

1. B. **"That she had to smuggle goods and Jews."** The narrator expresses disbelief that she has become someone who is capable of doing such things.

2. **Possible answers:** The narrator cannot believe that the Jewish people are being treated so poorly and is also surprised by her willingness to get involved, as it could be risky for her.

3. **Possible answers:** "A look over my shoulder showed the way was clear behind me." She also filled the wagon with hay for the escapees to hide under. This shows that she went to great lengths to help her friends even though it was not convenient and she could get into trouble if they were caught. Ultimately, it demonstrates that she feels that saving the lives of the innocent is important.

4. **Possible answer:** It reveals that she feels guilty for leaving her friends behind and not being able to do more to protect them.

5. **Answers will vary.** This point of view should include details about how the escapee sees, thinks, and feels during the escape and include details that are different from the original narrator. Examples would be; how he is feeling while waiting for the wagon, what it is like to be hiding under the hay, and how he feels when the wagon leaves him behind in the woods.

6. **Possible answers:** Anne's point of view is different because she is nervous about escaping whereas Irene Gut Opdyke is the one helping others escape. Anne mentions that she cries, packs memories that are important to her, and rushes to escape quickly and safely.

7. **Possible answers:** They do not open the door to anyone who is not their father. And they are quiet on the stairs. It is important to include these details because it shows how scared they were and how dangerous the situation was.

8. **Answers will vary.** The new account should include details about what it is like smuggling goods and people into the new hiding spot. It should also include details about what she is thinking and feeling.

Argument Writing (W.7.1), page 54

Students should use the following rubric to assess their success in answering the prompts for argument writing on page 54 of the workbook.

Rubric for Argument Writing

	Advanced	Proficient	Needs Improvement
Claims/ Organization	Introduces strong, clear claims, and acknowledges opposing claims. The reasoning and evidence is organized logically.	Claims are introduced but the writer does not acknowledge opposing claims. There are reasons and evidence in the essay but they are not organized logically.	Claims and opposing claims are not clear. The evidence and reasoning is weak and not clearly organized.
Support	Claims are fully supported with logical reasoning and relevant evidence. Uses accurate, credible sources. Demonstrates a clear understanding of the topic.	Claims are only generally supported with reasoning and relevant evidence. Uses weak sources. Demonstrates a limited understanding of the topic.	Claims are not fully supported with logical reasoning and relevant evidence. Does not use any accurate, credible sources. Does not demonstrate understanding of the topic.
Transitions	Uses transition words and phrases to organize ideas. The relationships between claims, reasoning, and evidence are clear.	Uses some transition words and phrases to organize ideas. The relationships between claims, reasoning, and evidence are somewhat clear.	Does not use transition words and phrases to organize ideas. The relationships between claims, reasoning, and evidence are unclear.
Style	Demonstrates full command of the conventions of English grammar and usage.	There are some mistakes in the conventions of English grammar and usage.	There are many mistakes in the conventions of English grammar and usage.
Conclusion	Provides a strong concluding statement or section. The conclusion supports the argument presented.	Provides a partial concluding statement or section. The conclusion somewhat supports the argument presented.	Does not provide a concluding statement or section. The conclusion does not support the argument presented.

Students should use the following rubric to assess their success in answering the prompts for informational writing on page 60 of the workbook.

Rubric for Informational Writing

	Advanced	Proficient	Needs Improvement
Ideas/ Organization	The topic is clearly introduced. Ideas, concepts, and/or information are organized logically.	The topic is somewhat clear. There are ideas, concepts, and/or information present in the essay but they are not organized logically.	The topic is not clear. The ideas, concepts, and/or information are weak and not clearly organized.
Development	The topic is fully developed with relevant facts, definitions, concrete details, and/or quotations.	The topic is only somewhat developed with relevant facts, definitions, concrete details, and/or quotations.	The topic is not developed. The piece does not include relevant facts, definitions, concrete details, and/or quotations.
Transitions	Uses transition words and phrases to organize ideas. The relationships between ideas and concepts are clear.	Uses some transition words and phrases to organize ideas. The relationships between ideas and concepts are somewhat clear.	Does not use transition words and phrases to organize ideas. The relationships between ideas and concepts are unclear.
Style	Demonstrates full command of the conventions of English grammar and usage.	There are some mistakes in the conventions of English grammar and usage.	There are many mistakes in the conventions of English grammar and usage.
Conclusion	Provides a strong concluding statement or section. The conclusion supports the information or explanation presented.	Provides a partial concluding statement or section. The conclusion somewhat supports the information or explanation presented.	Does not provide a concluding statement or section. OR The conclusion does not support the information or explanation presented.

ENGLISH LANGUAGE ARTS ANSWERS EXPLAINED

Students should use the following rubric to assess their success in answering the prompts for narrative writing on page 62 of the workbook.

	Advanced	Proficient	Needs Improvement
Introduction/ Organization	Narrators/characters, point of view, and context are clearly established. The sequence of events unfolds naturally and logically.	Narrators/characters, point of view, and context are somewhat established. The sequence of events only somewhat unfolds naturally and logically.	Narrators/characters, point of view, and context are not clearly established. The sequence of events does not unfold naturally or logically.
Narrative Techniques	The narrative includes effective dialogue, pacing, and description to develop experiences, events, and/or characters.	The dialogue, pacing, and description is somewhat effective in developing experiences, events, and/or characters.	The dialogue, pacing, and description do not develop experiences, events, and/or characters. OR There is no dialogue or description. OR The pacing is inappropriate for the essay.
Transitions	Uses transition words and phrases to organize ideas. The sequence of events and transitions in setting or time are clear and effective.	Uses some transition words and phrases to organize ideas. The sequence of events and transitions in setting or time are only somewhat clear and/or effective.	Does not use transition words and phrases to organize ideas. The sequence of events and transitions in setting or time are unclear and/or ineffective.
Word Choice	Uses precise words and phrases, relevant descriptive details, and sensory language to capture the action and convey experiences and events.	Uses only some precise words and phrases, relevant descriptive details, and sensory language to capture the action and convey experiences and events.	Does not use OR uses very few precise words and phrases, relevant descriptive details, and sensory language to capture the action and convey experiences and events.
Conclusion	Provides a strong concluding statement or section. The conclusion supports or reflects upon the narrated experiences or events.	Provides a partial concluding statement or section. The conclusion somewhat supports or reflects upon the narrated experiences or events.	Does not provide a concluding statement or section. OR The conclusion does not support or reflect upon the narrated experiences or events.

1. Students should keep in mind that they are addressing an authority figure in the e-mail. Therefore, the body of the e-mail should be somewhat formal. In addition, remember that this e-mail is persuasive and include the purpose and benefits of the trip in the e-mail. An e-mail is an electronic correspondence so it should be written in letter format and include a greeting, closing statement, and a signature. Be sure to include a subject line that establishes the purpose of the e-mail.

2. This is a friendly letter so it should include all of the following in the format: a heading with a return address, the date, a greeting, body paragraphs that state your purpose and intent, a closing, and a signature. The letter is to a potential employer so keep the tone and language somewhat formal. Be sure to list and explain the strengths that you will bring to the job if you were to get the position you are applying for. (Good with children, good grades in school, and being responsible are all ideas for you to consider while writing.)

3. When writing a speech you want to make sure that the language flows and your purpose is clear and fully accomplished by the conclusion of the talk. This speech is to your peers so the tone can be less formal. However, also keep in mind that you are talking about a topic that is important to you and requires some attention from them to correct so make sure that your fellow students take your ideas seriously. You should establish your topic, explain why it is important, and give recommendations on how to fix the problem.

4. A newspaper book or movie review includes the following information: the title of the movie or book, the author of the book or the director, producer, main actors of the film, and some basic information about the plot and the characters. Be sure to give a brief overview about what the story or movie is about in the beginning of the review but no spoilers! Once your readers have a basic understanding of the main points of the book or film, you should begin a new paragraph and explain what specific things you got out of the work. Be sure that your opinions are clearly stated but also that you explain your reasons for those opinions. A good way to end the review is by stating your overall opinion of the work and offering a recommendation.

5. A blog is a less formal style of writing so language can be casual. Your audience is a group of younger students, many who are nervous about middle school and some who have limited English skills so make sure that your writing is clear and reader friendly to those with lower comprehension skills. Since the blog entry is explaining a typical day, it should be descriptive and written in chronological order. It may also be helpful to offer tips or advice to your readers.

Grammar and Usage (L.7.1), page 66

1. B. **"Compound."** The sentence includes two independent clauses and they are joined by a coordinator, "so."

2. A. **"Simple."** The sentence has a subject and expresses a complete thought. There is no coordinator and does not contain any other dependent or independent clauses.

3. C. **"Complex."** The sentence contains the dependent clause, "When she arrived at the airport." It is dependent on the rest of the sentence, "Sarah realized that she would miss her flight because she forgot her passport."

4. C. **"Complex."** The sentence contains the phrase, "After working in the garden." It is dependent on the beginning of the sentence, "Lisa washed her hands thoroughly."

5. **Possible answers:** The sentence should read, "My friend Michelle and I both wanted to go to the movies, but she wanted to see the new comedy and I wanted to see a horror movie." *or* "My friend Michelle and I both wanted to go to the movies, but she wanted to see the new comedy, whereas I wanted to see a horror movie."

6. **Possible answers:** "*Instead of doing her homework*, Amanda spent four hours reading her favorite book so she was unprepared for her Spanish test." *or* "Amanda spent four hours reading her favorite book *instead of doing her homework*, so she was unprepared for her Spanish test."

7. **Possible answers:** "The family vacation was a disaster because none of us remembered to pack warm clothes or boots" *or* "The vacation was a disaster because the family did not remember to pack warm clothes or boots."

8. **Possible answers:** "When I arrived at the museum, a painting caught my attention" *or* "A painting caught my attention as I arrived at the museum." The subject "I" needs to be included to clarify who/what arrived at the museum.

9. **Possible answers:** "The farmer proudly showed off his prize pumpkin, which weighed four hundred pounds, at the fair" *or* "The farmer proudly showed off his four hundred pound prize pumpkin at the fair." Who/what weighs four hundred pounds? In this case the pumpkin needs to be clarified.

10. **Possible answers:** "Though he was only fourteen years old, the university offered José a scholarship." *or* "Though José was only fourteen years old, the university offered him a scholarship." Who/what was only fourteen years old needs clarification. In this case it is José, not the university.

Capitalization, Punctuation, and Spelling (L.7.2), page 70

1. **The corrected sentence should read:** "Slippery, icy road conditions can make driving during a snowstorm dangerous."

   Slippery and icy both describe the same noun (road conditions) so they must be separated by a comma.

2. **The corrected sentence should read:** "The blond-haired, blue-eyed girl was wearing a striped wool sweater."

   Blond-haired and blue-eyed both describe the same noun (girl) so they must be separated by a comma. However, striped and wool should not be separated by a comma because striped actually modifies the wool sweater, not just the sweater.

3. **The corrected sentence should read:** "After Juan's teacher told his parents that he was a smart, hard-working student, they took him out for a delicious chocolate flavored ice cream cone."

   Smart and hard-working both describe the same noun (student) so they must be separated by a comma. However, delicious and chocolate flavored should not be separated by a comma because delicious actually modifies the chocolate flavored ice cream, not just the ice cream.

4. **The corrected sentence should read:** "I don't like to **waste** time so I do my homework within **one** hour of getting home from school.

   The word waist refers to the middle part of the body between the ribs and the hips, not the intended meaning of letting time get away from you as should be used in the sentence. The word won is the past tense of win which means to come in first or have a victory. Due to the context of the sentence, the word used should be spelled, "one," like the number.

5. **The corrected sentence should read:** "There was a **deer** in Billy's back yard, and it had the cutest white **tail**."

   The word dear means precious or cherished, not the animal. The word tale means a story and it should be spelled tail, which is the back part of the animal.

6. **The corrected sentences should read:** "When my little sister hurt her arm she was in a lot of **pain** so we took her to the doctor. He said that it was a **break** and put her arm in a cast so it would **heal** properly.

   Pane should be spelled pain to convey hurt. Brake should be spelled break to show that there was an injury where the bone split or cracked. Heel refers to the back part of the foot but a cast would help an injury get better, or heal.

Using Precise Language (L.7.3), page 72

1. **The corrected paragraph should read:** "Even though many of the girls on the school council had little in <u>common</u>, they were able to <u>cooperate</u> to plan the <u>school</u> dance. <u>Each</u> of them had a specific job to do and all of them did their part to make the event a success.

   The phrase, *with each other* in the first sentence can be eliminated because saying that they had little in common fully expresses the idea. The word, *together,* also in the first sentence can be taken out as well. Cooperate implies that they worked together so it does not need to be clarified further. The whole second sentence, *They worked well with one another*, can be eliminated because it is essentially repeating what has already been stated in the first sentence. The words, *and every one,* can be removed from the third sentence. Using the word, *Each*, is enough to convey the idea.

2. **The corrected paragraph should read:** It is my opinion that school lunch periods should last longer. For example, if lunch starts at noon, instead of ending twenty minutes later, it should last forty-five minutes. It is a fact that many children do not have time to eat and digest their lunch in such a short time period. In the future, I hope that educational leaders will come to a consensus and the result will be longer lunch times for students.

The word *personal* can be eliminated from the first sentence. It is enough to say my opinion. Also the phrase, *a longer period of time*, can be condensed to one word: longer. There is no need to use both words, *twelve noon*. Noon can stand on its own. Also, the phrase, *twenty minutes later at 12:20*, should become twenty minutes later and the phrase, *last forty-five minutes and end at 12:45* should become *last forty-five minutes*. In the third sentence, *true fact* should just be fact. All facts are true so there is no need to include the word true. In the fourth sentence, the words *to come* can be eliminated and so future should just be used. Also in the last sentence, *of opinion*, can be taken out; consensus is enough. In addition the word, *end*, can be eliminated before the word result. It is implied that the result usually comes at the end of something.

3. **The corrected paragraph should read:** We had a test in History class today. During the test, we couldn't talk. I was worried that I might get something wrong but I wrote down all of the answers until my paper was filled. When we were finished answering the questions, there was a bonus question at the end.

The word *History* should only be used one time in the first sentence. In the second sentence *the course of* is redundant and should be eliminated. In the second sentence, *couldn't talk* is sufficient. In the third sentence, *possibly* is not needed with the word might. Might indicates probability so possibly does not need to be included. Also in the

third sentence, *to capacity*, should be omitted. Something filled is done to capacity, so describing something as "filled to capacity" is repetitive. In the last sentence *completely* and *added* should be eliminated. When something is finished, it is completed and a bonus indicated that something has been added. Therefore both of these words are redundant.

4. **The corrected paragraph should read:** I have a dilemma to solve. My dance recital is on the same day as my flute concert. I do not want to disappoint my choreographer or my music teacher. I know I have to make a decision soon but I wish I could postpone my decision.

In the first sentence, *problematic* should be omitted because it is understood that there is a problem if there is a dilemma. In the second sentence *very* should not be included because same does not need to be further clarified. The third sentence, *The recital and concert are on the same day so this is a big problem*, is a repetition of the first two sentences and should be eliminated. In the fourth sentence, the phrases *who taught me dance* and *who taught me the flute music* can be eliminated because it is not necessary to clarify what the teachers did. It should be understood that the choreographer created the dance and that the music teacher helped teach the music. In the last sentence, *definite* can be eliminated because decisions are definite, *in the near future* should be omitted because soon and in the near future have the same meaning, and *until later* is implied in the word postpone so these phrases are redundant.

5. **The corrected paragraph should read:** I love my new house. I want to live here forever. Moving was a surprise but I finally have my own room. I can decorate it exactly the way I always wanted to. The living room is so big that we could add a couch if we wanted to. I never did have a yard and now mine is big enough to play games with my friends. I am truly happy here.

It is redundant to use *love* and *adore* so choose only one of the verbs to include in the first sentence. In the second sentence *and ever* should be eliminated because it is repetitive. In the third sentence, *unexpected* should not be included because surprises are not expected.

Also in the third sentence, the phrase *that I don't have to share* does not need to be included because it is extraneous. It is enough to say *my own*. The word *same* should be omitted from the fourth sentence because exactly and the same are synonyms. The phrase *an additional* can be taken out of the fifth sentence. Add shows that there is something additional without clarification. In the sixth sentence, *before* is unnecessary and redundant. Really and truly are synonyms so only one of these words should be included in the last sentence.

Defining Unknown Words (L.7.4), page 74

1. B. **"Verb."** The word shows action because it affects Emma.

2. C. **"Trouble."** The sentence shows that Emma has little that can bother or trouble her.

3. **Possible answers:** Comfortable, happy, and blessings are all context clues because they show the opposite meaning of vex. Also, distress is a context clue because it has a similar meaning.

4. A. **"Noun."** Governess identifies a person in this sentence. Therefore it is a noun.

5. D. **"A woman who is employed to take charge of a child's upbringing"**

6. C. **"Of, pertaining to, or like a chief."** The word chiefly is used as an adverb in the sentence. Therefore the definition for the adjective form of the word is incorrect.

ENGLISH LANGUAGE ARTS PRACTICE TEST, page 76

1. A. Students should choose **"He tricked him by breaking his front legs and knocking him down."** In the sixth paragraph, Buck breaks Spitz's legs one at a time which causes him to become weak and then Buck is able to knock the dog down with his shoulder. Students should be able to cite directly from the text to support their answer.

2. B. **"He will become a leader of the other dogs because they will respect and fear him."** Although this is not implicitly stated in the pas-

sage, students should infer that by defeating this worthy adversary, the other dogs may be fearful of the champion and that he will gain the respect from the pack. Also, the sentence, "Buck stood and looked on, the successful champion, the dominant primordial beast who had made his kill and found it good," implies that Buck will have power (domination) over the other dogs.

3. A. **"One must be strong of both body and mind to survive in the wild."** In this excerpt, Buck learns that he must use both his strength and his intelligence to defeat his enemy. He not only possessed a powerful physical strength but also was quick-witted enough to change tactics in order to weaken his enemy and gain an advantage in the fight. The sentences, "He fought by instinct, but he could fight by head as well he rushed, as though attempting the old shoulder trick, but at the last instant swept low to the snow and in. His teeth closed on Spitz's left fore leg. There was a crunch of breaking bone, and the white dog faced him on three legs," imply that Buck used his brain as well as his body to win the fight.

4. D. **"The harsh climate and geography of the Arctic require strength and cunning to survive."** The setting, the cold climate of the Arctic, is described in the first several paragraphs of the passage. London mentions "powdery snow" (paragraph one), "frosty air" (paragraph two), and "Across Canada and the Barrens" (paragraph three) to show us the harsh weather conditions. The fact that Buck wins the fight with Spitz demonstrates Buck's mastery. Also, the last sentence of the passage shows that Buck was proud of his victory, "Buck stood and looked on, the successful champion, the dominant primordial beast who had made his kill and found it good."

5. **Answer:** The use of personification adds to the suspenseful tone of the passage. It adds imagery and the silence shows that the dogs were waiting for something to happen. It sets the scene for the big fight between the two dogs.

6. B. **"Relentless."** The fact that Buck does not stop attacking even though the other dog is about to fall and die shows that he does not give up. Students may be distracted by answer C because the word mercy is used in the following sentence, however, by using context clues, students should

understand that this is an antonym for the word inexorable.

7. D. **"Mercy was a thing reserved for gentler climes. He maneuvered for the final rush."** These sentences show that Buck did not have any sympathy for Spitz and continued to fight him even though he was hurting and desperate.

8. **Possible answers:** They both think that they will win the fight. In paragraph 6, Spitz has the upper hand. Spitz is an experienced fighter and is a strong, fierce dog. Buck is new to fighting and has never been in a fight before. Also, Buck is hurt and Spitz is untouched. However, in paragraph 7, Buck now believes that *he* will win the fight because he is using his imagination. He begins to gain the upper hand when he tricks Spitz by swooping low and breaking his leg.

9. C. **"But Buck possessed a quality that made for greatness—imagination. He fought by instinct, but he could fight by head as well he rushed, as though attempting the old shoulder trick, but at the last instant swept low to the snow and in."** These sentences indicate that while Spitz was previously winning the fight, Buck began to gain the upper hand by using his imagination and intelligence.

10. The summary should include only details from the passage and no opinions. Students should describe what prompted the fight between Buck and Spitz, how the other dogs reacted to the fight, the fight itself, and the results of the fight.

11. Students should use the Narrative Writing rubric as a guide for the story.

12. **Answer:** A, A, B, B, C, C, D, D. This is the traditional couplet rhyme scheme where two lines rhyme with one another and then the next two rhyme, and so on.

13. B. **"Nothing can stay pure forever."** The poet writes about how youth and innocence are fleeting.

14. D. **"Color."** In the first line, the poet uses "green" and "gold" as clues to the meaning of the word hue, which is found in the second line.

15. **Answers will vary.** All of the types of figurative language listed in parentheses are present in the poem. Students should identify the type of figurative language they chose and explain how

it contributes to the meaning. For example, the personification in the last line, "Nothing gold can stay," is used to convey that nothing stays in its purest form forever.

16. **Possible answers:** "By 1774, it seemed to the leaders of the revolutionary movement that there was 'a settled, fixed plan for *enslaving* the colonies, or bringing them under arbitrary government,'" "John Dickenson had written, '*Those who are taxed* without their consent… are *slaves*,' And "Josiah Quincy exclaimed, 'I speak it with grief—I speak it with anguish—Britons are our oppressors… we are slaves.'" "George Washington similarly expressed his conviction that the English government was 'endeavoring by every piece of art and despotism to fix the shackles of slavery upon us.'" All of these are quotes from the text that show that the patriots felt as though they were being treated like slaves.

17. D. **"It was a sensitive subject for the colonists to say they were enslaved when many owned slaves."** Answer A could be a distracter because the paragraph does state that there was slavery in colonial life. Although the paragraph alludes to the fact that some people thought that slaves deserve freedom, it is not explicitly stated in the passage until later paragraphs so answer B is incorrect. The word *rant* is also used in the paragraph so students could be distracted by answer C.

18. **Answers:** Rhode Island, Connecticut, Delaware, and Pennsylvania. Massachusetts also tried to make efforts to abolish slavery but they were vetoed by the governor.

19. A. **"To demonstrate that she believes that everyone has a right to freedom, even slaves."** Abigail Adams never comes out and says that she is not a slave owner so answer B is incorrect. The word *robbed* is used in the quote so students may be distracted by answer C.

20. **Answer:** The idea of the white Southerners being treated as poorly as their slaves scared them.

21. C. **"Dilemma."** Students should use context clues to help them determine that the word *plight* means *problem* or *dilemma*.

22. **Answer:** A textbook would stick to factual information about the Revolutionary War and most likely not offer opinions about slavery.

Most current textbooks also focus on the outcome of the war as positive and would not bring the negative view about slavery into their informational writing.

23. **B. "To emphasize that people believed they were enslaved by the British."** Although the ideas are repeated, students could be distracted by answer D, but that is not the author's main purpose.

24. **Answers will vary:** Students may write about how no one likes to have their rights taken away, how colonists felt mistreated, or the negative connotation behind the word *slavery* that ultimately drove the patriots to fight against British oppression.

25. If students agree that the colonists were enslaved, then they should cite evidence from the article that supports their opinion, especially from the first and last paragraphs of the excerpt. If students disagree with the statement, then the focus of their writing should be about how the colonists had freedoms that slaves did not have and so were not truly enslaved.

26. **C. "The Statue of Liberty."**

27. **Possible answers:** "A mighty woman with a torch," "From her beacon-hand/Glows world-wide welcome"; and "I lift my lamp beside the golden door!" These show that the structure is in the female form and that she is holding a torch in her hand just as the Statue of Liberty does.

28. The poet's use of personification shows that the structure is used as a symbol of welcoming immigrants to the United States.

29. **A. "She feels that she represents hope."**

30. **Answer:** Poems will vary but students should include all of the relevant information about their landmark. Students should also consider their audience of peers and teacher while writing.

31. **Answer:** Based on the fact that the character has wet shoes, socks, and feet, students should infer that he has either stepped in or fallen into cold water. It is also possible that students may infer that the snowy conditions have caused the character's feet to become wet.

32. **A. "Flowed."** Using context clues, students should be able to determine that the meaning of the word ebbed means traveled or flowed as

the warm blood moved down and away from the man's body.

33. **D. "Dangerous."** The extremely cold temperatures should indicate that the climate is dangerous for humans because they could freeze.

34. **Possible answers:** "But it was surprising, the rapidity with which his cheeks and nose were freezing," "And he had not thought his fingers could go lifeless in so short a time," "Lifeless they were, for he could scarcely make them move together to grip a twig, and they seemed remote from his body and from him," and "When he touched a twig, he had to look and see whether or not he had hold of it." All of these provide evidence that the negative temperatures have a threatening effect on the man.

35. **D. "He should not have built his fire underneath the spruce tree."** It is the location of the fire, under the spruce tree, that causes the fire to go out. Snow from the branches above extinguishes the fire.

36. **Answer:** The use of onomatopoeia (*snapping*, *crackling*) brings the fire to life. This use of language is meant to affect the reader because he or she should be able to visualize the fire and imagine feeling a sense of warmth. In addition, the use of personification (*promising life with every dancing flame*) has a positive connotation that shows that the character is feeling hopeful about the comfort and safety that the fire will bring to him.

37. **B. "His wet feet froze the faster, and his exposed fingers numbed the faster, though they had not yet begun to freeze."** The other evidence does not directly show the danger that the character was in.

38. **Answer:** Students should use the rubric for Informational Writing as a guide to complete this writing task.

39. **The corrected sentence should read:** "In order to get from the island to the shore, the family must take a long, tedious boat ride through wild, treacherous seas."

The words *long* and *tedious* both describe the same noun (*boat ride*) so they must be separated by a comma. In addition, *wild* and *treacherous* both describe *the seas* and should also be separated by a comma.

40. **Possible answers:** "When the little girl arrived at the carnival, a clown scared her." *or* "A clown scared the little girl as she arrived at the carnival." The subject *the little girl* needs to be included to clarify who/what arrived at the carnival.

41. **The corrected paragraph should read:** Rosie and Rebecca are identical twins. The twins used to do everything together but now that they are older they each want to be individual people. Their mother used to dress them in matching clothes but now they have unique senses of style. They used to have similar likes. However, now they prefer different activities.

   It is redundant to use *identical* and *who look alike* so choose only one of the descriptions to include in the first sentence. In the second sentence *their own* and *individual* have the same meaning so only one of the phrases should be used. In the third sentence, *alike* and *in matching clothes* have the same meaning so one can be eliminated. Similarly, *unique* and *personal* have the same meaning so only choose one to use here. In the fourth sentence, choose between *have similar likes* or *enjoyed the same things.* The word *different* or the phrase *activities that are dissimilar to each other* should be omitted from the fourth sentence because it is redundant to use both.

42. A. **"Simple."** The sentence has a subject and expresses a complete thought. There is no coordinator and does not contain any other dependent or independent clauses.

43. C. Students should choose *gloomy*. The paragraph describes a sad and gloomy occasion.

44. Some of the words that contribute to the meaning of despondent are *solemn*, *sadness*, *mourners*, *cry*, and *sobbing*.

45. A. **Strength** is the most appropriate answer.

46. **Answer:** The above allusion refers to Zeus, King of the gods, who possessed great physical strength. He was deemed the most powerful of the gods.

47. B. **"Pretend there is a problem when there is not in order to get attention"** is the most appropriate answer.

48. **Answer:** The above allusion is from the popular fairytale "The Boy Who Cried Wolf." In the tale, the main character repeatedly reports that a wolf has come to attack the village's flock of sheep. However, this was not true. After several such incidences, the townsfolk stopped believing the young boy so when a real wolf does come, no one believes him and the wolf attacks.

49. **The corrected sentence should read:** My sister Nicole went to the softball practice and I had dance class at 4:15, and since my mother had to drive us both, we had to rush.

50. **The corrected sentence should read:** My little cousin tried to bake a cake for my grandmother's birthday by himself but he used one cup of flour instead of two so it did not taste good.

MATH

The Common Core mathematics standards are created to be building blocks between grade levels. The concepts learned in grades 5 and 6 are foundational skills necessary for students to master grade 7 concepts. This allows teachers to make sure that achievement gaps are closed and that students have prior knowledge to continue their learning with more challenging concepts. The Common Core Standards in grade 6 allow students to connect ratio and rates to whole number multiplication and division as well as learn to divide fractions. New to students in grade 6 is the introduction of negative numbers, writing and solving expressions and equations, and statistical thinking. Concepts in grade 7 mathematics extend student schemata to include more advanced work with rates, proportions, and rational numbers. Seventh-grade students also explore more advanced geometric concepts and extend their knowledge of statistics to include making inferences based on two sets of data distributions. New to students in grade 7 is the introduction of probability and the advanced use of algebra in geometric concepts.

UNIT RATES

RP.A.1 Compute unit rates associated with ratios of fractions, including ratios of lengths, areas, and other quantities measured in like or different units.

1. Which of the following represents a unit rate for average speed of travel?
   - Ⓐ 40 miles in 50 minutes
   - Ⓑ 7 kilometers in 3 minutes
   - Ⓒ 250 meters per second
   - Ⓓ 502,080 feet in 2 days

2. Jim needs to move his firewood from his truck to the wood pile at his house. He estimates that he will move $\frac{1}{8}$ of the total wood in 45 minutes. Which unit rate can he use to help him plan how long it will take for him to move all the firewood?
   - Ⓐ $\frac{1}{6}$ of the wood in 1 hour
   - Ⓑ 0.25 of the wood in 90 minutes
   - Ⓒ $\frac{2}{8}$ of the wood in $1\frac{1}{2}$ hours
   - Ⓓ 0.125 of the wood per 1 minute

3. A new electronics manufacturer is able to produce 144 microchips in 6 days. Which of the following unit rates cannot be used by the engineers to plan the amount of time it will take to produce an order of 80,000 microchips?
   - Ⓐ 24 microchips/day
   - Ⓑ 168 microchips in a week
   - Ⓒ 1 microchip per 1 hour
   - Ⓓ 3,333 in 1 year

4. Andrew collected data over the course of 2 weeks and determined that he runs on average 1.5 miles in about 15 minutes. He would like to run a marathon this summer and wanted to plan how long it would take him to complete the marathon, so he could plan a training program to build his endurance.

Part A. Determine a unit rate based on this data that Andrew can use to help plan his training program.

Part B. Using the unit rate you found in part A, determine the amount of time that Andrew should plan he will have to run if he competes in a 26-mile marathon.

Part C. Andrew decides to run through a park to practice before entering the marathon. He maps out his course and notices that his path appears to be in the shape of a trapezoid as shown below.

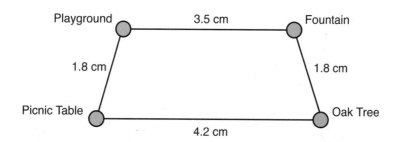

Determine how many full laps on his path he will need to run to practice for 26 miles if the map scale is 4 cm = 1,200 feet.

(Answers are on page 172.)

PROPORTIONAL
RELATIONSHIPS

RP.A.2 Recognize and represent proportional relationships between quantities. (See Appendix B for substandards 7.RP.A.2.a–2.d)

1. Kristyn babysits and was mixing baby formula to pour into a bottle using water and powdered milk. The baby drinks 250 ml of formula per bottle. It is important for the baby's health to make sure the formula is mixed in the correct proportions.

   The label on the back of the formula can had the following mixing directions:

Water	Formula powder
60 ml	8 g
100 ml	$13\frac{1}{3}$ g

   Which proportion would allow Kristyn to know how many grams to use to correctly make 250 ml of baby formula?

   Ⓐ $\dfrac{60}{8} = \dfrac{x}{250}$

   Ⓑ $\dfrac{2}{15} = \dfrac{x}{250}$

   Ⓒ $\dfrac{100}{3\frac{1}{3}} = \dfrac{250}{x}$

   Ⓓ $\dfrac{4}{60} = \dfrac{250}{x}$

2. On average, Jordan is able to collect money for 7 tolls in 2.5 minutes at a tollbooth on the interstate. Which equation can be used to calculate the number of tolls, t, Jordan can collect in a certain amount of minutes, m?

   Ⓐ $2.8m = t$ Ⓒ $m = 2.5t$

   Ⓑ $7m = t$ Ⓓ $m = 17.5t$

3. Which of the following graphs represents a proportional relationship?

Ⓐ
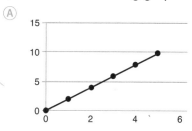

Ⓒ
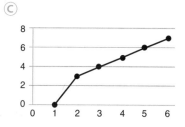

Ⓑ
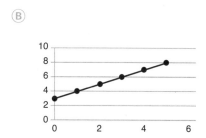

Ⓓ
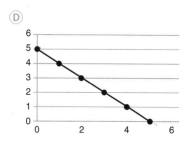

4. The graph below was made by a student who helps run the school store.

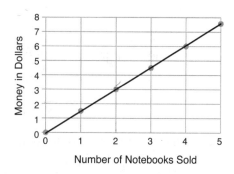

Part A. Describe what the point (2, 3) represents in the context of the graph?

Part B. What is the constant of proportionality represented by the graph? Explain the method that you used to determine this.

Part C. Write an equation that can represent the relationship between notebooks sold and the cost as shown in the graph.

5. Luke was trying to determine which vehicle gets the best gas mileage and each car manufacturer provided the information in a different format.

Vehicle A

$m = 35g$

Vehicle C

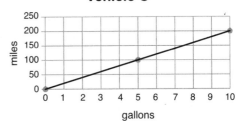

Vehicle B

Gallons	Miles
2	24
6	72
20	240

Vehicle D

10 miles per gallon

Which of the following vehicles has the best gas mileage?

Ⓐ Vehicle A   Ⓒ Vehicle C

Ⓑ Vehicle B   Ⓓ Vehicle D

6. Which of the following charts represents a proportional relationship?

Ⓐ

0	3
1	6
2	9
3	12
4	15

Ⓒ

0	2
1	6
2	10
3	14
4	18

Ⓑ

0	0
1	2
2	4
3	6
4	8

Ⓓ

0	0
1	3
2	4
3	5
4	6

7. One of the many statistics that is calculated in professional baseball is the number of games pitched and strikes thrown by pitchers. The chart below shows some of the collected data.

Games pitched (g)	Strikes thrown (s)
1	
2	124
5	310
10	620
	744

Part A. Write an equation based on the data in the table that represents the relationship between the number of games pitched and the amount of strikes thrown.

Part B. Using your equation, complete the table for the missing values. Show your work below.

> Constant of proportionality is the same as a scale factor.

Part C. Graph the data on the grid below.

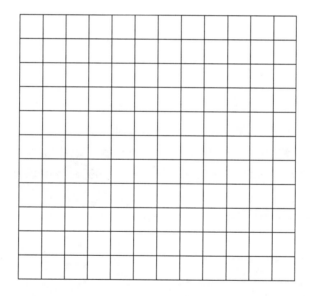

Part D. Is this graph proportional? How do you know?

Part E. Explain what the point (0, 0) represents in terms of the context of this situation.

(Answers are on page 173.)

PERCENT PROBLEMS
AND PROPORTIONS

> **RP.A.3** Use proportional relationships to solve multi-step ratio and percent problems. Examples: simple interest, tax, markups and markdowns, gratuities and commissions, fees, percent increase and decrease, and percent error.

1. Which of the following equations would directly result in finding the total, T, with 8% tax on a pair of sneakers, s?

   > 30% off is equivalent to 70% of the original price.

   Ⓐ $T = 0.08s$

   Ⓑ $T = 1.08s$

   Ⓒ $T = s + 0.08$

   Ⓓ $T = s - 0.08$

2. Emily went to the electronic store with a 20% off coupon and a $15 off coupon. If Emily can only use one coupon, which coupon should Emily use to save the most money if she wants to buy computer speakers for $50. Justify your answer by showing the discounted price for each coupon.

3. Andrew receives commission based on the type of electronic items he helps to sell to his customers as shown in the chart below. Determine the total amount of commission that he earns if he sells a computer for $598, a TV for $299.99, and batteries for $10.50.

Computers and Game Systems	5%
Televisions and Stereos	$3\frac{1}{2}\%$
Other Supplies	1%

4. Which of the following is a correct method to determine the sale price
   of a $25 shirt that is on sale for 40% off?

   Ⓐ 0.40(25)

   Ⓑ 25 − 0.40

   Ⓒ 0.60(25)

   Ⓓ 1.40 + 25

5. What is the original price of a dress that is on sale for $56.00 and is 30% off?

   Ⓐ $80.00

   Ⓑ $16.80

   Ⓒ $39.20

   Ⓓ $72.80

6. Gregory modified his racing snowmobile to produce 20%
   more horsepower. If the snowmobile normally produces
   8 horsepower, what does it now produce with the new
   modifications?

   > A percent can be changed
   > to a decimal by moving
   > the decimal point 2 places
   > to the left.

7. Keegan's 7th-grade math average went from an 80 to an 88. Which of the following
   represents the percent of increase in Keegan's grades?

   Ⓐ 8%

   Ⓑ 9%

   Ⓒ 10%

   Ⓓ 90%

8. Rich was trying to decide at what bank to invest his $5,000. The Bank of Pythagorus offers
   him a 4.75% rate for 3 years whereas Einstein's Bank will give a 2% rate for 7 years.
   Determine which bank will provide the most interest at the end of their offers, assuming no
   money is withdrawn from the bank. Justify your answer with work using $I = prt$.

(Answers are on page 174.)

ADDING AND
SUBTRACTING INTEGERS

NS.A.1 Apply and extend previous understandings of addition and subtraction to add and subtract rational numbers; represent addition and subtraction on a horizontal or vertical number line diagram. (See Appendix B for substandards 7.NS.A.1.a–1.d)

You should not be using a calculator for the following computational problems.

1. Using the number line, find the sums and differences of the following expressions. Explain the process for using the number line to assist you in solving the problems.

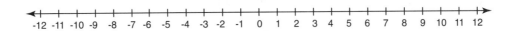

-12 -11 -10 -9 -8 -7 -6 -5 -4 -3 -2 -1 0 1 2 3 4 5 6 7 8 9 10 11 12

$-3 + -9 =$ _____

$-10 + 6 =$ _____

$2 + -8 =$ _____

$-7 + 12 =$ _____

2. On Saturday morning the temperature outside was –4 degrees Fahrenheit. By noon, the temperature had risen 12 degrees, and then at 9 P.M., it dropped 17 degrees.

Write an expression that this situation describes. _____

What was the temperature at 9 P.M.? _____

Explain how you could use the vertical number line as a tool to solve the problem.

Subtracting a negative is the same
as adding a positive (5 − −6 = 5 + 6).

3. What is the value of 4 + −10? Draw a number line to justify your answer.

If the signs are the same you add the
numbers. If the signs are different you
subtract. Always use the sign from the
number that has the larger absolute
value for the final answer.

4. Perform the given operations:

$-9 + -8 =$ $10 - 6 =$

$10 - -9 =$ $-6 + 12 =$

$26 - -12 =$ $120 + -30 =$

$5 - 7 + 3 - 10 =$ $-20 + -80 - -12 =$

$3 - 20 =$ $-15 - -8 =$

$-18 + 18 =$ $-16 - 7 =$

$-90 + -78 =$ $-90 - 78 =$

$4 - 6 - 10 =$ $32 + -16 - 16 =$

(Answers are on page 175.)

MULTIPLYING AND DIVIDING INTEGERS

> **NS.A.2** Apply and extend previous understandings of multiplication and division and of fractions to multiply and divide rational numbers. (See Appendix B for substandards NS.A.2.a– NS.A.2.c)

You should not be using a calculator for the following computational problems.

1. Find the products of the following expressions.

   $-3 \cdot -5 =$ _____ $(-10)(+6) =$ _____

   $(-2)(4) =$ _____ $-7 \cdot 12 =$ _____

2. Find the quotients of the following expressions.

   $-30 \div -5 =$ _____ $\dfrac{-10}{2} =$ _____

   $(-20) \div (4) =$ _____ $\dfrac{64}{-8} =$ _____

   > Multiplying and dividing integers use the same rules for determining the sign of the answer.

3. Which of the following is the answer to $\dfrac{-20}{0}$?

   (A) -20

   (B) 20

   (C) 0

   (D) Undefined

Often students find success when they draw arrows from the first factor to each of the numbers inside the parentheses.

$2(x + 8)$

4. Which expression is equivalent to $-7(y - 2)$?
   Ⓐ $-7y + 14$
   Ⓑ $-7y - 14$
   Ⓒ $7y - 14$
   Ⓓ $7y + 14$

5. Which expression is equivalent to $3(-4x - 9)$?
   Ⓐ $-12x + 27$
   Ⓑ $-12x - 27$
   Ⓒ $12x - 27$
   Ⓓ $12x + 27$

6. Which expression is the simplest form of $-x(4 + 11)$?
   Ⓐ $-4x - 11x$
   Ⓑ $-4x + 11x$
   Ⓒ $7x$
   Ⓓ $-15x$

7. David wrote five $10 checks and two checks for $100 each. Which of the following expressions represents this scenario?
   Ⓐ $5(-10) + 2(-100)$
   Ⓑ $-5(-10) + -2(-100)$
   Ⓒ $-5(10) + -2(100)$
   Ⓓ $5(-10) + -2(-100)$

(Answers are on page 176.)

RATIONAL NUMBERS AND LONG DIVISION

NS.A.2.d Convert a rational number to a decimal using long division; know that the decimal form of a rational number terminates in 0s or eventually repeats.

You should not use a calculator for these problems.

> The numerator becomes the dividend inside the long division box and the denominator is the divisor, which is outside the long division box.

1. Convert $\dfrac{2}{3}$ to a decimal.

2. Convert $\dfrac{1}{7}$ to a decimal.

3. Convert $\dfrac{9}{16}$ to a decimal.

4. Which of the following is not a definition of a rational number?
   - Ⓐ   A number that can only be written as a ratio of whole numbers.
   - Ⓑ   A number which in decimal form terminates in zeros.
   - Ⓒ   A number which in decimal form repeats.
   - Ⓓ   A decimal that does not repeat or terminate.

5. As a decimal $\dfrac{5}{9}$ is correctly written in which form?
   - Ⓐ   0.5
   - Ⓑ $0.\overline{5}$
   - Ⓒ   0.55
   - Ⓓ   0.555555555556

6. Convert $\frac{1}{8}$ to a decimal.

7. Based on the answer you calculated for $\frac{1}{8}$ in question 6, complete the chart to find the decimal values of the following fractions. *Do not use long division!*

Fraction	Work area	Decimal form	Strategy
$\frac{1}{8}$	——		——
$\frac{2}{8}$			
$\frac{3}{8}$			
$\frac{6}{8}$			
$\frac{7}{8}$			

8. Define a rational number and provide an example and a counterexample for your definition.

(Answers are on page 177.)

REAL-WORLD APPLICATION OF RATIONAL NUMBERS

NS.A.3 Solve real-world and mathematical problems involving the four operations with rational numbers.

The health inspector was monitoring freezer temperatures at 7 different restaurants. The data is recorded in the table below. Use this data to answer questions 1–3.

Fish N More	–12°C
MexTex	–18°C
Pasta Bowl	–17°C
Panini Pete's	0°C
Jim's Harbor	–20°C
Pizza King	2°C
Onofry's Deli	5°C

1. Which of the following represents the approximate mean temperature of the freezers?
    (A) –8.6°C
    (B) –60°C
    (C) 0°C
    (D) 10.6°C

2. The range can be calculated using which of the following expressions?
    (A) 5 – 20
    (B) 5 – –20
    (C) –20 – 5
    (D) –20 – –5

3. The average temperature of a freezer is –18°C. The health inspector says that an acceptable range is ±2 degrees.

    Part A. Determine the highest acceptable value.

    Part B. Determine the lowest acceptable value.

    Part C. How many of the restaurants meet the health inspector's requirements?

A volcanologist was monitoring the height of a volcano near the Galapagos Islands. The volcano continually erupts and the lava solidifies and adds to the height of the volcano. He recorded heights below sea level as a negative number. The data is shown in the table below. Use this data to answer questions 4–6.

Year	Height (meters)
1955	−28.3
1965	−14.8
1975	−7.9
1985	3.7
1995	12.1
2005	14.9

4. Which of the following represents the approximate average growth per year between 1965 and 1975?
   Ⓐ 2.27 meters per year
   Ⓑ 3.45 meters per year
   Ⓒ 6.9 meters per year
   Ⓓ 0.69 meters per year

5. Which of the following dates represent the greatest change in height of the volcano?
   Ⓐ 1955–1965
   Ⓑ 1975–1985
   Ⓒ 1985–1995
   Ⓓ 1995–2005

6. Before 1955, volcanologists predicted that the volcano had increased in height by 0.45 meters per year. If this rate is correct, what would have been the expected height of the volcano in 1941?

(Answers are on page 177.)

EQUIVALENT EXPRESSIONS

EE.A.1 Apply properties of operations as strategies to add, subtract, factor, and expand linear expressions with rational coefficients.

1. Which of the following expressions is equivalent to $-7x + 3 - 5x - 10$?

   Ⓐ $-12x - 7$

   Ⓑ $2x - 7$

   Ⓒ $12x + 13$

   Ⓓ $-2x - 13$

2. $8x + 16$ is equivalent to all of the following expressions except:

   Ⓐ $8(x + 2)$

   Ⓑ $2x + 5 + 6x + 11$

   Ⓒ $2(4x + 8)$

   Ⓓ $10x - 2x - 20 + 4$

3. Simplify: $-2(3a) - 2x + 3(2x^2) + 3x$

4. Explain using a property why $4r + 2v$ is equivalent to $2v + 4r$.

5. Simplify: $(3n^2 + n - 10) - (2n^2 + 8n - 2)$.

6. Complete the chart below and verify that the expressions you created are equivalent to the given expression. The first expression must be the most simplified expression and the other expression can be any other equivalent expression. Use $n = 3$ to verify.

	Simplified expression	Equivalent expression
$\frac{1}{2}(10n + 50)$		
$-10n - 30 - 5n$		
$4n - 9 + 6r - n - 4r - 2r$		

7. Find the difference of $(6n^2 - 10n - 10) - (3n^2 - 5n - 10)$.

8. Which of the following expressions is equivalent to $3x + 4x - 5$?

Ⓐ $2x$

Ⓑ $7x - 5$

Ⓒ $11x$

Ⓓ $x - 5$

(Answers are on page 178.)

RATIONAL NUMBER COMPUTATION

> **EE.B.3** Solve multi-step real-life and mathematical problems posed with positive and negative rational numbers in any form (whole numbers, fractions, and decimals), using tools strategically. Apply properties of operations to calculate with numbers in any form; convert between forms as appropriate; and assess the reasonableness of answers using mental computation and estimation strategies.

You should not use a calculator for these problems.

1. Explain if the following statement is true or false and justify your choice.

   A negative plus a positive is always a positive.

2. Complete the chart.

Exponential form	Factor form	Standard form
$(-2)^4$		
$(-2)^5$		
-2^4		
-2^5		
$-(-2)^4$		

3. Which of the following expressions is equivalent to $-2(10) + (-8)^2 - 4(1 - 10)$?

   (A) 80

   (B) 8

   (C) -21

   (D) -40

4. Richard made deposits and wrote checks in his bank account during the month of November as shown in the list below. If he started with $450.00 in his account, what is his ending balance?

Richard's Transactions in November	
Deposit	$325.95
Check written for	$ 75.82
Deposit	$ 45.25
Deposit	$500
Withdrawn	$125
Check written for	$ 97.32
Withdrawn	$600

5. David withdrew $50 on six different times from his bank account and deposited $25 on three different times. If these were the only changes in his account and his ending balance showed $750, how much money did his account have to begin with?

Ⓐ $375

Ⓒ $975

Ⓑ $525

Ⓓ $1,125

6. The temperature in Albany, NY started at 65 degrees and dropped 5 degrees every hour for 2 hours and then 3 degrees each hour for 4 hours. Keegan and Christian wrote the following equations to show this change. Determine whose equation is correct and justify your answer; be sure to discuss what the error is in the incorrect formula.

Keegan	Christian
$65 + 2(-5) + 4(-3) = t$	$t = 65 - 2(-5) - 4(-3)$

7. Determine the value of the following expression:

$$\frac{-2}{10} + \frac{-7}{12} \div 1\frac{1}{2} + |2.36 - 7.4|$$

(Answers are on page 179.)

WRITING EQUATIONS AND INEQUALITIES

EE.B.4 Use variables to represent quantities in a real-world or mathematical problem, and construct simple equations and inequalities to solve problems by reasoning about the quantities.

<	≤	>	≥
Less than	Less than or equal to	Greater than	Greater than or equal to
Under or below	At maximum or at most	More than	At minimum or at least

1. Which of the following equations represents "twice a number increased by 5 is equal to 4 less than the number"?
   - Ⓐ $5x = 4 - x$
   - Ⓑ $2x + 5 = 4 - x$
   - Ⓒ $(2 + 5)x = x - 4$
   - Ⓓ $2x + 5 = x - 4$

2. Bella wanted to buy 3 sodas, s, and 2 bags of popcorn, p, at the movies and not spend more than \$25. Which of the following inequalities represents this situation?
   - Ⓐ $3s + 2p = 25$
   - Ⓑ $2s + 3p < 25$
   - Ⓒ $3s + 2p ≤ 25$
   - Ⓓ $2s + 3p = 25$

3. Which of the following equations represents the total t when you are buying 2 pairs of pants that each cost p, a new shirt that costs \$23, and there is 8% sales tax?
   - Ⓐ $2p + 23 + .08 = t$
   - Ⓑ $1.08(2p + 23) = t$
   - Ⓒ $2p + 23 + 1.08 = t$
   - Ⓓ $.08(2p + 23) = t$

4. Troy wanted to know how many $49.99 video games he could buy if he had a $10 coupon and his grandparents typically give him at least $200 for his birthday. Write a mathematical sentence that he could use to help him determine this.

5. Write two different equations that could be used to find the perimeter of a square. Describe why the two equations you wrote are equivalent.

6. Geoff wanted to sell his car for 40% less than what he originally paid for it. Which of the following equations represents the price he will sell the car for, if it originally was $39,999?

   Ⓐ $(.60)(39,999) = s$

   Ⓑ $(0.40)(39,999) = s$

   Ⓒ $39,999 \div 0.40 = s$

   Ⓓ $39,999 \div 0.60 = s$

7. Tanya at the Fox Inn Bed and Breakfast charges $250 per day for the deluxe suite and an additional $20 for housekeeping. Which of the following equations could Tanya use to calculate the total bill (T) when her customers check out after staying a number of days (p)?

   Ⓐ $250 + 20p = T$

   Ⓑ $250p = T - 20$

   Ⓒ $p = (T - 20)250$

   Ⓓ $T = 250p - 20$

(Answers are on page 180.)

SOLVING EQUATIONS

EE.B.4.a Solve word problems leading to equations of the form $px + q = r$ and $p(x + q) = r$, where p, q, and r are specific rational numbers. Solve equations of these forms fluently. Compare an algebraic solution to an arithmetic solution, identifying the sequence of the operations used in each approach.

Try to solve these problems without a calculator to practice your computation skills. Some parts of tests will not allow a calculator.

1. Which of the following values is the solution to $-3n + 7.5 = 28.02$?

   Ⓐ   6.84

   Ⓑ   −6.84

   Ⓒ   11.84

   Ⓓ   −11.84

   > Get common denominators to add and subtract fractions.

2. Solve the following equation:

$$\frac{1}{2}x - -3.75 = -5\frac{1}{8}$$

   > When you divide fractions you are really multiplying by the reciprocal of the second fraction (divisor).

3. In order to solve the following equation, what is the first step?

   $3r + 87 + -5r = -150$

   Ⓐ Divide each side by 87

   Ⓑ Add 87 to each side

   Ⓒ Combine like terms of $3r$ and $-5r$

   Ⓓ Change the signs on each negative number

4. What properties and in what order would you solve the following equation?

   $-5(c - 10) + 3c = 25$

   Ⓐ Distributive property, combine like terms, multiplicative inverse

   Ⓑ Combine like terms, distributive property, additive inverse

   Ⓒ Combine like terms, additive inverse, distributive property

   Ⓓ Distributive property, multiplicative inverse, additive inverse

5. Solve the following equation:

    $-7(2x - 10) = -1120$

6. Solve the following equation and check your answer.

    $2(y - 20) -5y = 950$

7. Mimi was creating a trapezoidal patio as shown in the diagram. The entire
    area of the patio was 745 square feet. The bases are 28 feet and 22 feet.
    Find the value of the missing dimension.

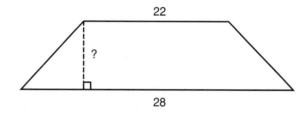

(Answers are on page 180.)

REAL-WORLD APPLICATION OF INEQUALITIES

EE.B.4.b Solve word problems leading to inequalities of the form $px + q > r$ or $px + q < r$, where p, q, and r are specific rational numbers. Graph the solution set of the inequality and interpret it in the context of the problem.

Greg wants to have his next birthday party at the bowling alley. Use the chart below to help you solve the following problems.

Age	Cost per person
$a < 5$	free
$5 \leq a < 10$	$5
$a \geq 10$	$7

1. If Greg has two brothers, ages 10 and 5, and Greg is turning 12, then which of the following will be the cost for the birthday party?
    - Ⓐ $17
    - Ⓑ $12
    - Ⓒ $18
    - Ⓓ $19

2. Greg decided only to have his friends come to the party, all of whom are older than 10. His mom has allotted no more than $60 to spend for the party. The Bowling Alley charges $15 for cake and ice cream.

    Part A. Write an inequality to represent how many total kids can be at the party.

    Part B. Solve the inequality to determine how many total kids can be at the party.

    Part C. Draw the solution on a number line.

3. How much money would his mother need to allow for the party if he wanted exactly 7 friends to come?

4. Greg's grandmother decides that she will give $25 to help with the cost of the party. His mom agrees but tells Greg that he now will have to account for the 8% tax also with the extra money.

Part A. Write an inequality to represent how many total kids can be at the party including tax.

Part B. Solve the inequality to determine how many total kids can be at the party.

Part C. Draw the solution on a number line.

(Answers are on page 182.)

SCALE DRAWINGS

> **G.A.1** Solve problems involving scale drawings of geometric figures, including computing actual lengths and areas from a scale drawing and reproducing a scale drawing at a different scale.

Use a ruler to help you with the following questions.

1. A graphic arts company is designing a billboard sign like the one below for alongside of a highway. Find the actual length and width of the rectangular billboard if the scale is 1 centimeter = 2.5 meters.

Meyers Landscaping is designing a backyard for a new house and drew the aerial plot plan as shown below to present to the homeowners. The scale of the diagram is 2 inches = 15 feet. Use this information to answer questions 2–5.

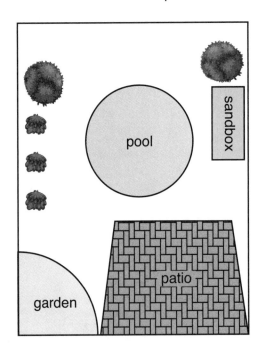

2. Find the area of the garden to the nearest tenth of a foot.

3. Determine the diameter of the pool, without using a ruler, if the circumference of the pool is 10π feet.

4. One paver stone covers approximately $\frac{1}{4}$ of a square foot and costs $1.25 per stone.

   Part A. Estimate the minimum amount of money it will cost to cover the trapezoidal patio.

   Part B. Landscapers will have to cut the paver stones to fit correctly and therefore order 10% more material to account for error. Calculate the number of paver stones and money with the 10% increase.

5. Which of the following scale factors could the landscaper use to maximize the fit on a standard size of $8\frac{1}{2}$ inch × 11 inch piece of paper.

   (A) 150%
   (B) 200%
   (C) 300%
   (D) 400%

(Answers are on page 182.)

DRAWING
GEOMETRIC SHAPES

Use a ruler and protractor to complete the following questions.

1. Draw a rectangle which measures 2.7 centimeters by 6.8 centimeters.

2. Construct a regular hexagon which has interior angles each measuring 120° and each side is $\frac{3}{4}$ of an inch in length.

3. Complete the chart below to determine the amount of triangles that can be made with the given measurements.

Measurement requirements	Draw space	# of unique triangles that can be formed
85°, 40°, 55°		
Length = 2.0 cm Width = 2.5 cm Height = 6.2 cm		
side = 3.0 cm side = 4.5 cm 90° angle included between the 2 given sides		
60° angle 40° angle 5.3 cm side included between the 2 given angles		
Sides of 3, 4 and 5 centimeters		
40° angle 2.2 cm side 4 cm side		

(Answers are on page 184.)

3-D FIGURES AND CROSS SECTIONS

G.A.3 Describe the two-dimensional figures that result from slicing three-dimensional figures, as in plane sections of right rectangular prisms and right rectangular pyramids.

1. Which two-dimensional figure results from a square pyramid being sliced horizontally and parallel to the base?
   - Ⓐ Triangle
   - Ⓑ Square
   - Ⓒ Circle
   - Ⓓ Pentagon

2. Which two-dimensional figure results from a square pyramid being sliced vertically and perpendicular to the base?
   - Ⓐ Triangle
   - Ⓑ Square
   - Ⓒ Circle
   - Ⓓ Pentagon

3. Which of the following measurements are the correct dimensions of the cross section resulting from a perpendicular slice to the base?

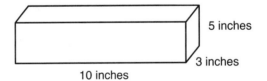

5 inches

3 inches

10 inches

   - Ⓐ 3 in. by 10 in.
   - Ⓑ 5 in. by 10 in.
   - Ⓒ 3 in. by 5 in.
   - Ⓓ 5 in. by 5 in.

4. A diagonal slice of a square pyramid will result in which two-dimensional figure?

- Ⓐ Triangle
- Ⓑ Square
- Ⓒ Rectangle
- Ⓓ Trapezoid

5. A diagonal slice of a cube will result in which two-dimensional figure?

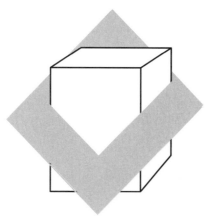

- Ⓐ Triangle
- Ⓑ Square
- Ⓒ Rectangle
- Ⓓ Trapezoid

(Answers are on page 186.)

AREA AND CIRCUMFERENCE OF CIRCLES

G.B.4 Know the formulas for the area and circumference of a circle and use them to solve problems; give an informal derivation of the relationship between the circumference and area of a circle.

1. What is the area of the given circle?

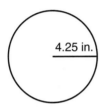

4.25 in.

- Ⓐ 18.0625π in.²
- Ⓑ 4.25π in.²
- Ⓒ 8.5π in.²
- Ⓓ 56.7π in.²

2. What is the circumference of the given circle?

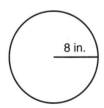

8 in.

- Ⓐ 8π in.
- Ⓑ 16π in.
- Ⓒ 4π in.
- Ⓓ 32π in.

Depending on if you use 3.14 or the Pi key on your calculator, your answers may vary in precision.

3. The circumference of a circle is 10π. Determine the area of the circle to the nearest hundredth.

4. Rich and Greg were buying new tires for their trucks. Greg decided to use low-profile tires that were 24 inches in diameter while Rich decided to use 35-inch tires. In one full rotation of the tires, what is the difference of the distance traveled to the nearest hundredth?

5. High school wrestling mats typically measure 38 feet by 38 feet with a 28-foot diameter circle as shown in the diagram below. Determine, to the nearest foot, the area of the mat outside the wrestling circle.

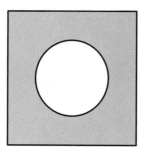

(Answers are on page 186.)

ANGLES AND ALGEBRA

G.B.5 Use facts about supplementary, complementary, vertical, and adjacent angles in a multi-step problem to write and solve simple equations for an unknown angle in a figure.

Use the following diagram, which shows parallel lines cut by transversals, to complete questions 1–4.

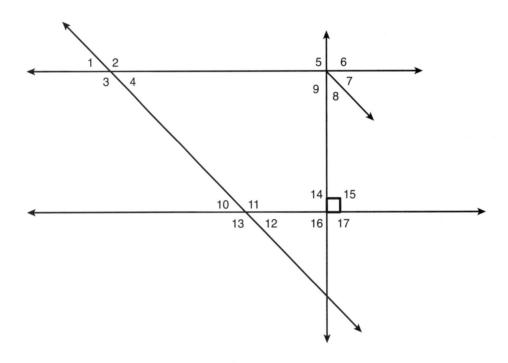

Complete the sentences using your knowledge of angle relationships.

1. If angle 1 measures 60 degrees then

    A. Angle 2 measures _____ because _____

    B. Angle 4 measures _____ because _____

2. If Angle 7 measures 40 degrees then

    A. Angle 8 measures _____ because _____

    B. Angle 6 measures _____ because _____

3. Angle 4 measures $y + 6$ degrees and angle 3 is twice angle 4.

Part A. Write an equation that would determine the measure of each angle.

Part B. Solve the equation for y.

Part C. Determine the measure of angle 3 and angle 4.

4. Angle 10 measures $2c + 30$ degrees and angle 12 is $5c$.

Part A. Write an equation that would determine the measure of each angle.

Part B. Solve the equation for c.

Part C. Determine the measure of angle 10 and angle 12.

(Answers are on page 187.)

SURFACE AREA AND VOLUME

> **G.B.6** Solve real-world and mathematical problems involving area, volume, and surface area of two- and three-dimensional objects composed of triangles, quadrilaterals, polygons, cubes, and right prisms.

1. What is the surface area of the rectangular prism shown below?

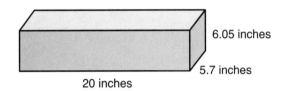

20 inches   6.05 inches   5.7 inches

Ⓐ   689.7 in.^{2} Ⓒ   538.97 in.^{2}

Ⓑ   383.485 in.^{2} Ⓓ   31.75 in.^{2}

2. What is the volume of the rectangular prism shown below?

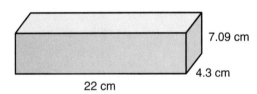

22 cm   7.09 cm   4.3 cm

Ⓐ   670.714 cm^2 Ⓒ   670.714 cm^3

Ⓑ   33.39 cm^2 Ⓓ   33.39 cm^3

3. What is the surface area of the cylinder shown below?

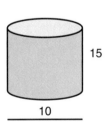

15   10

> Refer to your reference sheet for the formulas.

Ⓐ   628.3 units^2 Ⓒ   1099.6 units^2

Ⓑ   534.1 units^2 Ⓓ   1178.1 units^2

4. Which expression could correctly determine the surface area of a toilet paper tube that measures $1\frac{1}{2}$ inches in diameter by 4 inches in length?

   Ⓐ $2\pi r^2 + 2\pi rh$

   Ⓑ $\pi r^2 + \pi rh$

   Ⓒ $2\pi rh$

   Ⓓ $2\pi r^2$

5. While visiting Shambles Dairy Farm, you noticed that one of their silos was taller and skinner than the other, as shown below. Determine to the nearest cubic foot which silo has a larger volume.

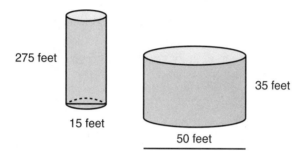

275 feet

15 feet

35 feet

50 feet

6. Troy and Reese were trying to decide what type of container to use to ship their new product. They want to minimize the surface area to reduce cost but maximize the volume so they can ship the most materials in it. Reese wants to use a cylinder but Troy suggests a triangular prism. Determine whose design fits the criteria and justify your choice.

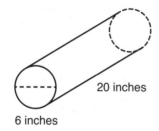

20 inches

6 inches

It is helpful to label the dimensions on the diagram so you remember what number corresponds to the variable in the formulas.

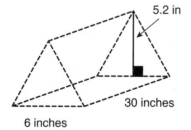

5.2 in

30 inches

6 inches

(Answers are on page 187.)

RANDOM SAMPLES AND INFERENCES

> **SP.A.1** Understand that statistics can be used to gain information about a population by examining a sample of the population; generalizations about a population from a sample are valid only if the sample is representative of that population. Understand that random sampling tends to produce representative samples and support valid inferences.
>
> **SP.A.2** Use data from a random sample to draw inferences about a population with an unknown characteristic of interest. Generate multiple samples (or simulated samples) of the same size to gauge the variation in estimates or predictions.

1. Which of the following methods of sampling would provide the most reliable data to analyze?

   Ⓐ Asking every third person you see at the mall.

   Ⓑ Mailing a questionnaire to home owners in your town.

   Ⓒ Randomly selecting people from a census list.

   Ⓓ Providing an online survey for a month.

2. Gregory wanted to determine the favorite brand of snowmobiles in his local area. Check all sampling methods that he could use to gather reliable data.

	Asking his friends with whom he rides snowmobiles		Surveying people at a snowmobile show
	Randomly selecting registered snowmobile drivers		Polling every winning driver at a snowmobile race
	Placing an online survey on a manufacturer's website		Observing the types of snowmobiles that are on the trails all season

3. After conducting a survey, Christian concluded that most American elementary students are interested in playing football. His Aunt Carrie told him that his conclusion was not valid. Circle all reasons that could apply to why his conclusion is not valid.

He asked mostly adults.   He surveyed kids at a
                                           football game.

He used a random sampling   He asked 500 people in
method.   NY and FL.

He selected people from   He asked questions that
each state.   omitted other sports.

4. A local politician polled 50 of his supporters and determined that it was a good idea to introduce a new law for the city. Determine if this conclusion is valid and justify your decision.

(Questions 5 and 6)

Jim wanted to analyze the amounts of colored candies that are in a typical bag from a candy company and his data is recorded below.

	Red	Green	Yellow	Blue
Bag 1	6	5	2	1
Bag 2	8	3	0	2
Bag 3	6	4	3	2

5. Which of the following inferences can be concluded from his data?
   Ⓐ   On average there are more yellow candies than blue.
   Ⓑ   Most bags have 15 candies in them.
   Ⓒ   On average 29% of the bag is green candies.
   Ⓓ   Red candies are most people's favorite.

6. To improve his analysis, Jim should
   Ⓐ   recount the candies in each bag.
   Ⓑ   sample more bags of candies.
   Ⓒ   sample a different candy company's bags.
   Ⓓ   only count the first five candies that shake out of each bag.

(Answers are on page 189.)

VISUAL OVERLAP OF TWO DATA DISTRIBUTIONS

> **SP.B.3** Informally assess the degree of visual overlap of two numerical data distributions with similar variabilities, measuring the difference between the centers by expressing it as a multiple of a measure of variability.

1. Data was collected on the fuel consumption on a trip from California to Washington, D.C. by two different truck drivers. Each truck driver averaged about 15 miles per gallon but their Mean Absolute Deviations were different. Jim's Mean Absolute Deviation was 3 miles per gallon and Richard's was 10 miles per gallon. Explain what the Mean Absolute Deviation represents in this particular situation.

Use the following dot plots for questions 2–4.

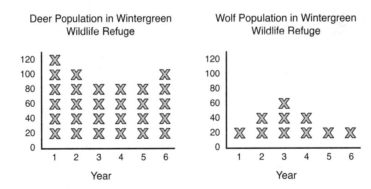

$$\mathbb{X} = 20$$

2. What conclusion can be drawn from these box plots?
   - Ⓐ Mean deer population is about 3 times larger than the mean wolf population.
   - Ⓑ Range in wolf population is larger than the range in the deer population.
   - Ⓒ In year 3 there were the same amount of deer and wolves.
   - Ⓓ Both graphs are not symmetric.

3. Which of the following inferences can be drawn from comparing the two data sets?
   - Ⓐ As the deer population increases, the wolf population increases.
   - Ⓑ There is an inverse relationship between the two populations.
   - Ⓒ As the deer population decreases, the wolf population decreases.
   - Ⓓ There is a skewed graph so no inference can be made.

4. Which of the following conclusions can be made based on the two graphs?
   - Ⓐ The shape of each graph is symmetric and therefore the populations have the same mean.
   - Ⓑ The shape of each graph is symmetric and therefore each population's mean and median are almost the same.
   - Ⓒ The shape of each graph is not symmetric and therefore each population's mean and median are almost the same.
   - Ⓓ The shape of each graph is not symmetric and therefore the populations have the same mean.

Use the two box plots, which show the ages of students in two different schools, to answer questions 5 and 6.

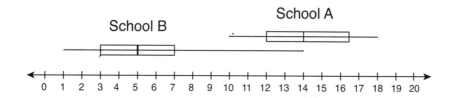

5. By analyzing the graphs, which of the following conclusions could be made?
   - Ⓐ There are more students at School A.
   - Ⓑ 50% of the students in School B are in high school.
   - Ⓒ Both schools have students that range in age from 1 to 18.
   - Ⓓ Students are typically older in School A than in School B.

6. After analyzing the graphs, which of the following conclusions cannot be made?
   - Ⓐ School A's median age is the same as School B's maximum age.
   - Ⓑ School B is skewed right and School A is symmetric.
   - Ⓒ School A has a potential outlier in its data and School B does not.
   - Ⓓ The age of students in School A is more evenly distributed whereas the distribution of the age of students in School B has more variability.

(Answers are on page 189.)

MEASURES OF CENTER AND VARIABILITY FOR TWO POPULATIONS

SP.B.4 Use measures of center and measures of variability for numerical data from random samples to draw informal comparative inferences about two populations.

Use the double stem and leaf plot, which show the yards ran by football players on two different teams, to answer the questions.

Canajoharie Cougars	Stem	Fonda Braves
3,3	0	2,4,5,5,6,8,9,9
0,8,9	1	0,0,1,3,3,3
3,6,7,7,8	2	0,1,1,1,1,2
0,1,2,3,6,8,9	3	1,5,5
2,2,3,4,4,5,9,9	4	1

For questions 1–7, determine if each statement is true or false. If false, correct the statement to make it true.

1. _____ The Cougars have a symmetric distribution of data.

2. _____ The Braves' data is skewed right.

3. _____ The Cougars have run more yards than the Braves.

4. _____ The median yards ran for the Braves is 3 and the Cougars is 36.

5. _____ The Braves' data will have a mean lower than the Cougars since it's skewed.

6. _____ 41 is an outlier in the Braves' data.

7. _____ The range for the Cougars is larger than the Braves' range.

In a stem and leaf plot, the stem is the tens digit and the leaf is the ones digit.

8. Using the data, compare and contrast the two football teams using the information you have concluded from answering questions 1–7.

(Answers are on page 190.)

PROBABILITY

1. Place the following probabilities correctly on the number line, use the letter and a dot to denote their placement.

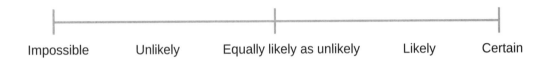

    Impossible   Unlikely   Equally likely as unlikely   Likely   Certain

    Ⓐ Flipping heads on a fair coin
    Ⓑ Getting an odd number when rolling a number cube
    Ⓒ Rolling a number on a number cube
    Ⓓ 8 out of 8 chance
    Ⓔ 0% chance
    Ⓕ 4 out of 5 chance in getting math homework
    Ⓖ 10% chance in winning the raffle at the park
    Ⓗ 50/50 chance

2. Christine is rolling a regular 6-sided number cube and wanted to predict the number of times she should get a 5 or 6. She decided to roll it 60 times. Determine how many 5s or 6s she should get.

3. On average, Jessica calculated that 17% of the time it snows during her drive to work. If she drives to work 180 days, how many days should it snow?

4. Troy and Theresa were playing a game and thought that the spinner was
not fair. They spun blue 20% of the time.

Part A. Determine the theoretical probability of spinning a blue.

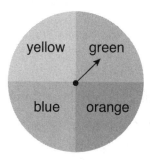

Part B. Determine a method to test if the spinner is fair or unfair and describe the
method of testing.

Part C. If Troy and Theresa were to spin the spinner 600 times, determine the expected
number of times that they should get a blue.

Part D. When Troy and Theresa spun it 600 times, blue was spun 147. Compare their
results to the expected results. Would this answer help prove or disprove that the
spinner was fair? Explain your reasoning.

(Answers are on page 190.)

PROBABILITY MODELS

1. The movie theater has five movies showing that Christian would like to watch and he can't decide which to go see. Which of the following probability models would help him determine what movie to go see?

   Ⓐ Flipping a fair coin

   Ⓑ Rolling a fair 6-sided die

   Ⓒ Picking one of 4 marbles out of a bag

   Ⓓ Spinning a spinner that is equally marked A, B, C, D, E

2. Which of the following spinners would represent the probability of picking an oatmeal cookie from a platter of cookies that has 40% chocolate, 40% oatmeal and 20% sugar cookies?

   Ⓐ

   Ⓒ

   Ⓑ

   Ⓓ

A geneticist was determining the probabilities of the seed color of a pea plant when she crossed two plant hybrids for seed color. Use the following Punnett Square to answer the following question; each square has equal likelihood of occurring.

YY	Yy
Yy	yy

3. A seed will be green if it has two lowercase letters in the Punnett Square; otherwise, it will be yellow. Given the Punnett Square shown, what is the probability that the seed will be yellow?

   Ⓐ $\dfrac{25}{100}$

   Ⓑ 0.5

   Ⓒ 75%

   Ⓓ 1

Keegan set up an experiment and placed 1 of each card, A, B, C, D, E, F, in a hat. He picked a card 20 times and replaced it after each pick. He recorded his results in the chart below.

Card	# times picked
A	6
B	1
C	3
D	3
E	3
F	4

4. Using Keegan's data, determine the probability that a vowel was chosen.

5. Determine the *theoretical* probability of picking one card from the hat, for example, picking the letter C.

6. Compare Keegan's data to the theoretical probability of picking each card and explain if Keegan's experimental results were what he should have expected. If they were not, suggest what may have happened to cause the discrepancy.

(Answers are on page 191.)

PROBABILITY OF COMPOUND EVENTS

> **SP.C.8** Find probabilities of compound events using organized lists, tables, tree diagrams, and simulation. (See Appendix B for substandards 8.SP.C.8.a, 8.SP.C.8.b, and 8.SP.C.8.c)

1. Which of the following is the probability of rolling an even number on a regular 8-sided number cube and then a number greater than 4 on a regular 6-sided number cube?

    Ⓐ $\dfrac{2}{12}$

    Ⓑ $\dfrac{6}{14}$

    Ⓒ $\dfrac{1}{2}$

    Ⓓ $\dfrac{6}{48}$

2. Theresa has 6 different color shirts and 4 different types of pants to wear to school. Which of the following models could she use to simulate the probability of randomly wearing a certain outfit that consists of one shirt and one pair of pants?
    Ⓐ Flipping a coin 6 times and rolling a 6-sided number cube
    Ⓑ Placing all the shirt colors in a hat and then flipping a coin for the pants
    Ⓒ Rolling a 6-sided number cube and then spinning a spinner divided into 25% sections
    Ⓓ Spinning a spinner that has 6 equal sections and then rolling a 6-sided number cube

3. There are 6 marbles in a bag. 3 are pink, 2 are purple, and 1 is clear.

    Part A. What is the probability of drawing a pink marble and then a clear marble if the first marble you pick is not replaced?

    Part B. What is the probability that you will draw both pink marbles if the first marble you pick is not replaced?

4. For his birthday, Gregory was able to pick one restaurant and one movie for his celebration. He could not decide between Carrie's Cucina or Mimi's Mexican restaurant and he couldn't decide between a comedy or horror movie.

Part A. Describe a probability model that would simulate the different combinations that he could potentially have for his celebration.

Part B. Make a tree diagram and then list all the combinations that he could have for his celebration.

Part C. Find the probability of the following:

Probability that he will eat at Mimi's Mexican restaurant and see a comedy.

5. Jim was going to make a pizza for dinner. He decided that he was only going to use 1 type of dough, 1 type of cheese, and 1 type of topping. He had regular or wheat dough. He had mozzarella, cheddar, or parmesan cheeses and pepperoni, sausage, mushrooms, or olives for a topping.

Part A. Describe a probability model that would simulate the different combinations that he could potentially have for his pizza.

Part B. Make a tree diagram and then list all the combinations that he could have for his pizza.

Part C. Find the probability of the following:

Probability that he will make a wheat pizza with cheddar cheese and mushrooms.

Probability that he will not use regular dough.

Probability that he will have a pizza with mozzarella and olives.

(Answers are on page 192.)

MATH PRACTICE TEST

My Name: _____

Today's Date: _____

1. Andrew needs to install new programs onto multiple computers at his job. He estimates that he installed 6 programs onto a computer in 2 hours and 18 minutes. Which rate can he use to help him plan how long it will take to install all the programs he has onto all the computers he has on his list?
   - Ⓐ 23 minutes per program
   - Ⓑ 6 programs in 2.3 hours
   - Ⓒ 2.3 programs per 1 hour
   - Ⓓ 2.3 programs per 1 minute

2. Which of the following graphs represents a proportional relationship?

   Ⓐ

   Ⓒ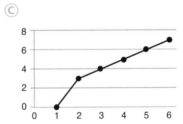

   Ⓑ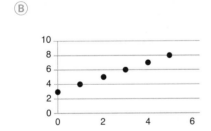

   Ⓓ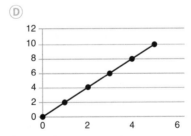

3. On average, Richard is able to plow 4 driveways in 1 hour and 45 minutes. Which equation can be used to calculate the number of driveways, d, Richard can plow in a certain amount of minutes, m?
   - Ⓐ $26.25m = d$
   - Ⓑ $.03m = d$
   - Ⓒ $m = 26.25d$
   - Ⓓ $m = .03d$

The graph below was made by a truck driver to help predict the total miles he will drive if he maintains a constant speed. Refer to the graph for questions 4–7.

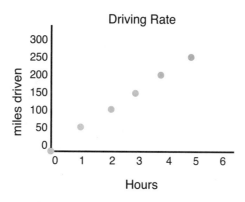

4. Describe what the point (3, 150) represents in the context of the graph.

5. What is the constant of proportionality represented by the graph? Explain the method that you used to determine this.

6. Where is the constant of proportionality located on the graph?

7. Write an equation that can represent the relationship between miles and hours as shown in the graph.

8. Which of the following charts represents a proportional relationship?

Ⓐ

0	4
1	8
2	12
3	16
4	20

Ⓒ

0	2
1	6
2	10
3	14
4	18

Ⓑ

0	0
1	3
2	6
3	9
4	12

Ⓓ

0	4
1	5
2	6
3	7
4	8

9. Which of the following equations would directly result in finding the discounted price, P, if there is a 30% off sale when you buy a kayak, k?

    Ⓐ $P = 0.70k$

    Ⓑ $P = 0.30k$

    Ⓒ $P = k - 0.70$

    Ⓓ $P = k - 0.30$

10. What is the original price of a television for which the total cost with 7% tax is $481.50?

    Ⓐ $33.70

    Ⓑ $474.50

    Ⓒ $450.00

    Ⓓ $515.21

11. Chris's spelling scores went from a 75 to an 87. Which of the following represents the percent of increase in Chris's scores?

    Ⓐ 12%

    Ⓑ 13%

    Ⓒ 14%

    Ⓓ 16%

12. Determine the monthly payments that Theresa will have to pay when she borrows $12,000 for 4 years at a 5.6% interest rate to buy her first car. Use the simple interest formula $I = prt$ to help.

13. Perform the given operations without a calculator:

$$-9 + -7 = \underline{\hphantom{XXXX}}$$

$$18 - -9 = \underline{\hphantom{XXXX}}$$

$$3 - 27 = \underline{\hphantom{XXXX}}$$

$$-20 + -8 - -50 + 18 = \underline{\hphantom{XXXX}}$$

$$1 - 6 = \underline{\hphantom{XXXX}}$$

$$-6 + 15 = \underline{\hphantom{XXXX}}$$

$$-10 - -8 = \underline{\hphantom{XXXX}}$$

$$-32 - 8 - 7 = \underline{\hphantom{XXXX}}$$

14. Perform the given operations without a calculator:

$$-38 \cdot -50 = \underline{\hphantom{XXXX}}$$

$$(-88) \div (-4) = \underline{\hphantom{XXXX}}$$

$$(-122)(24) = \underline{\hphantom{XXXX}}$$

$$\frac{-115}{5} = \underline{\hphantom{XXXX}}$$

15. Which of the following is the answer to $\frac{-70}{0}$?

(A) −70

(B) 0

(C) Undefined

(D) 70

16. Which expression is equivalent to $-3(y - 10)$?

(A) $3y - 10$

(B) $-3y - 10$

(C) $-3y + 30$

(D) $-3y - 30$

17. Which expression is the simplest form of $-x(9 - 8)$?

(A) $-9x + 8x$

(B) $9x - 8x$

(C) x

(D) $-x$

18. Bella calculated that one out of three babysitters helped with homework. Without using a calculator, what percent of the babysitters did not help with homework?

19. Which of the following expressions is equivalent to $7x - 10x - 5$?
   Ⓐ $-8x$
   Ⓑ $-3x - 5$
   Ⓒ $17x - 5$
   Ⓓ $3x - 5$

20. $4x + 24$ is equivalent to all of the following expressions except:
   Ⓐ $4(x + 6)$
   Ⓑ $x + 12 + 3x + 12$
   Ⓒ $2(2x + 12)$
   Ⓓ $10x - 6x - 20 + 4$

21. Find the difference of $(5n^2 + 3n - 1) - (2n^2 + 8n - 20)$.

22. Troy wanted to buy 3 apples, a, and 4 papayas, p, at the farmer's market and not spend more than \$12. Which of the following inequalities represents this situation?
   Ⓐ $3a + 4p > 12$
   Ⓑ $4a + 3p < 12$
   Ⓒ $3a + 4p \leq 12$
   Ⓓ $4a + 3p \geq 12$

23. Write an equation that represents the values in the chart below:

x	y
-2	-7
-1	-3
0	1
1	5
2	9

24. Solve the following equation:

$$-\frac{1}{2}x - -3.75 = -10\frac{1}{4}$$

25. Solve the following equation:

$$-2(-5c - 2) + 3c = 55$$

26. Jim has at most $150 to buy chlorine to take care of his pool this summer. He has a $10 coupon and each bucket, *b*, of chlorine costs $7.50.

Part A. Write an inequality to represent how many total buckets of chlorine he can buy.

Part B. Solve the inequality to determine how many buckets of chlorine he can buy.

Part C. Draw the solution on a number line.

27. A T-shirt graphic arts company is creating a design to be silkscreened onto shirts. The design is an upside down equilateral triangle that says "Chocolate Pi makes me Irrational!" The perimeter of the triangle has as many numbers of pi that can wrap around it and when measured results in a perimeter of 6.9 centimeters. Determine the length of one side of the triangle when the design is increased by 40% to fit on the shirts.

28. Which of the following measurements result in one unique triangle?
    Ⓐ 85°, 60°, 35°
    Ⓑ Length = 1.0 cm, Width = 2.5 cm, Height = 10.2 cm
    Ⓒ 40° angle, 2.2 cm side, 4 cm side
    Ⓓ 60° angle, 40° angle, 5.3 cm side included between the 2 given angles

29. Which two-dimensional figure results from a pentagonal pyramid being sliced vertically and perpendicular to the base?
    Ⓐ Triangle
    Ⓑ Square
    Ⓒ Circle
    Ⓓ Pentagon

30. What is the circumference of the given circle?

Ⓐ 5.72π in.

Ⓑ 11.44π in.

Ⓒ 2.86π in.

Ⓓ 33π in.

5.72 in.

31. The circumference of a circle is 21π. Determine the area of the circle to the nearest hundredth.

Use the following diagram, which shows intersecting lines, to complete questions 32 and 33.

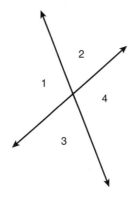

32. What type of angle relationship is between angle 2 and angle 3?

33. Angle 2 is represented by $3x + 5$ and Angle 3 is $4x - 10$.

Part A. Write an equation that would determine the measure of each angle.

Part B. Solve the equation for x.

Part C. Determine the measure of angle 2 and angle 3.

34. What is the volume of the rectangular prism shown below?

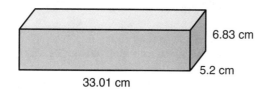

6.83 cm

5.2 cm

33.01 cm

- Ⓐ 1172.38316 cm²
- Ⓑ 15.04 cm²
- Ⓒ 15.04 cm³
- Ⓓ 1172.38316 cm³

35. What is the surface area of the cylinder shown below?

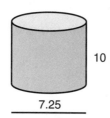

10

7.25

- Ⓐ 273.3 units²
- Ⓑ 310.3 units²
- Ⓒ 501.1 units²
- Ⓓ 412.8 units²

36. Which of the following methods of sampling would provide the most reliable data to analyze?
- Ⓐ Use a computer to randomly generate numbers that represent people.
- Ⓑ Ask every fourth person you see at the park.
- Ⓒ Mail a survey to taxpayers in your town.
- Ⓓ Provide an online questionnaire for a month.

Andy wanted to analyze the different colored cars that people have bought in the last few months and his data is recorded below. Use the table for questions 37 and 38.

	Red	White	Black	Blue
Used Cars R Us	9	3	1	1
Papa's Chevrolet	10	0	0	7
JR's Auto Center	1	6	3	2

37. Which of the following inferences can be concluded from his data?
    Ⓐ On average there are more black cars sold than blue.
    Ⓑ About 47% of the cars sold are red.
    Ⓒ Most car dealers sell used cars.
    Ⓓ JR's Auto Center sold more cars than the other two dealers combined.

38. To best improve his analysis, Andy should
    Ⓐ recount the cars sold at each dealer.
    Ⓑ sample a different car dealer.
    Ⓒ only count the first five cars sold each month.
    Ⓓ sample more car dealers for a longer amount of time.

Use the dot plot for question 39.

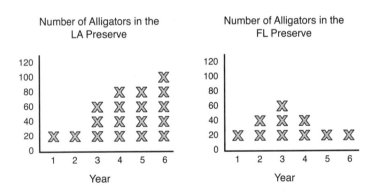

$\mathbb{X} = 20$

39. What conclusion can be drawn from these dot plots?
    Ⓐ The range in the LA alligator population is larger than the range in the FL alligator population.
    Ⓑ The mean LA alligator population is larger than the mean FL alligator population.
    Ⓒ In year 2 there were the same amount of alligators in both FL and LA.
    Ⓓ Both graphs are symmetric.

Use the double-box plot which show the ages of children at two different soccer fields to answer questions 40 and 41.

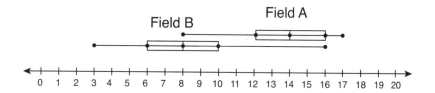

40. By analyzing the graphs, which of the following conclusions could be made?
- Ⓐ There are more children at Field B.
- Ⓑ 50% of the children at Field B are younger than 10 and older than 6.
- Ⓒ Both fields have children that range in age from 0 to 20.
- Ⓓ Most children are older at Field B than at Field A.

41. By analyzing the graphs, which of the following conclusions cannot be made?
- Ⓐ Field A's minimum age is the same as Field B's median age.
- Ⓑ Field A has an outlier in its data and Field B most likely does not.
- Ⓒ Field B is skewed right and Field A is symmetric.
- Ⓓ The age of children at Field B is more evenly distributed as the distribution of the age of children in Field A has more variability.

Use the double stem and leaf plot which show the home runs hit by players on two different baseball teams to answer the questions.

High Hitters	Stem	Sunny Sluggers
2, 3	0	2, 4, 5, 8, 9, 9
0, 8, 9	1	0, 0, 1, 3, 3
3, 6, 7, 7, 8	2	0, 1, 1, 2
0, 1, 2, 3, 6, 8, 9	3	1, 5, 5

42. Which conclusions can be made about the two data sets?
- Ⓐ Hitters outperform the Sluggers in home runs.
- Ⓑ Sluggers hit more home runs than the Hitters.
- Ⓒ Sluggers have a larger range than the Hitters.
- Ⓓ Sluggers have an equal range with the Hitters.

43. Determine which team has the larger median. Explain your process.

44. Bill is rolling a regular 6-sided number cube and wanted to predict the number of times he should get a 3 or 4. He decided to roll it 120 times. Determine how many 3's or 4's he should get.

45. On average, Chuck recorded that 9.5% of the time it is raining when he wakes up at 7 A.M. If Chuck records the weather at 7 A.M. for 186 mornings, how many mornings should it be raining?

Use the following information to answer questions 46 and 47. Aaron and Jenny were arguing about whose turn it was to wash the dishes and, to decide who should wash the dishes, Aaron suggested they flip a coin. Jenny thought her brother may try to trick her and thought it was an unfair coin.

46. **Part A**. Determine the theoretical probability of flipping heads.

    Part B. Determine a method to test if the coin is fair or unfair and describe the method of testing.

47. **Part A**. If Aaron and Jenny were to flip the coin 20 times, determine the expected amount of times that they should get heads.

    Part B. When Aaron and Jenny flipped it 20 times, heads occurred 12 times. Compare their results to the expected results from Part A. Based on your answer, would you tell Aaron and Jenny that the coin was fair or unfair? Explain your reasoning.

48. Melissa has six different fruits that she could eat, and she man't make up her mind about which one she wants. Which of the following probability models would you recommend that she use to make her decision?

Ⓐ Flipping a fair coin

Ⓑ Rolling a fair 6-sided die

Ⓒ Picking one of 4 marbles out of a bag

Ⓓ Spinning a spinner that is equally marked A, B, C, D, E

49. Which of the following is the probability of rolling a number less than 4 on a regular 8-sided number cube and then a number greater than 4 on a regular 6-sided number cube?

Ⓐ $\dfrac{6}{36}$

Ⓑ $\dfrac{6}{14}$

Ⓒ $\dfrac{1}{8}$

Ⓓ $\dfrac{5}{48}$

50. There are 7 pieces of candy in a jar. 4 are blue, 2 are purple, and 1 is green. You reach in for one piece of candy to eat, and then you take out another piece. What is the probability of drawing a blue candy and then a purple candy if the first candy you pick is not replaced?

(Answers are on page 193.)

MATH ANSWERS EXPLAINED

RATIOS AND PROPORTIONAL RELATIONSHIPS

Unit Rates (R.P.A.1), page 110

1. **C** A unit rate represents an amount per 1 unit. In this case for speed, all of these are distances over a course of time; however the correct answer must be reduced to the distance traveled in 1 unit. The unit may be a day, hour, minute, or second. Choice C is the only option that is reduced to the unit of 1, "per second" means per one second.

2. **A** A unit rate represents an amount per 1 unit. Choices B and C are equivalent rates for the given information, but are not reduced to 1 hour or 1 minute. To find the unit rate in this situation you would need to get the time to 1 hour.

   45 minutes out of 60 minutes reduces to $\frac{3}{4}$ of an hour. You must get $\frac{3}{4}$ of an hour to equal 1 hour by dividing by $\frac{3}{4}$. If you divide one part of the unit rate by $\frac{3}{4}$, you also must divide $\frac{1}{8}$ by $\frac{3}{4}$. You can also solve this problem using decimals by converting $\frac{1}{8} = 0.125$ and $\frac{3}{4} = 0.75$ using long division. Then you can solve the problem similarly to the previous method that used fractions. You would then need to divide 0.125 by 0.75. This would result in $0.1\overline{666666}$ which is equivalent to $\frac{1}{6}$.

3. **D** Although all of these appear to be unit rates as they all have an amount per 1 unit (day, week, hour, and year), choice D is not an equivalent unit rate to the given data. Also remember that this question asks you to choose the one that CANNOT be used.

4. **Part A:** $\frac{6\text{ miles}}{1\text{ hour}}$ or $\frac{0.1\text{ mile}}{1\text{ min}}$ 1.5 miles in about 15 minutes needs to be reduced to miles in 1 minute or projected to miles in 1 hour for it to be a unit rate.

$\frac{1.5\text{ miles}}{15\text{ min}} \frac{\div 15}{\div 15} = \frac{0.1\text{ mile}}{1\text{ min}}$ Or you can determine how many miles in 1 hour by multiplying by 4 since 4 groups of 15 min equals 1 hour.

$\frac{1.5\text{ miles}}{15\text{ min}} \frac{\times 4}{\times 4} = \frac{6\text{ miles}}{60\text{ min}} = \frac{6\text{ miles}}{1\text{ hour}}$

Part B: $4\frac{1}{3}$ hours or 4 hours 20 minutes

Since you found the unit rate in part A, you should use it in a proportion to predict the amount of time it will take to run 26 miles. After you set up the proportion you will cross multiply and solve for x.

$\frac{6\text{ miles}}{1\text{ hour}} = \frac{26\text{ miles}}{x\text{ hours}}$ $\frac{6x}{6} = \frac{26}{6}$ $x = 4\frac{1}{3}$ hour or 4 hours 20 minutes

Part C: 41 full laps

Step 1: In order to find the perimeter of the path, you need to convert the map to actual lengths. You can do this with proportions or by finding the constant of proportionality or the unit rate by reducing 4 cm = 1,200 feet to 1 cm = 300 feet.

$4.2 \times 300 = 1,260$ ft

$1.8 \times 300 = 540$ ft

$3.5 \times 300 = 1,050$ ft

Step 2: The perimeter of the trapezoid is found by adding all the sides:

$1,050 + 540 + 540 + 1,260 = 3,390$ feet.

3,390 feet is 1 lap.

Step 3: Finally, you need to determine how many laps he must run total for 26 miles if 1 lap is 3,390 feet. There are 5,280 feet in 1 mile. You can set up a proportion to help determine how many feet are in 26 miles and then divide by 3,390. Remember that the question asks for full laps. Since 40 laps will be a little short of 26 miles, you must round up to 41 laps to ensure you practice at least 26 miles.

$\frac{1\text{ mi}}{5,280\text{ ft}} = \frac{26\text{ mi}}{x\text{ ft}}$ $x = 137,280$ ft

$137,280 \div 3,390 = 40.495575$ laps

1. **B** When looking at each proportion, it is helpful if you label what each number represents and see if the labeling is consistent. In the proportion in choice B, the grams are in the numerator and the milliliters are in the denominator. So when setting up the second ratio, grams must stay in the numerator and milliliters must be in the denominator. Therefore the x is in the numerator and the 250 ml is in the denominator. Choice B is using the simplified form of the fraction:

$$\frac{8 \text{ grams}}{60 \text{ ml}} = \frac{2 \text{ grams}}{15 \text{ ml}}.$$

2. **A** Finding the unit rate or constant of proportionality can help when writing an equation. Jordan can collect 7 tolls in 2.5 minutes, so if you reduce it to the amount per minute, you can then find the constant of proportionality.

$$\frac{7 \text{ tolls}}{2.5 \text{ min}} \cdot \frac{\div 2.5}{\div 2.5} = \frac{2.8 \text{ tolls}}{1 \text{ min}}$$

Knowing that 2.8 tolls are collected in 1 minute, all you would need to do is multiply 2.8 by how many minutes Jordan is there collecting to calculate the amount of tolls in that time period. Since the minutes can change, you will use m for minutes and t for tolls as stated in the problem.

3. **A** Proportional relationships when graphed are straight lines (which show a constant of proportionality) that pass through the point (0, 0). The only graph that does this is choice A.

Choices B and D are straight, but do not pass through (0, 0). Choice C doesn't pass through (0, 0) and is not straight.

4. **Part A:** The point (2, 3) represents the relationship between the number of notebooks sold and the cost. In this particular case 2 notebooks were sold for $3. You can determine this by reading the x-axis label and the y-axis label. When writing ordered pairs (x, y) the first number is the x value for the horizontal axis and the second number is the y value corresponding to the vertical axis.

Part B: The constant of proportionality is 1.5 or 1.50. Explanations of methods to determine this will vary. Suggested response: Constant

of proportionality is also known as unit rate, which is the rate for 1 item. One method is to go along the x-axis to the number 1, then go up until you hit the line drawn. Once you hit the line, look to the left and read what number is on the y-axis at that height. This is the unit rate since it is the cost for 1 notebook. Another method is to take the ratio of $3 for 2 notebooks and divide to find the cost of 1 notebook. You could also look on the graph and notice that to go from one point to each of the next points, you would rise 1.5 units vertically for every 1 unit you go over horizontally.

Part C: $y = 1.5x$ or another equivalent equation like $y = \frac{3}{2}x$. Once you find the constant of proportionality, you can use that to help write your equation. For every value of x you would multiply it by 1.5 to result in the y value. So in other words, y equals x times 1.5, or $y = 1.5x$.

5. **A** You should reduce them to their unit rates or constant of proportionality to help you compare. Vehicle A uses an equation. If you substitute 1 gallon for g (gallons) and perform order of operations, you get $m = 35$, so on 1 gallon you can go **35 miles** in vehicle A. You can also see from the equation that the constant of proportionality is 35. Vehicle B's information is provided as a chart. Since 1 gallon is not in the chart, you need to find the constant of proportionality by dividing the miles by the gas. $24 \div 2 = 12$ *and* $240 \div 20 = 12$. Therefore for 1 gallon of gas you can only go **12 miles**. Vehicle C is graphed. To find the unit rate, you go over 1 and go up $\frac{1}{2}$ line. Each line is worth 50, so you can only go **25 miles** in vehicle C. Vehicle D is provided to you in words and 10 miles per gallon means you can go **10 miles** for 1 gallon. As you compare each, you will see vehicle A go more miles. Therefore it is the best on gas.

6. **B** A proportional relationship can be found in a table if there is a constant of proportionality that holds true for each input and output pair. Choice B is the only chart that has a constant of proportionality. If you multiply the first number of the chart by 2, it results each time in the second value in the chart.

7. **Part A:** $s = 62g$ or other equivalent equation like $g = s \div 62$. For every amount of games pitched you would multiply that number by 62 to result in the amount of strikes. So, strikes equals games pitched times 62, or $s = 62g$. Since 1 game is not in the chart, you need to find the constant of proportionality by dividing the strikes by the games.

$$124 \div 2 = 62 \text{ and } 620 \div 10 = 62.$$

Part B: When $g = 1$, $s = 62$ and when $s = 744$, $g = 12$. Substitute the values into the correct variables and solve as shown below.

When $g = 1$: use order of operations	When $s = 744$: use inverse operations
$s = 62g$	$s = 62g$
$s = 62(1)$	$\dfrac{744}{62} = \dfrac{62g}{62}$
$s = 62$	$12 = g$

Part C: Graph the data on the grid below.

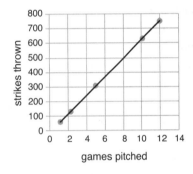

Part D: This graph is proportional since it is a straight line and would go through (0, 0) if the pattern continued.

Part E: Exact explanations will vary but should be similar to: (0, 0) represents that when 0 games are pitched then 0 strikes are thrown. (0, 0) holds true for the context and, when substituted into the equation, is an important requirement for it to be proportional.

Percent Problems and Proportions (RP.A.3), page 116

1. **B** To find the total with tax, you need to multiply by 108% or 1.08. Tax is found by adding the price of the item and the amount of tax but this method takes two steps. Note that the question asks for one equation resulting directly in the total. The quick method to find the total is to add the tax to 100%. The 100% represents the total amount of the item and the 8% represents the tax rate, together it is 108%. Choice A is a distractor since that is the first step of the typical way to calculate tax, but it requires another step of adding the tax and item together. Remember this question asked for an equation that directly results in the total.

2. **$15.00 coupon** To justify your answer, show work for both 20% off and $15 off.

$50 – $15 = $35. Set up a proportion to help find the value of 20% of 50, then subtract it from 50.

$$\frac{20}{100} = \frac{x}{50}$$

$$\frac{100x}{100} = \frac{1000}{100}$$

$$x = 10$$

$$\$50 - \$10 = \$40$$

3. **$40.51** First, find the commission for each item sold using proportions. The percent is placed over 100. The other ratio is written as the part over the whole. The part is what you are looking for and the whole is the cost of the item. Since it is money, round to the hundredth place. Add all three commissions together to find the total commission earned. 29.90 + 10.50 + 0.11 = 40.51

Computer at 5%
$\dfrac{5}{100} = \dfrac{x}{598}$
$\dfrac{100x}{100} = \dfrac{2990}{100}$
$x = 29.90$
TV at $3\frac{1}{2}$% or 3.5%
$\dfrac{3.5}{100} = \dfrac{x}{299.99}$
$\dfrac{100x}{100} = \dfrac{1049.965}{100}$
$x = 10.49965$
$x \approx 10.50$
Batteries at 1%
$\dfrac{1}{100} = \dfrac{x}{10.50}$
$\dfrac{100x}{100} = \dfrac{10.50}{100}$
$x = 0.105$
$x \approx 0.11$

4. **C** If an item is 40% off the price, then you are really paying 60% on the item as shown in choice C. This method allows you to directly result in the sale price without having to do the typical subtraction step that would normally come after multiplying 40% by the item. Choice A is a good distractor since it multiplies 40% by the cost of the shirt, however that only gives the discount, not the sale price.

5. **A** This question asks for the original price and therefore you need to know that if it is 30% off, then 70% is paid on it. You can either set up a proportion or use the equation method to help solve the problem. In either method, $56 is the part and you are finding the whole.

$$\frac{percent}{100} = \frac{part}{whole}$$

$$\frac{70}{100} = \frac{56}{x}$$

$$\frac{70x}{70} = \frac{5600}{70}$$

$$x = 80$$

$$percent \cdot whole = part$$

$$0.70n = 56$$

$$\frac{0.70n}{0.70} = \frac{56}{0.70}$$

$$n = 80$$

6. **9.6 horsepower** There are two methods to solving this problem. You can think of it as a markup problem.

Method 1	Method 2
$percent \cdot whole = part$	Think of it as 100%
$0.20(8) = p$	of the original power
$1.6 = p$	+20% of the power so
Then add the part to	120% in total.
the original to get the	$percent \cdot whole = part$
new amount.	$1.20(8) = p$
$8 + 1.6 = 9.6$	$9.6 = p$

7. **C** To find percent of increase or percent of decrease or percent error, use the formula:

$$\frac{percent}{100} = \frac{part\ (difference\ in\ amounts)}{whole\ (original\ amount)}$$

$$\frac{x}{100} = \frac{88 - 80}{80}$$

$$\frac{x}{100} = \frac{8}{80}$$

$$\frac{80x}{80} = \frac{800}{80}$$

$$x = 10$$

8. **Bank of Pythagorus** $5,000 is the principle, the *r* represents rate which is the percent rate and *t* is for time in years.

Bank of Pythagorus	Einstein's Bank
$I = prt$	$I = prt$
$I = 5000(0.0475)(3)$	$I = 5000(0.02)(7)$
$I = 712.50$	$I = 700$

THE NUMBER SYSTEM

Adding and Subtracting Integers (NS.A.1), page 118

1. **−3 + −9 = −12; 2 + −8 = −6; −10 + 6 = −4; −7 + 12 = 5** Explanations will vary but should be similar to the following. To use the number line, you start at the first number given in the problem and move to the left if the second number is a negative number and to the right if it is a positive number. You can think of the middle plus sign as the word "and" and read the problems as "negative 3 and negative 9."

2. **−4 + 12 − 17; −9 degrees; explanations will vary.** The vertical number line is just like an outdoor thermometer. Start at −4 and go up 12 marks for rising 12 degrees. This brings you to +8. Then from 8, go down the number line 17 marks (dropping 17 degrees) which leaves you at −9. Go up the vertical number line for a positive number and go down the vertical number line for negatives.

3. **−6** Models can vary.

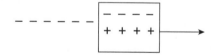

Draw 10 negative signs and 4 positive signs. The 4 positive signs will cancel with 4 negative signs and be removed, leaving you with 6 negative signs.

4. You can use a number line to help, draw pictures, or think that if the signs are the same, you add and if the signs are different you subtract. Always use the sign of the number with the greater absolute value. When there are more than two numbers, you can add and subtract in order from left to right as in the order of operations. You could also use the commutative and associative properties to change the order and grouping to make it easier for you.

$$-9 + -8 = \mathbf{-17}$$
$$10 - -9 = \mathbf{19}$$
$$26 - -12 = \mathbf{38}$$

$$5 - 7 + 3 - 10$$
$$-2 + 3 - 10$$
$$1 - 10$$
$$\mathbf{-9}$$

$$3 - 20 = \mathbf{-17}$$
$$-18 + 18 = \mathbf{0}$$
$$-90 + -78 = \mathbf{-168}$$

$$4 - 6 - 10$$
$$4 - 16$$
$$\mathbf{-12}$$

Associative property was used to group both negatives first.

$$10 - 6 = \mathbf{4}$$
$$-6 + 12 = \mathbf{6}$$
$$120 + -30 = \mathbf{90}$$

$$-20 + -80 - -12$$
$$-100 + 12$$
$$\mathbf{-88}$$

$$-15 - -8 = \mathbf{-7}$$
$$-16 - 7 = \mathbf{-23}$$
$$-90 - 78 = \mathbf{-168}$$

$$32 + -16 - 16$$
$$32 + -32$$
$$\mathbf{0}$$

Multiplying and Dividing Integers (NS.A.2), page 120

1. $-3 \cdot -5 = 15$; $(-2)(4) = -8$; $(-10)(+6) = -60$; $-7 \cdot 12 = -84$ To find the products, multiply the number as you would normally. To decide on the product's sign use the following rules: negative times a negative equals a positive. Negative times a positive or a positive times a negative is a negative.

2. $-30 \div -5 = 6$; $(-20) \div (4) = -5$; $\dfrac{-10}{2} = -5$; $\dfrac{64}{-8} = -8$ To find the quotients, divide the number as you would normally. To decide on the quotient's sign use the following rules: negative divided by a negative equals a positive. Negative divided by a positive or a positive divided by a negative is a negative.

3. **D** Division by zero is undefined. On a calculator you will get an error message. It is undefined since you cannot take something and divide it into nothing.

4. **A** This problem requires you to use the distributive property to simplify the expression to form an equivalent expression. When using the distributive property, you are multiplying the front factor over the entire quantity of the second factor. Be sure to multiply the first factor over each part of the second factor. The second factor has 2 terms inside the parentheses. So in this case you are multiplying -7 and y and then -7 and -2. Be sure to keep the terms separate. Since they are NOT like terms, you cannot combine them. You could think of this problem as $-7(y + -2)$. Remember your multiplication integer rules, a positive times a negative is a negative and a negative times a negative is a positive.

5. **B** This problem requires you to use the distributive property to simplify the expression to form an equivalent expression. When using the distributive property, you are multiplying the front factor over the entire quantity of the second factor. Be sure to multiply the first factor over each part of the second factor. The second factor has 2 terms inside the parentheses. So in this case you are multiplying 3 and $-4x$ and then 3 and -9. Be sure to keep the terms separate. Since they are NOT like terms, you cannot combine them. You could think of this problem as $3(-4x + -9)$. Remember your multiplication integer rules, a positive times a negative is a negative and a negative times a negative is a positive.

6. **D** This problem requires you to use the distributive property and then you must combine like terms to simplify the expression to form an equivalent expression. When using the distributive property, you are multiplying the front factor over the entire quantity of the second factor. Be sure to multiply the first factor over each part of the second factor. The second factor has 2 terms inside the parentheses. So in this case you are multiplying $-x$ and 4 to get $-4x$ and then $-x$ and 11 to get $-11x$. This results in $-4x - 11x$ or $-4x + -11x$. Since both terms have the variable x, they are like terms and should be combined to be $-15x$.

7. **A** Writing a check is taking money from your checking account so it can be represented by a negative number. Multiplication shows repeated

addition so you can use multiplication to shorten the expression.

Rational Numbers and Long Division (NS.A.2.d), page 122

Remember that you should not use a calculator for these problems. Numerator becomes the dividend inside the long division box and the denominator is the divisor which is outside the long division box.

1. $0.\overline{666666}$
2. $0.\overline{142857}$
3. 0.5625
4. **D** This question asks for the answer that is not correct. A rational number is a number that can only be written as a ratio of whole numbers, in decimal form terminates in zeros or repeats in decimal form.
5. **B** As a decimal $\frac{5}{9}$ is correctly written as $0.\overline{5}$. Often times some calculators will round repeating decimals, do not get tricked by this and choose choice D. The proper way to write repeating decimals is with a repeater bar.
6. 0.125
7. Based on the answer you calculated for $\frac{1}{8}$ in question 6, complete the chart to find the decimal values of the following fractions. *Do not use long division!*

8. A rational number is a number that can only be written as a ratio of whole numbers, in decimal form it terminates in zeros or repeats. A few examples are 0.125, –7, $\frac{1}{2}$. A counterexample is an irrational number like Pi or 1.3463897... be sure to leave the 3 dots....

Real-World Application of Rational Numbers (NS.A.3), page 124

1. **A** To find the mean, add all of the numbers and divide the sum by the amount of numbers you added. The question asks for approximately so your answer will be rounded. Choice B is a distractor since it is the sum of the values. Choice D is also a distractor and is the mean if only absolute values were used.

$$\frac{-12 + -18 + -17 + 0 + -20 + 2 + 5}{7}$$
$$\frac{-60}{7} \approx -8.6$$

2. **B** To find the range, you subtract the highest and lowest numbers. The highest is 5 and the lowest is –20. Choice A is a distractor since it does not show subtracting a negative.

Fraction	Work area	Decimal form	Strategy
$\frac{1}{8}$	——	0.125	——
$\frac{2}{8}$	0.125 + 0.125 ——— 0.250	0.25	Since $\frac{1}{8}$ is 0.125, then $\frac{2}{8}$ is two sets of 0.125 added together. Or you can reduce $\frac{2}{8} = \frac{1}{4}$ and know that is 0.25.
$\frac{3}{8}$	0.125 + 0.125 ——— 0.250 + 0.125 ——— 0.375	0.375	$\frac{3}{8} = \frac{2}{8} + \frac{1}{8}$ $\frac{3}{8}$ is one more group of $\frac{1}{8}$ added on. Since $\frac{2}{8}$ is 0.25, then you add 0.125 to that.
$\frac{6}{8}$	0.375 + 0.375 ——— 0.750	0.75	$\frac{6}{8}$ is $\frac{3}{8}$ doubled so you can add 0.375 to 0.375. Or you can reduce $\frac{6}{8} = \frac{3}{4}$ and know that is 0.75.
$\frac{7}{8}$	1.000 −0.125 ——— 0.875	0.875	$\frac{7}{8}$ is $\frac{1}{8}$ less than $\frac{8}{8}$. $\frac{8}{8}$ is worth 1 whole, subtract 0.125 from 1.

3. **Part A: −16°C** To find the highest value, you need to add 2 degrees, −18 + 2 = −16.

   Part B: −20°C To find the lowest value, you subtract 2 degrees off, −18 − 2 = −20.

   Part C: 3 restaurants. MexTex, Pasta Bowl, and Jim's Harbor fall within −16°C and −20°C.

4. **D** This question asks for the mean growth per year. There are ten years between 1965 and 1975. You need to find the change in height from −14.8 to −7.9 meters. Although the numbers are negative you need to think of their absolute value. 14.8 − 7.9 = 6.9 meters. 6.9 meters ÷ 10 years is 0.69 meters per year.

5. **A** To find the greatest change, you need to subtract the heights in each of the date ranges given. 1955–1965 is the greatest change 28.3 − 14.8 = 13.5. 1975–1985 is a change of 4.2. 1985–1995 is a change of 8.4 and 1995–2005 is a change of 2.8.

6. **−34.6 meters.** 1955–1941 is 14 years. 14 years times 0.45 is 6.3 meters. Since you need to go back 14 years, you need to take off another 6.3 meters from −28.3. −28.3 − 6.3 = −34.6.

EXPRESSIONS AND EQUATIONS

Equivalent Expressions (EE.A.1), page 126

1. **A** To find an equivalent expression, you can start with combining like terms. $-7x$ and $-5x$ are like terms and should be added together, +3 and −10 are also alike and can be combined to result in −7. You could also substitute a value for x into the original expression and then into each of the choices, picking the choice that results in the same value as the original expression. For example you can randomly pick $x = 2$ and substitute it into $-7x + 3 - 5x - 10$ to result in −31. Substituting 2 into x in choice A also results in −31, therefore they are equivalent.

2. **D** When like terms are combined in choice D they result in $8x − 16$ not $8x + 16$. This question asked for the one that is not equivalent. You could also substitute a value for x into the original expression and then into each of the choices, noting which ones also result in the same value as the original expression. Choice D is the only

one that does not result in the same value when 2 is substituted for x.

3. **$-6a + x + 6x^2$** First multiply then combine like terms

$$-2(3a) - 2x + 3(2x^2) + 3x$$
$$-6a - 2x + 6x^2 + 3x$$
$$-6a + x + 6x^2$$

4. Answers will vary. A suggested response is given.

   Both of the expressions are equivalent because of the commutative property of addition. This property lets you flip the order and still result in the same answer. If $r = 2$ and $v = 5$, you can also substitute those values into both expressions and show that both values are equal.

$4r + 2v$	$2v + 4r$
$4(2) + 2(5)$	$2(5) + 4(2)$
$8 + 10$	$10 + 8$
18	18

5. **$n^2 − 7n − 8$** Use the distributive property to distribute the negative sign in the middle of the parentheses to each term in the second set of parentheses. Then combine like terms. Remember that n^2 and n terms are not alike.

$$(3n^2 + n - 10) - (2n^2 + 8n - 2)$$
$$(3n^2 + n - 10) + (-2n^2 - 8n + 2)$$
$$n^2 - 7n - 8$$

6. Answers will vary for the second expression. Make sure the expression you created is equivalent to the original by substituting 3 in where you have any variable.

	Simplified expression	Equivalent expression
$\frac{1}{2}(10n + 50)$	$5n + 25$ $5(3) + 25$ $15 + 25$ 40	$5(n + 5)$ or $2n + 3n + 25$ $5(3 + 5)$ $5(8)$ 40
$-10n - 30 - 5n$	$-15n - 30$ $-15(3) - 30$ $-45 - 30$ -75	$5(-3n - 6)$ or $-15(n + 2)$ $5(-3(3) - 6)$ $5(-9 - 6)$ $5(-15)$ -75
$4n - 9 + 6r - n - 4r - 2r$	$3n - 9$ $3(3) - 9$ $9 - 9$ 0	$3(n - 3)$ $3(3 - 3)$ $3(0)$ 0

7. **$3n^2 - 5n$** Use the distributive property to distribute the negative sign in the middle of the parentheses to each term in the second set of parentheses. Then combine like terms, remember that n^2 and n terms are not alike.

$(6n^2 - 10n - 10) - (3n^2 - 5n - 10)$

$(6n^2 - 10n - 10) + (-3n^2 + 5n + 10)$

$3n^2 - 5n$

8. B To find an equivalent expression, you can start with combining like terms. $3x$ and $4x$ are like terms and should be added together. -5 does not have anything alike and cannot be combined with the other terms. You could also substitute a value for x into the original expression and then into each of the choices, picking the choice that results in the same value as the original expression. For example, you can randomly pick $x = 2$ and substitute it into $3x + 4x - 5$ to result in 9. Substituting 2 into x in choice B also results in 9. Therefore they are equivalent.

Rational Number Computation (EE.B.3), page 128

1. **False.** Justifications can vary. However, you should discuss the following. Sometimes a negative plus a positive results in a positive, but only if the more dominant number is positive. For example $-9 + +30$. A negative plus a positive can result in a negative if the dominant number is negative. For example $6 + -50$.

2. Answers are given in the table. Remember that when given in "exponential form," and the negative sign is inside the parentheses, then you write the negative sign with the number each time as the factor; this is shown in the first two problems under the "Factor form" column. If the negative is outside the parentheses as shown in the third and fourth problems, you bring the negative to the final answer, "Standard form." The last problem shows both the negative inside and outside the parentheses. The negative is written each time with the number and is also brought to the final product. When multiplying, 2 negatives cancel each other.

Exponential form	Factor form	Standard form
$(-2)^4$	$(-2) \cdot (-2) \cdot (-2) \cdot (-2)$	16
$(-2)^5$	$(-2) \cdot (-2) \cdot (-2) \cdot (-2) \cdot (-2)$	-32
-2^4	$-(2 \cdot 2 \cdot 2 \cdot 2)$	-16
-2^5	$-(2 \cdot 2 \cdot 2 \cdot 2 \cdot 2)$	-32
$-(-2)^4$	$-(-2) \cdot (-2) \cdot (-2) \cdot (-2)$	-16

3. A You must perform the order of operations to solve this problem as shown below.

$-2(10) + (-8)^2 - 4(1 - 10)$

$-2(10) + (-8)^2 - 4(-9)$

$-2(10) + 64 - 4(-9)$

$-20 + 64 - 4(-9)$

$-20 + 64 + 36$

$44 + 36$

80

4. **$423.06** Deposits are considered positive numbers and withdrawals are considered negative numbers. Set up the problem by aligning the decimal points and adding and subtracting each of the values starting with $450. To be quicker, group all the deposits and group all the withdrawals, then only add on the one total deposit amount and only subtract the one total withdrawal amount.

Deposits	Withdrawals	Final
325.95	$-$ 75.82	450.00
45.25	$-$ 125.00	$+$ 871.20
+500.00	$-$ 97.32	1321.20
871.20	$+ -$ 600.00	$+ -$898.14
	$-$ 898.14	$+$ 423.06

5. C To make this problem quicke, think of the six $50 withdrawals as $6 \times -\$50 = -\$300$. Withdrawals can be considered negative numbers. Think of the three $25 deposits as $3 \times \$25 = \$75$. Since they gave you the final balance, you need to work backwards to determine the stating balance. Working backwards required inverse operations. So instead of $-\$300$, add 300 and instead of $+\$75$, subtract 75 from $750. Remember to line up the decimal points.

```
  750.00
 +300.00
 1050.00
+ - 75.00
 +975.00
```

6. **Keegan's equation.** This equation is correct since dropping in temperature represents a negative number. Keegan used multiplication to shorten the equation. He could also have used this equation $65 + -5 + -5 + -3 + -3 + -3 + -3 = t$. Christian is incorrect because he used subtraction signs in the problem along with the negative signs. Remember that subtracting a negative is really adding a positive.

7. $4\dfrac{203}{450}$ Perform the order of operations. First complete the absolute value bars. Then divide the fractions. Remember to change to improper fractions and then multiply by the reciprocal of the divisor. Then complete the adding of the two negative fractions by adding them together, first getting common denominators. Finally change the decimal to a fraction and subtract those fractions, be sure to get another common denominator. Remember to simplify your final answer.

$$\frac{-2}{10} + \frac{-7}{12} \div 1\frac{1}{2} + \left|2.36 - 7.4\right|$$

$$\frac{-2}{10} + \frac{-7}{12} \div 1\frac{1}{2} + \left|-5.04\right|$$

$$\frac{-2}{10} + \frac{-7}{12} \div \frac{3}{2} + 5.04$$

$$\frac{-2}{10} + \frac{-7}{12} \times \frac{2}{3} + 5.04$$

$$\frac{-2}{10} + \frac{-14}{36} + 5.04$$

$$\frac{-72}{360} + \frac{-140}{360} + 5.04$$

$$\frac{-212}{360} + 5.04$$

$$\frac{-212}{360} + 5\frac{4}{100}$$

$$\frac{-212}{360} + \frac{504}{100}$$

$$\frac{-2120}{3600} + \frac{18144}{3600}$$

$$\frac{16024}{3600}$$

$$4\frac{1624}{3600}$$

$$4\frac{203}{450}$$

1. **D** Twice a number is multiplying by 2 and increased by 5 means to add 5. Be careful on 4 less, this means subtract 4 from the number. Often times there will be a distractor choice like choice B that has the subtraction in the incorrect order.

2. **C** The words "not more than" means you must be less than or equal to the amount. This is only given in choice C.

3. **B** Consider a smaller problem first, just writing an equation without tax: $2p + 23 = t$. Then from there think about how you would insert tax into the equation to get the total. Notice it asked for the total and not for just the tax. Total is found by multiplying the entire amount of the purchase by 108% = 1.08 (100% is the purchase and the tax 8%). So to the equation you just wrote multiply the purchase by 1.08. Choice D would only result in the amount of tax, not the total with tax.

4. **$49.99v - 10 \geq 200$** Since the question asked for a mathematics sentence and the description said "at least" you should be writing an inequality using the $\geq$ symbol. Coupons are used to deduct or subtract money off, therefore be sure to write minus 10.

5. **Answers and explanations will vary, most common equations are $P = s + s + s + s$ or $P = 4s$** Perimeter is found by adding all the sides. Squares have all sides equal in measure so you can use one variable. These equations are equivalent because you can combine like terms since they are all the same variable.

6. **A** If the car is 40% off the original price then it can be considered 60% on the original price. You should multiply 60% by the original price. Choice B is a good distractor since it uses 40%, however the question asks for one equation that results in the actual price. Choice B will give the discount amount not the final amount of the car.

7. **B** The typical equation that is generally made from this situation is $250p + 20 = T$, however that choice is not given. Instead, a partially solved equation that is equivalent to that is given, choice B. If you start to solve and subtract 20 from each side of the equation, it would result in choice B.

1. **B** To solve equations, you need to perform inverse operations. In this problem you should subtract 7.5 from each side and then divide each side by negative 3.

$$-3n + 7.5 = 28.02$$
$$\underline{-7.5 = -7.5}$$
$$\frac{-3n}{-3} = \frac{20.52}{-3}$$
$$n = -6.84$$

2. $x = -17\frac{3}{4}$ To solve equations, you need to perform inverse operations. In this problem you should change the negative sign to an addition sign. Then subtract $3\frac{3}{4}$ from each side after you get common denominators. Since you are subtracting $3\frac{3}{4}$ from a negative you really are adding the two fractions together. Then divide each side by $\frac{1}{2}$. Remember when you divide fractions you need to change to improper fractions and multiply by the reciprocal of the divisor.

$$\frac{1}{2}x - -3.75 = -5\frac{1}{8}$$
$$\frac{1}{2}x + 3\frac{3}{4} = -5\frac{1}{8}$$
$$\underline{-3\frac{6}{8} = -3\frac{6}{8}}$$
$$\frac{\frac{1}{2}x}{\frac{1}{2}} = \frac{-8\frac{7}{8}}{\frac{1}{2}}$$
$$x = -17\frac{3}{4}$$

How to divide fractions:

$$-8\frac{7}{8} \div \frac{1}{2}$$
$$-\frac{71}{8} \times \frac{2}{1}$$
$$-\frac{71}{4} \times \frac{1}{1}$$
$$-\frac{71}{4}$$
$$-17\frac{3}{4}$$

3. **C** The first step is to simplify the problem and combine like terms. You should combine $3r$ and $-5r$ to make $-2r$. The other choices are completely incorrect steps.

4. **A** The process is shown below starting with the distributive property

$$-5(c - 10) + 3c = 25$$
$$-5c + 50 + 3c = 25$$
$$-2c + 50 = 25$$
$$\underline{-50 = -50}$$
$$\frac{-2c}{-2} = \frac{-25}{-2}$$
$$c = 12.5$$

5. **85** To solve the equation, you need to perform the distributive property, then use inverse operations to solve. Be careful when performing your operations with negative integers.

$$-7(2x - 10) = -1120$$
$$-14x + 70 = -1120$$
$$\underline{-70 = \quad -70}$$
$$\frac{-14x}{-14} = \frac{-1190}{-14}$$
$$x = 85$$

6. $y = -330$ **and check below.** To solve the equation, you need to perform the distributive property, combine like terms, and then use inverse operations to solve. Be careful when performing your operations with negative integers. To perform a check, take the solution and substitute it for every place you see the variable. Then perform the order of operations to see if the left side of the equation equals the right side of the equation. If it does then you have the correct solution. If it does not then it is not a solution and you had an error. Try to solve the equation again.

$$2(y - 20) - 5y = 950$$
$$2y - 40 - 5y = 950$$
$$-40 - 3y = 950$$
$$\underline{+40 \qquad = +40}$$
$$\frac{-3y}{-3} = \frac{990}{-3}$$
$$y = -330$$

MATH ANSWERS EXPLAINED

Check

$$2(y - 20) - 5y = 950$$
$$2(-330 - 20) - 5(-330) = 950$$
$$2(-350) - 5(-330) = 950$$
$$-700 + 1650 = 950$$
$$950 = 950$$

7. **29.8 feet.** Substitute the numbers for the correct variables and then simplify the parentheses. $\frac{1}{2}$ and 50 are like terms so combine them to make 25. Then use inverse operations to get the variable alone.

$$A = \frac{1}{2}h(b_1 + b_2)$$
$$745 = \frac{1}{2}h(28 + 22)$$
$$745 = \frac{1}{2}h(50)$$
$$\frac{745}{25} = \frac{25h}{25}$$
$$29.8 = h$$

Real-World Application of Inequalities (EE.B.4.b), page 134

1. **D** The one brother falls into the $5 category since five year olds are included in that category as denoted by the $\leq$. Both Greg and his other brother will fall into the $7 category since $a \geq 10$ represents 10 and older. $5 + 7 + 7 = 19$

2. **Part A: 7s + 15 $\leq$ 60** Since all his friends are older than 10, you must use the $7 cost per person. The $15 charge should be added on. You must use the $\leq$ since the quesiton says no more than 60 dollars. This inequality is $7s + 15 \leq 60$.

   Part B: 6 kids Use inverse operations to solve the inequality. Since you can't have a part of a person, you need to round down.

$$7s + 15 \leq 60$$
$$\underline{-15 \quad -15}$$
$$\frac{7s}{7} \leq \frac{45}{7}$$
$$s \leq 6\frac{3}{7}$$

3. **$64.** 7 kids times $7 is $49. $49 plus the $15 cake and ice cream fee equals $64.

4. **Part A: (7s + 15)1.08 $\leq$ 85** Since all his friends are older than 10, you must use the $7 cost per person. The $15 charge should be added on. You must use the $\leq$ since the question says Greg cannot spend more than $85, which is the total of the original $60 and the extra $25.

   Part B: 9 kids Perform the distributive property, then use inverse operations to solve the inequality. Since you can't have a part of a person, you need to round down. He will only be able to have 9 friends.

$$(7s + 15)1.08 \leq 85$$
$$(7.56s + 16.2) \leq 85$$
$$\underline{-16.2 \quad -16.2}$$
$$\frac{7.56s}{7.56} \leq \frac{68.8}{7.56}$$
$$s \leq 9.1005$$

Part C:

GEOMETRY

Scale Drawings (G.A.1), page 136

1. **10 meters by 4 meters.** If the scale is 1 centimeter = 2.5 meters, you can set up proportions or use the constant of proportionality (unit rate) to convert the scale measurements to the actual measurements. Both methods are shown. You should have measured the rectangle to be 4 cm by 1.6 cm. Be sure to convert each dimension.

$$\frac{1 \text{ cm}}{2.5 \text{ m}} = \frac{4}{x}$$
$$\frac{1x}{1} = \frac{10}{1}$$
$$x = 10 \text{ meters}$$

Constant of proportionality is 2.5 so 1.6 times 2.5 is another method.

$$2.5 \times 1.6 = 4 \text{ meters}$$

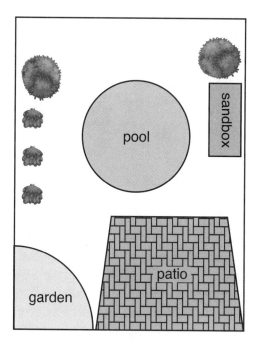

2. **17.3 ft²** First measure the radius of the garden and you should get $\frac{10}{16}$ of an inch. Then using the scale to convert, you can set up a proportion or you can use the constant of proportionality. Use 1 in. = 7.5 feet.

$$\frac{10}{16} \text{ of } 7.5 = r$$

$$\frac{10}{16} \cdot 7.5 = r \text{ or } 0.625(7.5) = r$$

$$r = 4.6875 \text{ feet}$$

Next use the area of a circle formula to calculate the actual square feet. You need to divide your final answer by 4, since it's a quarter of a circle. You should use the Pi key on your calcualtor for more precision and you should not be rounding any numbers until the very end.

$$A = \pi r^2$$
$$A = \pi 4.6875^2$$
$$A = 21.97265625\pi$$
$$A = 69.02913545 \text{ ft}^2$$
$$A = \frac{69.02913545}{4}$$
$$A = 17.25728386 \text{ ft}^2$$
$$A \approx 17.3 \text{ ft}^2$$

3. **10 feet.** The formula for circumference is $C = \pi d$ and given to you was $C = 10\pi$; therefore d must be 10.

4. **Part A: = $721.25**

First you must measure the height and the two bases of the trapezoid. The height measures $1\frac{1}{8}$ of an inch, the largest base is $2\frac{9}{16}$ and the shortest is 2 inches. You must then convert each of these to the actual measurements.

$1\frac{1}{8} \times 7.5$
$\frac{9}{8} \times 7.5$
$\frac{67.5}{8}$
= 8.4375 feet
$2\frac{9}{16} \times 7.5$
$\frac{41}{16} \times 7.5$
$\frac{307.5}{16}$
= 19.21875 feet
$2 \times 7.5 = 15$ feet

Then use the trapezoid formula to calculate the area, use the actual dimensions you just calculated.

$$A = \frac{1}{2}h(b_1 + b_2)$$
$$A = \frac{1}{2}8.4375(15 + 19.21875)$$
$$A = \frac{1}{2}8.4375(34.21875)$$
$$A = \frac{1}{2}(288.720731)$$
$$A = 144.3603516 \text{ feet}$$

Since the information given is that one paver covers one-fourth of a square foot, you will need 4 pavers per square foot. So you must multiply your answer by 4.

$$144.3603516 \times 4 = 577.4414063$$
$$\text{or } 577 \text{ pavers}$$

Each paver costs a $1.25 so,

$$577 \times 1.25 = \$721.25.$$

Part B: 635 pavers and $793.75. A 10% increase means you need all of the pavers (100%) plus 10% more so you can use 110% to make your calculations easier. Remember to recalculate the amount of money also.

$$577 \times 1.10 = 634.7 \text{ pavers or } 635 \text{ pavers}$$
$$635 \times \$1.25 = \$793.75$$

5. C **The entire backyard measures $2\frac{1}{2}$ by $3\frac{1}{4}$ inches.** If you take each choice and multiply the percent by each dimension, you can see which dimensions stay within the standard size of $8\frac{1}{2}$ inch $\times$ 11 inch piece of paper. Only 300% stays in the paper size without going over and uses most of the paper.

$2\frac{1}{2} \times 300\%$
$2\frac{1}{2} \times 3 = 7.5$ inches
$3\frac{1}{4} \times 300\%$
$3\frac{1}{4} \times 3 = 9.75$ inches

1.

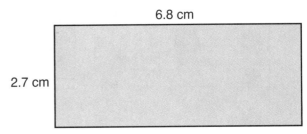

Start with your ruler and draw a 6.8 cm horizontal line across your paper. Then use your protractor to make a 90° angle at the end of the 6.8 cm line, do this by placing a mark on the paper at the 90° point on the protractor. Use your ruler to then measure from the end of the 6.8 cm line up vertically 2.7 cm in length, making sure you maintain the 90° angle. Do the same for the other side of the rectangle.

2.

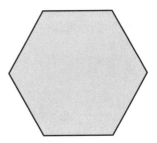

A hexagon is a closed polygon with 6 connected sides. A regular hexagon has all sides with the same lengths and all angles with the same degrees. Start with your ruler and draw a $\frac{3}{4}$ inch horizontal line across your paper. Then use your protractor to make a 120° angle at the end of the line, do this by placing a mark on the paper at the 120° point on the protractor. Use your ruler to then measure from the same end of the first line another $\frac{3}{4}$ inch line toward the 120° mark you left, making sure you maintain the 120° angle. Continue to do this for the other sides as well, basing each new line off of the previously drawn line. You may find it helpful to rotate your paper as you go so each new line is horizontal in front of you.

3.

Measurement requirements	Draw space	# of unique triangles that can be formed
85°, 40°, 55°		Infinite amount of triangles since the sides can be any lengths
Length = 2.0 cm Width = 2.5 cm Height = 6.2 cm		0 triangles since given these 3 lengths there is no way for the shape to be closed with the correct lengths
side = 3.0 cm side = 4.5 cm 90° angle included between the 2 given sides		1 triangle since the 90° must be in between the 2 given sides
60° angle 40° angle 5.3 cm side included between the 2 given angles		1 triangle since the side must be in between the 2 given angles
Sides of 3, 4 and 5 centimeters		1 triangle since with these 3 specific lengths there is only one way for it to be closed
40° angle 2.2 cm side 4 cm side		Multiple triangles since it does not specify where the angle and sides must be located

Note: Figures are not drawn to scale.

3-D Figures and Cross Sections (G.A.3), page 140

1. **B** A horizontal and parallel slice to the base of a square pyramid is a square. Choice A is a distractor, and would be the answer if there was a vertical, perpendicular slice.

2. **A** A vertical and perpendicular slice to the base of a square pyramid is a triangle. Choice B is a distractor, and would be the answer if there was a horizontal, parallel slice.

3. **C** The cross section resulting from a perpendicular, vertical slice to the base is a square just like the right or left side of the prism. Look for the right side's measurements in the picture.

4. **D** A diagonal slice of a square pyramid will result in a trapezoid. Since the plane slices diagonally, the upper left measurement will be shorter than the lower right measurement.

5. **C** A diagonal slice of a cube will result in a rectangle. Since the plane slices diagonally, the diagonal measurement is longer than the cube's original measurement resulting in a rectangle.

Area and Circumference of Circles (G.B.4), page 142

> NOTE to student: depending on if you use 3.14 or the Pi key on your calculator, your answers may vary in precision.

1. **A** This problem gave the answers in terms of π, which means you do not need to actually multiply the radius squared by π. Each of the other choices are good distractors as they all have common errors in them.
$$A = \pi r^2$$
$$A = \pi \cdot 4.25^2$$
$$A = 18.0625\pi$$

2. **B** To find the circumference of the circle, you must use the correct formula $C = \pi d$ or $C = 2\pi r$. This problem gave the answers in terms of π, which means you do not need to actually multiply the diameter by π. Each of the other choices are good distractors as they all have common errors in them. The picture labeled only the radius, so if you use the $C = \pi d$ formula be sure to double the radius for the diameter; $8 \times 2 = 16$.
$$C = \pi d$$
$$C = 16\pi$$

3. **78.54 units^2.** Using the formula $C = \pi d$ and the information $C = 10\pi$ you can tell that the diameter must be 10, therefore the radius is half or 5. Then use the radius measurement in the area formula $A = \pi r^2$. Be sure to round to the hundredth.
$$A = \pi r^2$$
$$A = \pi \cdot 5^2$$
$$A = 25\pi$$
$$A \approx 78.53981633974483$$
$$A \approx 78.54$$

4. **34.56 inches.** Rotation of a tire would be calculated by using the circumference formula. The question asks for the difference in the distance a tire would travel, so you must calculate the circumference of each tire and subtract your answers. If you get a negative difference, use the absolute value as distance is not negative. Directions tell you to round to the hundredth. You should do this after you subtract to be more precise.

Rich's 35-inch tires	Greg's 24-inch tires
$C = \pi d$	$C = \pi d$
$C = 35\pi$	$C = 24\pi$
$C \approx 109.9557428756428$	$C \approx 75.39822368615504$

5. **828 square feet.** The area of the mat outside the wrestling circle would be found by subtracting the area of the circle from the area of the total square mat. Calculate each area separately and then subtract. Remember to divide the 28 foot circular diameter in half for the radius; $28 \div 2 = 14$. The question asks you to the nearest foot, which means you must round to the whole number.

Square mat area	Circle ring area
$A = bh$	$A = \pi r^2$
$A = 38 \cdot 38$	$A = \pi \cdot 14^2$
$A = 1444$	$A = 196\pi$
	$A \approx 615.7521601035995$

$1444 - 615.7521601035995 = 828.2478398964005$

Angles and Algebra (G.B.5), page 144

1. A. Angle 2 measures 120 degrees because angles 1 and 2 are supplemental and must add up to 180 degrees. $180 - 60 = 120$

   B. Angle 4 measures 60 degrees because angles 1 and 4 are vertical angles and are congruent by definition. Congruent means equal in measure.

2. A. Angle 8 measures 50 degrees because angles 7 and 8 are complementary. Complementary angles add up to 90 degrees. $90 - 40 = 50$

   B. Angle 6 measures 90 degrees because angles 7 and 6 are supplemental and must add up to 180 degrees. $180 - 90 = 90$

3. **Part A:** $y + 6 + 3(y + 6) = 180$ These are supplemental angles. Therefore you need to set up your equation so they add up to 180 degrees. Angle 3 is three times the entire amount of angle 4 so you must use the distributive property.

   Part B: Remember to distribute and then combine like terms. Then use inverse operations to solve.

$$y + 6 + 3(y + 6) = 180$$
$$y + 6 + 3y + 18 = 180$$
$$4y + 24 = 180$$
$$\underline{-24 \quad -24}$$
$$\frac{4y}{4} = \frac{156}{4}$$
$$y = 39$$

   Part C: Angle 4 is 45 degrees since angle 4 equals the y you just solved for in Part B plus 6. Angle 3 is 135 degrees since it is three times that of angle 4's measure. You can check yourself by making sure they add up to 180; $45 + 135 = 180$.

4. **Part A:** $2c + 30 = 5c$ These are vertical angles. Therefore you need to set up your equation so they are equal to each other since the definition of vertical angles says they are congruent.

   Part B: Remember to get variables to one side of the equation. Then use inverse operations to solve.

$$2c + 30 = 5c$$
$$\underline{-2c \qquad -2c}$$
$$\frac{30}{3} = \frac{3c}{3}$$
$$10 = c$$

   Part C: Angle 10 and angle 12 are both 50 degrees. Substitute 10 into each expression to get the degree value.

$2c + 30$	$5c$
$2(10) + 30$	$5(10)$
$20 + 30$	50
50	

Surface Area and Volume (G.B.6), page 146

1. C The length is 20, width is 5.7, and height is 6.05. Substitute these values for the corresponding variable and use order of operations to solve.

   $SA = 2lh + 2lw + 2wh$
   $SA = (2 \cdot 20 \cdot 6.05) + (2 \cdot 20 \cdot 5.7) + (2 \cdot 5.7 \cdot 6.05)$
   $SA = 242 + 228 + 68.97$
   $SA = 538.97$

2. C The length is 22, width is 4.3 and height is 7.09. Substitute these values for the corresponding variable and use order of operations to solve. Be careful and read the labels. Choice A is centimeters squared which is the label for area and surface area.

   $V = lwh$
   $V = 22 \cdot 4.3 \cdot 7.09$
   $V = 670.714$

3. **A** The radius is 5 since the diameter is 10. The height is 15. Substitute these values for the corresponding variable and use order of operations to solve. You should use the Pi key on your calculator to have a more precise calculation.

$$SA = 2\pi r^2 + 2\pi rh$$
$$SA = 2\pi 5^2 + 2\pi 5 \cdot 15$$
$$SA = 2\pi 25 + 2\pi 75$$
$$SA = 50\pi + 150\pi$$
$$SA = 200\pi$$
$$SA \approx 628.3185307179586$$

4. **C** The expression for the total surface area of a cylinder is $2\pi r^2 + 2\pi rh$, but a toilet paper tube does not have a top or a bottom. Therefore you must remove the part of the expression that represents the area of the 2 circles which is $2\pi r^2$.

5. **Shorter/Wider Silo.** Remember that the radius is half of the diameter, the pictures give you the diameters, and you need to use half of it in the formula. Substitute these values for the corresponding variable and use order of operations to solve. You should use the Pi key on your calculator to have a more precise calculation. Remember to round to the nearest cubic foot, which is to the whole number. Your work is your justification as long as you have shown all your steps.

Tall/Skinnier Silo
$V = \pi r^2 h$
$V = \pi 7.5^2 \cdot 275$
$V = \pi 56.25 \cdot 275$
$V = 15,468.75\pi$
$V \approx 48,596.51136021711$
$V \approx 48,597$

Shorter/Wider Silo
$V = \pi r^2 h$
$V = \pi 25^2 \cdot 35$
$V = \pi 625 \cdot 35$
$V = 21,875\pi$
$V \approx 68,722.33929727673$
$V \approx 68,722$

6. Reese's cylinder best fits the criteria. You must determine the surface area and volume for each of the containers and then determine which one is the smallest surface area with the largest volume. For the cylinder remember that the radius is 3 since the diameter is 6. Substitute these values for the corresponding variable and use order of operations to solve. You should use the Pi key on your calculator to have a more precise calculation. For the triangular prism the length is 30, the width is 6, and the height is 5.2; s and p are 6 also. Your work is your justification if you have shown all steps.

Cylinder
$V = \pi r^2 h$
$V = \pi 3^2 \cdot 20$
$V = \pi 9 \cdot 20$
$V = 180\pi$
$V \approx 565.5$
$SA = 2\pi r^2 + 2\pi rh$
$SA = 2\pi 3^2 + 2\pi 3 \cdot 20$
$SA = 2\pi 9 + 2\pi 60$
$SA = 18\pi + 120\pi$
$SA = 138\pi$
$SA \approx 433.7$

Triangular Prism
$V = \frac{1}{2}lwh$
$V = \frac{1}{2}30 \cdot 6 \cdot 5.2$
$V = 15 \cdot 6 \cdot 5.2$
$V = 468$
$SA = wh + lw + lp + ls$
$SA = (6 \cdot 5.2) + (30 \cdot 6) + (30 \cdot 6) + (30 \cdot 6)$
$SA = 31.2 + 180 + 180 + 180$
$SA = 571.2$

STATISTICS AND PROBABLITITY

Random Samples and Inferences (SP.A.1 and SP.A.2), page 148

1. **C** Random sampling would provide the most reliable data as it removes bias and prejudice that may occur in collecting the data and it does not allow anyone to be excluded. Choice A may seem like a good method however it doesn't allow everyone to have an equal chance and it always excludes the first and second people. Mailing a questionnaire could be good but it's only to homeowners and an online survey would exclude people that do not have access to the Internet.

2. Each of the checked options provides reliable results as they are the most random, covering the most time and have a good amount of data in the sample size. They also do not exclude people. Also remember that he wants to make an inference based on his local area, so he does not need to ask people outside his area. The choices that are not checked can lead to biased samples.

Asking his friends with whom he rides snowmobiles	✔	Surveying people at a snowmobile show	
✔	Randomly selecting registered snowmobile drivers	Polling every winning driver at a snowmobile race	
Placing an online survey on a manufacturer's website	✔	Observing the types of snowmobiles that are on the trails all season	

3. Since Christian wanted to conclude that most American elementary students are interested in playing football, he should be asking students across America that are not biased to football. This question asks for what he may have done incorrectly which could lead to invalid conclusions. You should have circled:

   He asked mostly adults.

   He surveyed kids at a football game.

   He asked 500 people in NY and FL.

   He asked questions that omitted other sports.

4. Answers will vary. A suggested response is provided: A local politician's conclusion is not valid since he asked his supporters who are biased and only 50 people which is not a good sample size to represent an entire city.

5. **C** Choice C is the only true statement that can be concluded. Choice A is incorrect since on average the yellow and blue have the same amount. Choice B says most bags have 15 candies, yet there is only one bag with 15 in it. Although red candies are the most common in each bag, you cannot conclude that it is because it's the people's favorite, so choice D is also incorrect.

6. **B** To improve his analysis, Jim should sample more bags as it is important to have a good amount in your sample size to be a good representative sample of the entire population.

Visual Overlap of Two Data Distributions (SP.B.3), page 150

1. Answers will vary. A suggested response is provided: Jim's MAD is smaller than Richard's which means that Jim's miles per gallon are all clustered nearer to the mean of 15 whereas Richard's are more spread out. This could show that Jim is more of a consistent driver and typically stays close to 15 miles per gallon while Richard is less consistent and often times gets very low gas mileage and other times gets very high, but is often spread. Remember the Mean Absolute Deviation (MAD) is a number that shows the spread or dispersion in your data. Since the mean was the same for both drivers, the MAD can show us how spread or clustered the data is.

2. **A** The mean deer population is about 3 times larger than the mean wolf population if you calculate that the mean of the deer is about 93.3 and the wolf's mean is 33.3. Each of the other choices is incorrect: the ranges are the same for the data, both graphs are relatively symmetric. For year 3, the deer population was 80 and the wolf population was 60.

3. **B** By comparing the overlap of the graphs, you can see that when the deer population is high, the wolf population is low and vice versa. Therefore you call this an *inverse relationship*. You can see this on the graph: as wolf bars are high, the deer population bars are low.

4. **B** Both of these graphs are relatively symmetric. When the graphs are symmetric, it means the mean and median are centered; and if perfectly symmetric, they are the same value. The beginning of choice A is a correct statement, however the means are not the same. One is 93.3 and the other is 33.3.

5. **D** By comparing the overlaps of these two graphs on the same number line, you can see that School A's graph is more to the right on the number line. Since the number line represents ages, you can conclude the students are older, especially since School B ends at age 14. Choice A is a good distractor since School A is over larger numbers but the numbers do not represent the amount of students, rather just their ages.

6. **C** By comparing the overlaps of these two graphs on the same number line, you can see that School A's graph is symmetric and School B's is skewed because of the long tail on the right of the box. This long tail typically means the data is more spread and that is usually caused by an outlier. The other choices are all plausible conclusions. This question asked for the one that could not be considered.

Measures of Center and Variability for Two Populations (SP.B.4), page 152

1. **False** The Cougars have a **skewed to left** distribution of data.

2. **True** The Braves' data is skewed right since the tail is to the right when the stem is written horizontally.

3. **True** The Cougars have run more yards than the Braves and you can verify this by adding up all the yards or by noticing the shape of the data is heavier to the right where the numbers are higher as compared to the Braves' data.

4. **False** The median yards ran for the Braves is **13** and the Cougars is **32**. Remember to use the Stem as the tens digit in all the numbers.

5. **False** The Braves' data will have a mean **higher** than the median since its skewed **right**. Remember that data distributions that are skewed have mean and medians that are different. If it is skewed right, the mean will typically

be higher than the median. You can verify this by calculating the mean and the median.

6. **False** 41 is **the maximum** in the Braves' data. There is no outlier in this data as there are no gaps on the graphs and no one piece of data is far away from the other data points.

7. **True** The range for the Cougars is larger than the Braves' range. $41 - 2 = 39$ for Braves and $49 - 3 = 46$ for the Cougars.

8. Answers will vary. A suggested response is given. The Cougars' data is skewed left (tail to the left) making most of their data points with the higher yards ran. Since the Braves' data is skewed right (tail to the right) this makes most of their data points toward the left and therefore they have run less yards. Since the Cougar graph is skewed left we can generalize that the median is higher for them than their mean and the reverse of that is true for the Braves. The range can also tell us that the Cougars vary slightly more than the Braves as their range is larger. Although they are all within 2 to 49 points, which implies both teams are within the same range and can typically run the same distances, the Cougars seem to run more yards more often.

Probability (SP.C.5 and SP.C.6), page 154

1.

| E G | | B H A | | F C |

Impossible   Unlikely   Equally likely as unlikely   Likely   Certain

Probabilities are from 0 to 1, or 0% (impossible) to 100% (certain).

A. Flipping heads on a fair coin is $\frac{1}{2}$ the time or 50% which is in the middle at equally like as unlikely to occur.

B. Getting an odd number when rolling a number cube is $\frac{1}{2}$ the time or 50% which is in the middle at equally likely as unlikely to occur.

C. Rolling a number on a number cube is always going to happen so it's certain, 100%.

D. 8 out of 8 chance is 1, which is 100 percent or certain.

E. 0% chance also means impossible.

F. 4 out of 5 chance in getting math homework is 80% which is close to 5 out of 5 so it's likely to happen but not certain.

G. 10% chance in winning the raffle at the park is 1 out of 10 and very close to 0 out of 10 so it is close to impossible but not impossible. Place it more towards the 0 endpoint.

H. 50/50 chance is same as 50% which is in the middle as equally likely as unlikely to occur.

2. **20.** There are a few methods that you could use to determine the answer. The probability of getting a 5 or 6 is $\frac{2}{6}$. You could set up a proportion using the probability of the event in fraction form, $\frac{2}{6} = \frac{x}{60}$ and then cross multiply. The most common way though is to just multiply the probability in fractional form by the amount of times you are doing the event.

$$\frac{2}{6} \cdot 60$$

$$\frac{2}{6} \cdot \frac{60}{1}$$

$$\frac{120}{6}$$

$$20$$

3. **30.6 days.** There are a few methods that you could use to determine the answer. The probability is 17% or $\frac{17}{100}$. You could set up a proportion using the probability of the event in fraction form, $\frac{17}{100} = \frac{x}{180}$ and then cross multiply. You could just multiply the probability in fraction form by the amount of times you are doing the event $\frac{17}{100} \cdot 180$. The easiest way for this though is just to multiply the percent by the amount of times you are doing the event:

$$17\% \text{ of } 180 = \text{days}$$
$$.17(180) = \text{days}$$
$$30.6 \text{ days}$$

4. **Part A:** $\frac{1}{4}$ Theoretical Probability is the amount of times the event should occur over the total possible outcomes. Since there is 1 blue and 4 total colors the P (blue) = $\frac{1}{4}$.

Part B: Answers vary. Troy and Theresa could have only spun the spinner a few times, giving them experimental probabilities that could be off. Experimental Probability typically reaches the Theoretical Probability as more trials are conducted. So they should spin the spinner about 100 times (or more) and keep track of how many times each appears and determine the fraction and percent forms. They then can compare their experimental data with the theoretical data to see if the spinner is unfair. They need to remember that they probably will not get the exact theoretical answer, but it should be close. If the experimental data for blue is far off as compared to the other colors, then they may conclude it's unfair.

Part C: 150 times. The most common way to determine the amount of times is to multiply the probability in fraction form by the amount of times you are doing the event.

$$\frac{1}{4} \cdot 600$$

$$150$$

Part D: Answers can vary but should be similar to: The expected result was 150 times, and they got 147 which is very close. I think this would disprove that the spinner is unfair, they were only 3 off from the expected. When converting the probabilities from fractions to percents, the expected is $\frac{1}{4} = 0.25 = 25\%$ and the data they gathered results in $\frac{147}{600} = 0.245 = 24.5\%$. This is very close and also helps to prove that the spinner is probably fair.

Probability Models (SP.C.7), page 156

1. D Since the movie theater has five movies showing, any model that has five equal sections or sides would be appropriate. In this case only the spinner has 5 equal sections.

2. A You need to look for the spinner that has 2 sectors of equal size (40%) and one sector that is half the size of the larger sizes (20%). Choice B is a good distractor since it has 3 options, like each flavor cookie, but the sectors are all equal in choice B and should not be equal.

3. **C** A seed will be green if it has two lowercase letters in the Punnett Square, yy. The questions asks for yellow though, so you can either count the ones that are not yy, which is YY and Yy. This gives you 3 out of 4 or 75%. You could also choose to calculate the one part that is green, yy, and get 25% and subtract it from 100% to get the complement of green.

4. **P(vowel) is $\frac{9}{20}$.** Cards that are vowels are A and E. There are 6 A's and 3 E's totaling 9 out of 20 picks.

5. $\frac{1}{6} = 16.\overline{6}\%$ To determine the theoretical probability of picking one specific card from the hat, you would notice that there is 1 of each out of 6. You can divide 1 by six and get $0.1\overline{6}$ and then change to a percent. Theoretical probability is determining what you should get, not what the experiment resulted in.

6. There is a discrepancy. Explanations will vary but should be similar to: Keegan should have gotten $16.\overline{6}\%$ each letter an equal number of times, but when you calculate the percent from the chart you can see there is a large discrepancy. You can also see that Keegan should have gotten 1 for every 6 but only got 1 B for every 20 times; this is too low. A also occurred 6 times which is too high. This could be due to cards being different sizes and/or not being shaken in the hat.

Probability of Compound Events (SP.C.8), page 158

1. **A** To answer this question you can create a tree diagram or list the combinations in a sample space and count how many times you see an even number (2,4,6,8) on an 8-sided cube and then a number greater than 4 (5 and 6) on a 6-sided cube in the tree or the list. You can also multiply the probability of rolling an even number by the probability of rolling a number greater than a 4.

2. **C** Theresa has 6 different color shirts and 4 different types of pants to wear to school. Her model must have something that has 6 equal sections (like a 6-sided number cube) and something with 4 equal sections (like a spinner divided into 25% sectors).

3. There are 6 marbles in a bag. 3 are pink, 2 are purple, and 1 is clear. The easiest method is to multiply the two events' probability. Remember you are not replacing a marble when you draw, so you will have one less marble in the bag, thus resulting in one less in the second fraction's denominator.

Part A: $\frac{3}{30}$

P(pink then clear) = $\frac{3}{6} \times \frac{1}{5} = \frac{3}{30}$.

You could reduce it to $\frac{1}{10}$.

Part B: $\frac{6}{30}$. Remember that you are not replacing the marble you first drew. Since the question asks for both being pink, you have to take into account that you could have drawn a pink the first time and therefore there is also one less pink in the bag as well, thus the numerator is 2 and not 3 for the second fraction.

P(pink then pink) = $\frac{3}{6} \times \frac{2}{5} = \frac{6}{30}$.

You could reduce it to $\frac{1}{5}$.

4. **Part A**: Answers will vary as long as two items are used each with only 2 options. Since Gregory can choose out of 2 each time, a coin has 2 sides and could be used, assigning heads to one restaurant and tails to the other. He would do the same for the other coin, assigning heads to comedy and tails to horror. He could also write the names of the restaurants on paper and draw out of a hat and then do the same for the movies.

Part B: Make a tree diagram and then list all the combinations that he could have for his celebration.

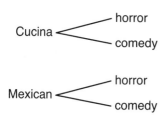

Part C: Use your list or tree diagram to see how many combinations there are for each of the questions. This will be your denominator. The denominator is 4 since there are 4 total combinations.

Probability that he will eat at Mimi's Mexican restaurant and see a comedy is $\frac{1}{4}$.

5. Remember that he is only going to use 1 type of dough, 1 type of cheese, and 1 type of topping. He had regular or wheat dough (2 choices). He had mozzarella, cheddar, or parmesan cheeses (3 choices), and pepperoni, sausage, mushrooms, or olives for a topping (4 choices).

Part A: Answers will vary. He could use a coin to determine the type of dough since there are 2 types. He could put the names of the cheeses on the same size papers and put them in a hat. For the toppings he could use 4 cards in a bowl, each marked with a letter for each type of topping.

Part B:

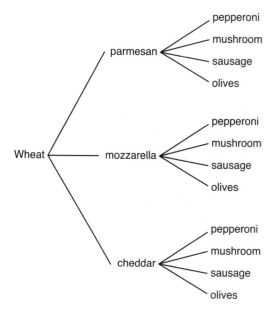

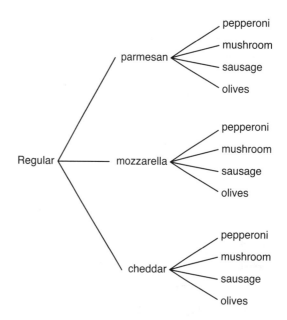

Part C: Use your list or tree diagram to see how many combinations there are for each of the questions, this will be your denominator. The denominator is 24 since there are 24 total combinations.

Probability that he will make a wheat pizza with cheddar cheese and mushrooms is $\frac{1}{24}$.
Probability that he will not use regular dough is $\frac{12}{24} = \frac{1}{2}$.
Probability that he will have a pizza with mozzarella and olives is $\frac{2}{24} = \frac{1}{12}$. This includes either regular or wheat dough.

MATH PRACTICE TEST, page 160

1. **A** A unit rate represents an amount per 1 unit. In this case the only rate that is correct is that Andrew can install 1 program every 23 minutes. He could use this to determine the total time it will take based on how many programs he has. Convert the time to all minutes, 2 hours is 120 minutes (60 minutes times 2). Next divide the 138 minutes by 6 programs to get 23 minutes per program. (RP.A.1)

2. **D** Proportional relationships when graphed are straight lines (shows a constant of proportionality) that pass through the point (0, 0). The only graph that does this is choice D. (RP.A.2)

3. **C** If you find the unit rate or constant of proportionality it can help to write the equations. Richard can plow 4 driveways in 1 hour and 45 minutes which is a total of 105 minutes. If you reduce it to the amount of minutes per driveway, you can then find the constant of proportionality.

$$\frac{4 \text{ driveways}}{105 \text{ min}} = \frac{\div 4}{\div 4} = \frac{1 \text{ driveway}}{26.25 \text{ min}}$$

Knowing that 1 driveway is plowed in 26.25 minutes, all you would need to do is multiply 26.25 by how many driveways, d, there are to be plowed to result in the amount of minutes it should take. (RP.A.2)

4. The point (3, 150) represents the relationship between the number of hours and miles driven. In this particular case, in 3 hours the truck driver will drive 150 miles. You can determine this by reading the x-axis label and the y-axis label. When writing ordered pairs (x, y) the first number is the x value for the horizontal axis and the second number is the y value corresponding to the vertical axis. (RP.A.2)

5. The constant of proportionality is 50. Explanations of methods to determine will vary. Suggested response: Constant of proportionality is also known as unit rate, which is the rate for 1 item. One method is to go along the x-axis to the number 1 then go up until you hit the dot drawn. Once you hit the dot, look to the left and read what number is on the y-axis at that height. This is the unit rate since it is the miles driven for 1 hour. Another method is to take the ratio of 150 miles in 3 hours and divide to find the miles for 1 hour. You could also look on the graph and notice that to go from one point to each of the next points, you would rise 50 units vertically for every 1 unit you go over horizontally. (RP.A.2)

6. The constant of proportionality can be found by going along the x-axis to the number 1 then go up until you hit the dot drawn. Once you hit the line, look to the left and read what number is on the y-axis at that height. This is the unit rate since it is the miles driven for 1 hour. (RP.A.2)

7. **$y = 50x$** Once you find the constant of proportionality you can use that to help write your equation. For every value of x you would multiply it by 50 to result in the y value. So in other words, y equals x times 50, or $y = 50x$. (RP.A.2)

8. **B** Proportional relationships when graphed must go through the origin (0, 0), be a straight line, and have a constant of proportionality (slope) which maintains a repeated pattern from point to point (over and up). (RP.A.2)

9. **A** To find the discounted price you need to multiply by 0.70 since 30% off is equivalent to 70% of the original price. This question wants a direct result in the discounted price so you must have one equation that gives the direct answer. The other method is to multiply by 0.30 and then subtract that product from the original price, but that is a 2-step method and would need 2 equations. Choice B is a distractor since that is the first step of the 2-step method to calculate discount. (RP.A.3)

10. **C** This question asks for the original price and therefore you need to know that you can use 107% since 7% tax onto the total is 107% or 1.07. You can either set up a proportion or use the equation method to help solve. In either method, $481.50 is the part and you are finding the whole. It is the part since you are using a percent greater than 100%. (RP.A.3)

$$\frac{\text{percent}}{100} = \frac{\text{part}}{\text{whole}}$$
$$\frac{107}{100} = \frac{481.50}{x}$$
$$\frac{107x}{107} = \frac{48150}{107}$$
$$x = 450$$

$$\text{percent} \cdot \text{whole} = \text{part}$$
$$1.07n = 481.50$$
$$\frac{1.07n}{1.07} = \frac{481.50}{1.07}$$
$$n = 450$$

11. **D** To find percent of increase or percent of decrease or percent error, use the formula:

$$\frac{\text{percent}}{100} = \frac{\text{part (difference in amounts)}}{\text{whole (original amount)}}$$
$$\frac{x}{100} = \frac{87 - 75}{75}$$
$$\frac{x}{100} = \frac{12}{75}$$
$$\frac{75x}{75} = \frac{1200}{75}$$
$$x = 16\%$$

(RP.A.3)

12. **$306** Remember that the question asks for the monthly payments, not just the interest. Use the formula to find the interest and then add the interest to the amount she needs to repay (12,000) and then divide that by the 48 months that she will have in 4 years. 4 years times 12 months per year is 48 months total. Remember that 5.6% can be written as the decimal 0.056.

    I = prt

    I = 12,000(0.056)(4)

    I = 2,688

    12,000 + 2,688 = 14,688 to be repaid

    14,688 ÷ 48 = 306

13. You can use a number line to help, draw pictures, or think that if the signs are the same, you add and if the signs are different you subtract. Always use the sign of the number with the greater absolute value. When there are more than two numbers, you can add and subtract in order from left to right as in the order of operations. You could also use the commutative and associative properties to change the order and grouping to make it easier for you. (NS.A.1.a–NS.A.1.d)

$-9 + -7 = -16$	$1 - 6 = -5$
$18 - -9 = 27$	$-6 + 15 = 9$
$3 - 27 = -24$	$-10 - -8 = -2$
$-20 + -8 - -50 + 18 = 40$	$-32 - 8 - 7 = -47$

14. $-38 \cdot -50 = 1900$; $(-122)(24) = -2928$;

    $(-88) \div (-4) = 22$; $\dfrac{-115}{5} = -23$

    (NS.A.2.a–NS.A.2.c)

15. C Division by zero is undefined. On a calculator you will get an error message. It is undefined since you cannot take something and divide it by nothing. (NS.A.2.b)

16. C This problem requires you to use the distributive property to simplify the expression to form an equivalent expression. When you use the distributive property you are multiplying the front factor over every part of the factor inside the parentheses (addend). So in this case you are multiplying -3 and y and then -3 and -10. Be sure to keep the terms separate because they are NOT like terms and you cannot combine them. Remember your multiplication rules for integers, a positive times a negative is a negative and a negative times a negative is a positive. Often students find success when they draw arrows from the first factor to each of the terms inside the parentheses. (NS.A.2.b)

17. D This problem requires you to use the distributive property and then you must combine like terms to simplify the expression to form an equivalent expression. When you use the distributive property you are multiplying the front factor over every part of the other factor. So in this case you are multiplying $-x$ and 9 to get $-9x$ and then $-x$ and -8 to get $+8x$. This results in $-9x + 8x$. Since both terms have the variable x they are like terms and should be combined to be $-1x$ or just $-x$. (NS.A.2.b)

18. **$66.\overline{6}$%** Remember that 1 out of 3 do help, so 2 out of 3 do not help therefore you should be dividing 2 by 3. (NS.A.2.d)

19. B To find an equivalent expression you can start with combining like terms. $7x$ and $-10x$ are like terms and should be combined together, resulting in $-3x$, -5 does not have anything alike and cannot be combined with the other terms. (EE.A.1)

20. D When like terms are combined in choice D they result in $4x - 16$, not $4x + 24$; this question asked for the one that is not equivalent. You could also substitute a value for x into the original expression and then into each of the choices, noting which ones also result in the same value as the original expression. Choice D is the only one that does not result in the same value when 2 is substituted for x. (EE.A.1)

21. **$3n^2 - 5n + 19$** Use the distributive property to distribute the negative sign in the middle of the parentheses to each term in the second set of parentheses. Then combine like terms, remembering that n^2 and n terms are not alike. (EE.A.1)

    $$(5n^2 + 3n - 1) - (2n^2 + 8n - 20)$$
    $$(5n^2 + 3n - 1) + (-2n^2 - 8n + 20)$$
    $$3n^2 - 5n + 19$$

22. C The words "not more than" means the cost must be less than or equal to the amount. This is only given in choice C. Also notice that you need 3 apples or $3a$ and $4p$ for 4 papayas. (EE.B.4)

23. **$y = 4x + 1$** You could try the guess and check method however this may take you a long time.

Since the x values are in order you can look down the y column and see that the numbers are increasing by 4 or +4; this becomes the number you multiply the x by. Since the value when $x = 0$ is given, you can look to see what the y value is. This becomes the value you either add on or subtract off. In this case it's +1. The equation is $y = 4x + 1$ (EE.B.4)

24. **$x = 28$** To solve equations you need to perform inverse operations. In this problem you should change the negative signs to an addition sign. Then subtract $3\frac{3}{4}$ from each side after you get common denominators. Since you are subtracting $3\frac{3}{4}$ from a negative you really are adding the two fractions together. $-13\frac{4}{4} = -14$. Then divide each side by $-\frac{1}{2}$. Remember when you divide fractions you need to change to improper fractions and multiply by the reciprocal of the divisor. (EE.B.4.a)

$$-\frac{1}{2}x - -3.75 = -10\frac{1}{4}$$
$$-\frac{1}{2}x + 3\frac{3}{4} = -10\frac{1}{4}$$
$$\underline{-3\frac{3}{4} = -3\frac{3}{4}}$$
$$\frac{-\frac{1}{2}x}{-\frac{1}{2}} = \frac{-14}{-\frac{1}{2}}$$
$$x = 28$$

How to divide fractions:

$$-14 \div -\frac{1}{2}$$
$$-14 \times -\frac{2}{1}$$
$$\frac{28}{1}$$
$$28$$

25. **$c = 3\frac{12}{13}$** Start by using the distributive property followed by combining like terms then inverse operations. It is easiest to leave the final answer as a mixed number instead of trying to divide it. (EE.B.4.a)

$$-2(-5c - 2) + 3c = 55$$
$$10c + 4 + 3c = 55$$
$$13c + 4 = 55$$
$$\underline{-4 = -4}$$
$$\frac{13c}{13} = \frac{51}{13}$$
$$c = 3\frac{12}{13}$$

(EE.B.4.b)

26. **Part A: $7.50b - 10 \leq 150$** Since each bucket costs \$7.50, you must use the \$7.50 cost per bucket. The \$10 coupon should be subtracted off. You must use the $\leq$ symbol since the question states that Jim cannot spend more than \$150.

Part B: 21 buckets Use inverse operations to solve the inequality. Since you can't have a part of a bucket, you need to round down. (EE.B.4.b)

$$7.50b - 10 \leq 150$$
$$\underline{+10 \quad +10}$$
$$\frac{7.5b}{7.5} \leq \frac{160}{7.5}$$
$$b \leq 21.\overline{3333}$$

Part C:

27. **3.22 cm.** If the triangle is equilateral, then it has 3 sides of equal measure and therefore we can divide 6.9 by 3 to result in 1 side, which is 2.3 cm. Then increase 2.3 cm by 40%. The quickest way to do this is to multiply by 140% or 1.40 (G.A.1)

$$1.40 \times 2.3 = 3.22 \text{ cm}$$

28. **D** To have a unique triangle you must be given a side dimension between two different angles. This will result in only 1 possible triangle. Choice A will make an infinite number of triangles. Since the lengths of the sides can be anything, the triangles made would all be similar to each other and would be related by a constant of proportionality. Choice B does not close to make a triangle because the two sides are much too short to meet when drawn off a 10.2 cm side. However, be careful. There are some dimensions

that would work and only produce one triangle. Choice C would not make only one. There would be multiple triangles that could be made since it didn't specify the exact location of the sides and angles. (G.A.2)

29. A A vertical and perpendicular slice of a pentagonal pyramid is a triangle. Choice D is a distractor, and would be the answer if there was a horizontal, parallel slice. (G.A.3)

30. B To find the circumference of the circle you must use the correct formula, $C = \pi d$ or $C = 2\pi r$. This problem gave the answers in terms of π which means you do not need to actually multiply the diameter by π. The picture labeled only the radius, so if you use the formula, be sure to double the radius for the diameter; $5.72 \times 2 = 11.44$. (G.B.4)

$$C = \pi d$$
$$C = 11.44\pi$$

31. **346.36 units²** Using the formula $C = \pi d$ and the information $C = 21\pi$, you can tell that the diameter must be 21, therefore the radius is half or 10.5. Then use the radius measurement in the area formula, $A = \pi r^2$. Be sure to round to the nearest hundredth. (G.B.4)

$$A = \pi r^2$$
$$A = \pi \cdot 10.5^2$$
$$A = 110.25\,\pi$$
$$A \approx 346.3605901$$
$$A \approx 346.36$$

32. **Vertical Angles**. Vertical angles are opposite angles which are congruent and are formed when any 2 lines intersect. (G.B.5)

33. **Part A: $3x + 5 = 4x - 10$** These are vertical angles; therefore, you need to set up your equation so they are equal to each other since the definition of vertical angles says they are congruent.

Part B: $15 = x$ Remember to get variables to one side of the equation. Then use inverse operations to solve.

$$3x + 5 = 4x - 10$$
$$\underline{+10 = \qquad +10}$$
$$3x + 15 = 4x$$
$$\underline{-3x \qquad = -3x}$$
$$\frac{15}{1} = \frac{1x}{1}$$
$$15 = x$$

Part C: Angle 2 and angle 3 are both 50 degrees. Substitute 15 into each expression to get the degree value.

$3x + 5$	$4x - 10$
3(15) + 5	4(15) −10
45 + 5	60 − 10
50	50

(G.B.5)

34. D The length is 33.01, width is 5.2, and height is 6.83. Substitute these values for the corresponding variable in the volume formula and use order of operations to solve. Be careful and read the labels. Choice A is centimeters squared which is for area and surface area. (G.B.6)

$$V = lwh$$
$$V = 33.01 \cdot 5.2 \cdot 6.83$$
$$V = 1172.38316$$

35. B The radius is 3.625 since the diameter is 7.25. The height is 10. Substitute these values for the corresponding variable in the correct surface area formula and use order of operations to solve. You should use the Pi key on your calculator to have a more precise calculation. Remember to round to the tenth. (G.B.6)

$$SA = 2\pi r^2 + 2\pi rh$$
$$SA = 2\pi 3.625^2 + 2\pi 3.625 \cdot 10$$
$$SA = 2\pi 13.140625 + 2\pi 36.25$$
$$SA = 26.28125\pi + 72.5\pi$$
$$SA = 98.78125\pi$$
$$SA \approx 310.3301871875$$

36. A Random sampling would provide the most reliable data as it removes bias and prejudice that may occur in collecting the data and it does not

allow anyone to be excluded. Computers can do this without bias. (SP.A.1 and SP.A.2)

37. **B** Choice B is the only true statement that can be concluded. (SP.A.1 and SP.A.2)

38. **D** To improve his analysis, Andy should sample more car dealers for a longer time. It is important to have a good amount in your sample size to be a good representative sample of the entire population over a period of time. (SP.A.1 and SP.A.2)

39. **B** Mean LA alligator population is larger than the mean FL alligator population

    Each of the other choices are incorrect as the ranges are the same for the data, both graphs are not symmetric, and year 2 on each graph are not the same numbers. (SP.B.3)

40. **B** By comparing the overlaps of these two graphs on the same number line, you can see that Field B's box is from 6 to 10, and the box represents 50%. (SP.B.3)

41. **C** By comparing the overlaps of these two graphs on the same number line, you can see that Field A's graph is not symmetric and Field B's is not really skewed. The other choices are all plausible conclusions. This question asked for the one that could not be considered. (SP.B.3)

42. **A** The only answer that can be concluded is that the Hitters outperform the Sluggers since the data is skewed toward higher homeruns for the Hitters. (SP.B.4)

43. **Sluggers' median is 12 and Hitters' median is 27.** Processes can vary; I counted that there were 18 scores for the Sluggers which means the median is between the 9th and 10th value point. I noticed with the Hitters there are 17 values. Therefore the middle number is the 9th value. (SP.B.4)

44. **40.** There are a few methods that you could use to determine the answer. The probability of getting a 3 or 4 is $\frac{2}{6}$. You could set up a proportion using the probability of the event in fraction form, $\frac{2}{6} = \frac{x}{120}$ and then cross multiply. The most common way though is to just multiply the probability in fractional form by the amount

of times you are doing the event. (SP.C.5 and SP.C.6)

$$\frac{2}{6} \cdot 120$$

$$\frac{2}{6} \cdot \frac{120}{1}$$

$$\frac{240}{6}$$

$$40$$

45. **17.67 mornings.** There are a few methods that you could use to determine the answer. The probability is 9.5% or $\frac{9.5}{100}$. You could set up a proportion using the probability of the event in fraction form, $\frac{9.5}{100} = \frac{x}{186}$ and then cross multiply. The quickest way for this though is just to multiply the percent by the amount of times you are doing the event: (SP.C.5 and SP.C.6)

$$9.5\% \text{ of } 186 = \text{days}$$

$$.095(186) = \text{days}$$

$$17.67 \text{ days}$$

46. **Part A:** $\frac{1}{2}$ *Theoretical probability* is the amount of times the event should occur over the total possible outcomes. Since there is 1 head and 2 total sides, the P(head) = $\frac{1}{2}$.

    Part B: Answers vary. Aaron and Jenny should flip the coin several times and see what appears. Experimental Probability typically reaches the Theoretical Probability as more trials are conducted. So they should flip the coin about 100 times (or more) and keep track of how many times each appears and determine the fraction and percent forms. They then can compare their experimental data with the theoretical data to see if the coin is unfair. They need to remember that they probably will not get the exact theoretical answer, but it should be close. If the experimental data for heads is far off as compared to tails, then they may conclude it's unfair. (SP.C.5 and SP.C.6)

47. **Part A: 10 times.** The most common way to determine the amount of times is to multiply the

probability in fraction form by the amount of times you are doing the event.

$$\frac{1}{2} \cdot 20$$

$$\frac{20}{2}$$

$$10$$

Part B: Answers can vary but should be similar to: The expected result was 10 times, and they got 12 which is very close. I think this would disprove that the coin is unfair because they were only 2 off from the expected. (SP.C.5 and SP.C.6)

48. B Since there are 6 fruits to choose from, any model that has six equal sections or sides would be appropriate. In this case only the dice has 6 equal sections. (SP.C.7.a and SP.C.7.b) (SP.C.8.a–SP.C.8.c)

49. C To answer this question, you can create a tree diagram or list the combinations in a sample space and count how many times you see a number less than 4 (3, 2, or 1) on an 8-sided cube and then a number greater than 4 (5 and 6) on a 6-sided cube in the tree or the list. You can also multiply the probability of rolling a number less than 4 by the probability of rolling a number greater than 4.

$$\frac{3}{8} \times \frac{2}{6} = \frac{6}{48} \text{ or } \frac{1}{8}$$

(SP.C.8.a–SP.C.8.c)

50. $\frac{8}{42}$ There are 7 pieces of candy in a jar. Four are blue, 2 are purple, and 1 is green. The easiest method is to multiply the probability of the two events. Remember, you are not replacing a piece of candy when you draw, so you will have one fewer piece of candy in the jar, thus resulting in one less in the second fraction's denominator. (SP.C.8.a–SP.C.8.c)

$$P(\text{blue then purple}) = \frac{4}{7} \times \frac{2}{6} = \frac{8}{42}$$

You could also reduce it to $\frac{4}{21}$.

APPENDIX A
ENGLISH LANGUAGE ARTS STANDARDS

Reading: Literature
CCSS.ELA-Literacy.RL.7.1 Cite several pieces of textual evidence to support analysis of what the text says explicitly as well as inferences drawn from the text.
CCSS.ELA-Literacy.RL.7.2 Determine a theme or central idea of a text and analyze its development over the course of the text; provide an objective summary of the text.
CCSS.ELA-Literacy.RL.7.3 Analyze how particular elements of a story or drama interact (e.g., how setting shapes the character or plot).
CCSS.ELA-Literacy.RL.7.4 Determine the meaning of words and phrases as they are used in a text, including figurative and connotative meanings; analyze the impact of rhymes and other repetitions of sounds (e.g., alliteration) on a specific verse or stanza of a poem or section of a story or drama.
CCSS.ELA-Literacy.RL.7.5 Analyze how a drama's or poem's form or structure (e.g. soliloquy, sonnet) contributes to its meaning.
CCSS.ELA-Literacy.RL.7.6 Analyze how an author develops and contrasts the points of view of different characters or narrators in a text.
CCSS.ELA-Literacy.RL.7.7 Compare and contrast a written story, drama, or poem to its audio, filmed, staged, or multimedia version, analyzing the effect of techniques unique to each medium (e.g., lighting, sound, color, or camera focus and angles in a film).
CCSS.ELA-Literacy.RL.7.9 Compare and contrast a fictional portrayal of a time, place, or character and a historical account of the same period as a means of understanding how authors of fiction use or alter history.
CCSS.ELA-Literacy.RL.7.10 By the end of the year, read and comprehend literature, including stories, dramas, and poems, in the grades 6–8 text-complexity band proficiently, with scaffolding as needed at the high end of the range.
Reading: Informational Text
CCSS.ELA-Literacy.RI.7.1 Cite several pieces of textual evidence to support analysis of what the text says explicitly as well as inferences drawn from the text.
CCSS.ELA-Literacy.RI.7.2 Determine two or more central ideas in a text and analyze their development over the course of the text; provide an objective summary of the text.
CCSS.ELA-Literacy.RI.7.3 Analyze the interactions between individuals, events, and ideas in a text (e.g., how ideas influence individuals or events, or how individuals influence ideas or events).
CCSS.ELA-Literacy.RI.7.4 Determine the meaning of words and phrases as they are used in a text, including figurative, connotative, and technical meanings; analyze the impact of a specific word choice on meaning and tone.
CCSS.ELA-Literacy.RI.7.5 Analyze the structure an author uses to organize a text, including how the major sections contribute to the whole and to the development of the ideas.
CCSS.ELA-Literacy.RI.7.6 Determine an author's point of view or purpose in a text and analyze how the author distinguishes his or her position from that of others.
CCSS.ELA-Literacy.RI.7.7 Compare and contrast a text to an audio, video, or multimedia version of the text, analyzing each medium's portrayal of the subject (e.g., how the delivery of a speech affects the impact of the words).

CCSS.ELA-Literacy.RI.7.8 Trace and evaluate the argument and specific claims in a text, assessing whether the reasoning is sound and the evidence is relevant and sufficient to support the claims.

CCSS.ELA-Literacy.RI.7.9 Analyze how two or more authors writing about the same topic shape their presentations of key information by emphasizing different evidence or advancing different interpretations of facts.

CCSS.ELA-Literacy.RI.7.10 By the end of the year, read and comprehend literary nonfiction in the grades 6–8 text-complexity band proficiently, with scaffolding as needed at the high end of the range.

Writing

CCSS.ELA-Literacy.W.7.1 Write arguments to support claims with clear reasons and relevant evidence.

CCSS.ELA-Literacy.W.7.1.A Introduce claim(s), acknowledge alternate or opposing claims, and organize the reasons and evidence logically.

CCSS.ELA-Literacy.W.7.1.B Support claim(s) with logical reasoning and relevant evidence, using accurate, credible sources and demonstrating an understanding of the topic or text.

CCSS.ELA-Literacy.W.7.1.C Use words, phrases, and clauses to create cohesion and clarify the relationships among claim(s), reasons, and evidence.

CCSS.ELA-Literacy.W.7.1.D Establish and maintain a formal style.

CCSS.ELA-Literacy.W.7.1.E Provide a concluding statement or section that follows from and supports the argument presented.

CCSS.ELA-Literacy.W.7.2 Write informative/explanatory texts to examine a topic and convey ideas, concepts, and information through the selection, organization, and analysis of relevant content.

CCSS.ELA-Literacy.W.7.2.A Introduce a topic clearly, previewing what is to follow; organize ideas, concepts, and information, using strategies such as definition, classification, comparison/contrast, and cause/effect; include formatting (e.g., headings), graphics (e.g., charts, tables), and multimedia when useful to aiding comprehension.

CCSS.ELA-Literacy.W.7.2.B Develop the topic with relevant facts, definitions, concrete details, quotations, or other information and examples.

CCSS.ELA-Literacy.W.7.2.C Use appropriate transitions to create cohesion and clarify the relationships among ideas and concepts.

CCSS.ELA-Literacy.W.7.2.D Use precise language and domain-specific vocabulary to inform about or explain the topic.

CCSS.ELA-Literacy.W.7.2.E Establish and maintain a formal style.

CCSS.ELA.W.7.2.F Provide a concluding statement or section that follows from and supports the information or explanation presented.

CCSS.ELA-Literacy.W.7.3 Write narratives to develop real or imagined experiences or events using effective technique, relevant descriptive details, and well-structured event sequences.

CCSS.ELA-Literacy.W.7.3.A Engage and orient the reader by establishing a context and point of view and introducing a narrator and/or characters; organize an event sequence that unfolds naturally and logically.

CCSS.ELA-Literacy.W.7.3.B Use narrative techniques, such as dialogue, pacing, and description, to develop experiences, events, and/or characters.

CCSS.ELA-Literacy.W.7.3.C Use a variety of transition words, phrases, and clauses to convey sequence and signal shifts from one time frame or setting to another.

CCSS.ELA-Literacy.W.7.3.D Use precise words and phrases, relevant descriptive details, and sensory language to capture the action and convey experiences and events.

CCSS.ELA-Literacy.W.7.3.E Provide a conclusion that follows from and reflects on the narrated experiences or events.

CCSS.ELA-Literacy.W.7.4 Produce clear and coherent writing in which the development, organization, and style are appropriate to task, purpose, and audience. (Grade-specific expectations for writing types are defined in standards 1–3 above.)

CCSS.ELA-Literacy.W.7.5 With some guidance and support from peers and adults, develop and strengthen writing as needed by planning, revising, editing, re-writing, or trying a new approach, focusing on how well purpose and audience have been addressed. (Editing for conventions should demonstrate command of Language standards 1–3 up to and including grade 7.)
CCSS.ELA-Literacy.W.7.6 Use technology, including the Internet, to produce and publish writing and link to and cite sources as well as to interact and collaborate with others, including linking to and citing sources.
CCSS.ELA-Literacy.W.7.7 Conduct short research projects to answer a question, drawing on several sources and generating additional related, focused questions for further research and investigation.
CCSS.ELA-Literacy.W.7.8 Gather relevant information from multiple print and digital sources, using search terms effectively; assess the credibility and accuracy of each source; and quote or paraphrase the data and conclusions of others while avoiding plagiarism and following a standard format for citation.
CCSS.ELA-Literacy.W.7.9 Draw evidence from literary or informational texts to support analysis, reflection, and research.   CCSS.ELA-Literacy.W.7.9.A Apply *grade 7 Reading standards* to literature (e.g., "Compare and contrast a fictional portrayal of a time, place, or character and a historical account of the same period as a means of understanding how authors of fiction use or alter history").   CCSS.ELA-Literacy.W.7.9.B Apply *grade 7 Reading standards* to literary nonfiction (e.g., "Trace and evaluate the argument and specific claims in a text, assessing whether the reasoning is sound and the evidence is relevant and sufficient to support the claims").
CCSS.ELA-Literacy.W.7.10 Write routinely over extended time frames (time for research, reflection, and revision) and shorter time frames (a single sitting or a day or two) for a range of discipline-specific tasks, purposes, and audiences.
Speaking and Listening
CCSS.ELA-Literacy.SL.7.1 Engage effectively in a range of collaborative discussions (one-on-one, in groups, and teacher-led) with diverse partners on grade 7 topics, texts, and issues, building on others' ideas and expressing their own clearly.   CCSS.ELA-Literacy.SL.7.1.A Come to discussions prepared, having read or researched material under study; explicitly draw on that preparation by referring to evidence on the topic, text, or issue to probe and reflect on ideas under discussion.   CCSS.ELA-Literacy.SL.7.1.B Follow rules for collegial discussions, track progress toward specific goals and deadlines, and define individual roles as needed.   CCSS.ELA-Literacy.SL.7.1.C Pose questions that elicit elaboration and respond to others' questions and comments with relevant observations and ideas that bring the discussion back on topic as needed.   CCSS.ELA-Literacy.SL.7.1.D Acknowledge new information expressed by others and, when warranted, modify their own views.
CCSS.ELA-Literacy.SL.7.2 Analyze the main ideas and supporting details presented in diverse media and formats (e.g., visually, quantitatively, orally) and explain how the ideas clarify a topic, text, or issue under study.
CCSS.ELA-Literacy.SL.7.3 Delineate a speaker's argument and specific claims, evaluating the soundness of the reasoning and the relevance and sufficiency of the evidence.
CCSS.ELA-Literacy.SL.7.4 Present claims and findings, emphasizing salient points in a focused, coherent manner with pertinent descriptions, facts, details, and examples; use appropriate eye contact, adequate volume, and clear pronunciation.
CCSS.ELA-Literacy.SL.7.5 Include multimedia components and visual displays in presentations to clarify claims and findings and emphasize salient points.
CCSS.ELA-Literacy.SL.3.6 Adapt speech to a variety of contexts and tasks, demonstrating command of formal English when indicated or appropriate. (See grade 7 Language standards 1 and 3 for specific expectations.)

CCSS.ELA-Literacy.L.7.1 Demonstrate command of the conventions of standard English grammar and usage when writing or speaking.

CCSS.ELA-Literacy.L.7.1.A Explain the function of phrases and clauses in general and their function in specific sentences.

CCSS.ELA-Literacy.L.7.1.B Choose among simple, compound, complex, and compound-complex sentences to signal differing relationships among ideas.

CCSS.ELA-Literacy.L.7.1.C Place phrases and clauses within a sentence, recognizing and correcting misplaced and dangling modifiers.

CCSS.ELA-Literacy.L.7.2 Demonstrate command of the conventions of standard English capitalization, punctuation, and spelling when writing.

CCSS.ELA-Literacy.L.7.2.A Use a comma to separate coordinate adjectives (e.g., *It was a fascinating, enjoyable movie* but not *He wore an old [,] green shirt*).

CCSS.ELA-Literacy.L.7.2.B Spell correctly.

CCSS.ELA-Literacy.L.7.3 Use knowledge of language and its conventions when writing, speaking, reading, or listening.

CCSS.ELA-Literacy.L.7.3.A Choose language that expresses ideas precisely and concisely, recognizing and eliminating wordiness and redundancy.

CCSS.ELA-Literacy.L.7.4 Determine or clarify the meaning of unknown and multiple-meaning words and phrases based on *grade 7 reading and content*, choosing flexibly from a range of strategies.

CCSS.ELA-Literacy.L.7.4.A Use context (e.g., the overall meaning of a sentence or paragraph; a word's position or function in a sentence) as a clue to the meaning of the word or phrase.

CCSS.ELA-Literacy.L.7.4.B Use common, grade-appropriate Greek or Latin affixes and roots as clues to the meaning of a word (e.g., *belligerent, bellicose, rebel*).

CCSS.ELA-Literacy.L.7.4.C Consult general and specialized reference materials (e.g., dictionaries, glossaries, thesauruses), both print and digital, to find the pronunciation of a word or determine or clarify its precise meaning or its part of speech.

CCSS.ELA-Literacy.L.7.4.D Verify the preliminary determination of the meaning of a word or phrase (e.g., by checking the inferred meaning in context or in a dictionary).

CCSS.ELA-Literacy.L.7.5 Demonstrate understanding of figurative language, word relationships, and nuances in word meanings.

CCSS.ELA-Literacy.L.7.5.A Interpret figures of speech (e.g., literary, biblical, and mythological allusions) in context.

CCSS.ELA-Literacy.L.7.5.B Use the relationship between particular words (e.g., synonym/antonym, analogy) to better understand each of the words.

CCSS.ELA-Literacy.L.7.5.C Distinguish among the connotations (associations) of words with similar denotations (definitions) (e.g., *refined, respectful, polite, diplomatic, condescending*).

CCSS.ELA-Literacy.L.7.6 Acquire and use accurately grade-appropriate general academic and domain-specific words and phrases; gather vocabulary knowledge when considering a word or phrase important to comprehension or expression.

APPENDIX B

MATH STANDARDS

Ratios and Proportional Relationships

CCSS.Math.Content.7.RP.A.1 Compute unit rates associated with ratios of fractions, including ratios of lengths, areas, and other quantities measured in like or different units. *For example, if a person walks 1/2 mile in each 1/4 hour, compute the unit rate as the complex fraction $\frac{\frac{1}{2}}{\frac{1}{4}}$ miles per hour, equivalently 2 miles per hour.*

CCSS.Math.Content.7.RP.A.2 Recognize and represent proportional relationships between quantities.
  CCSS.Math.Content.7.RP.A.2.a Decide whether two quantities are in a proportional relationship, e.g., by testing for equivalent ratios in a table or graphing on a coordinate plane and observing whether the graph is a straight line through the origin.
  CCSS.Math.Content.7.RP.A.2.b Identify the constant of proportionality (unit rate) in tables, graphs, equations, diagrams, and verbal descriptions of proportional relationships.
  CCSS.Math.Content.7.RP.A.2.c Represent proportional relationships by equations. *For example, if total cost t is proportional to the number n of items purchased at a constant price p, the relationship between the total cost and the number of items can be expressed as t = pn.*
  CCSS.Math.Content.7.RP.A.2.d Explain what a point (x, y) on the graph of a proportional relationship means in terms of the situation, with special attention to the points $(0, 0)$ and $(1, r)$ where r is the unit rate.

CCSS.Math.Content.7.RP.A.3 Use proportional relationships to solve multi-step ratio and percent problems. Examples: simple interest, tax, markups and markdowns, gratuities and commissions, fees, percent increase and decrease, percent error.

The Number System

CCSS.Math.Content.7.NS.A.1 Apply and extend previous understandings of addition and subtraction to add and subtract rational numbers; represent addition and subtraction on a horizontal or vertical number line diagram.
  CCSS.Math.Content.7.NS.A.1.a Describe situations in which opposite quantities combine to make 0. *For example, a hydrogen atom has 0 charge because its two constituents are oppositely charged.*
  CCSS.Math.Content.7.NS.A.1.b Understand $p + q$ as the number located a distance $|q|$ from p, in the positive or negative direction depending on whether q is positive or negative. Show that a number and its opposite have a sum of 0 (are additive inverses). Interpret sums of rational numbers by describing real-world contexts.
  CCSS.Math.Content.7.NS.A.1.c Understand subtraction of rational numbers as adding the additive inverse, $p - q = p + (-q)$. Show that the distance between two rational numbers on the number line is the absolute value of their difference, and apply this principle in real-world contexts.
  CCSS.Math.Content.7.NS.A.1.d Apply properties of operations as strategies to add and subtract rational numbers.

CCSS.Math.Content.7.NS.A.2 Apply and extend previous understandings of multiplication and division and of fractions to multiply and divide rational numbers.
  CCSS.Math.Content.7.NS.A.2.a Understand that multiplication is extended from fractions to rational numbers by requiring that operations continue to satisfy the properties of operations, particularly the distributive property, leading to products such as $(-1)(-1) = 1$ and the rules for multiplying signed numbers. Interpret products of rational numbers by describing real-world contexts.
  CCSS.Math.Content.7.NS.A.2.b Understand that integers can be divided, provided that the divisor is not zero, and every quotient of integers (with non-zero divisor) is a rational number. If p and q are integers, then $-(p/q) = (-p)/q = p/(-q)$. Interpret quotients of rational numbers by describing real-world contexts.
  CCSS.Math.Content.7.NS.A.2.c Apply properties of operations as strategies to multiply and divide rational numbers.
  CCSS.Math.Content.7.NS.A.2.d Convert a rational number to a decimal using long division; know that the decimal form of a rational number terminates in 0s or eventually repeats.

CCSS.Math.Content.7.NS.A.3 Solve real-world and mathematical problems involving the four operations with rational numbers.

CCSS.Math.Content.7.EE.A.1 Apply properties of operations as strategies to add, subtract, factor, and expand linear expressions with rational coefficients.

CCSS.Math.Content.7.EE.A.2 Understand that rewriting an expression in different forms in a problem context can shed light on the problem and how the quantities in it are related. *For example, a + 0.05a = 1.05a means that "increase by 5%" is the same as "multiply by 1.05."*

CCSS.Math.Content.7.EE.B.3 Solve multi-step real-life and mathematical problems posed with positive and negative rational numbers in any form (whole numbers, fractions, and decimals), using tools strategically. Apply properties of operations to calculate with numbers in any form; convert between forms as appropriate; and assess the reasonableness of answers using mental computation and estimation strategies. *For example: If a woman making $25 an hour gets a 10% raise, she will make an additional 1/10 of her salary an hour, or $2.50, for a new salary of $27.50. If you want to place a towel bar 9 3/4 inches long in the center of a door that is 27 1/2 inches wide, you will need to place the bar about 9 inches from each edge; this estimate can be used as a check on the exact computation.*

CCSS.Math.Content.7.EE.B.4 Use variables to represent quantities in a real-world or mathematical problem, and construct simple equations and inequalities to solve problems by reasoning about the quantities.

CCSS.Math.Content.7.EE.B.4.a Solve word problems leading to equations of the form $px + q = r$ and $p(x + q) = r$, where p, q, and r are specific rational numbers. Solve equations of these forms fluently. Compare an algebraic solution to an arithmetic solution, identifying the sequence of the operations used in each approach. *For example, the perimeter of a rectangle is 54 cm. Its length is 6 cm. What is its width?*

CCSS.Math.Content.7.EE.B.4.b Solve word problems leading to inequalities of the form $px + q > r$ or $px + q < r$, where p, q, and r are specific rational numbers. Graph the solution set of the inequality and interpret it in the context of the problem. *For example: As a salesperson, you are paid $50 per week plus $3 per sale. This week you want your pay to be at least $100. Write an inequality for the number of sales you need to make, and describe the solutions.*

CCSS.Math.Content.7.G.A.1 Solve problems involving scale drawings of geometric figures, including computing actual lengths and areas from a scale drawing and reproducing a scale drawing at a different scale.

CCSS.Math.Content.7.G.A.2 Draw (freehand, with ruler and protractor, and with technology) geometric shapes with given conditions. Focus on constructing triangles from three measures of angles or sides, noticing when the conditions determine a unique triangle, more than one triangle, or no triangle.

CCSS.Math.Content.7.G.A.3 Describe the two-dimensional figures that result from slicing three-dimensional figures, as in plane sections of right rectangular prisms and right rectangular pyramids.

CCSS.Math.Content.7.G.B.4 Know the formulas for the area and circumference of a circle and use them to solve problems; give an informal derivation of the relationship between the circumference and area of a circle.

CCSS.Math.Content.7.G.B.5 Use facts about supplementary, complementary, vertical, and adjacent angles in a multi-step problem to write and solve simple equations for an unknown angle in a figure.

CCSS.Math.Content.7.G.B.6 Solve real-world and mathematical problems involving area, volume, and surface area of two- and three-dimensional objects composed of triangles, quadrilaterals, polygons, cubes, and right prisms.

CCSS.Math.Content.7.SP.A.1 Understand that statistics can be used to gain information about a population by examining a sample of the population; generalizations about a population from a sample are valid only if the sample is representative of that population. Understand that random sampling tends to produce representative samples and support valid inferences.

CCSS.Math.Content.7.SP.A.2 Use data from a random sample to draw inferences about a population with an unknown characteristic of interest. Generate multiple samples (or simulated samples) of the same size to gauge the variation in estimates or predictions. *For example, estimate the mean word length in a book by randomly sampling words from the book; predict the winner of a school election based on randomly sampled survey data. Gauge how far off the estimate or prediction might be.*

CCSS.Math.Content.7.SP.B.3 Informally assess the degree of visual overlap of two numerical data distributions with similar variabilities, measuring the difference between the centers by expressing it as a multiple of a measure of variability. *For example, the mean height of players on the basketball team is 10 cm greater than the mean height of players on the soccer team, about twice the variability (mean absolute deviation) on either team; on a dot plot, the separation between the two distributions of heights is noticeable.*

CCSS.Math.Content.7.SP.B.4 Use measures of center and measures of variability for numerical data from random samples to draw informal comparative inferences about two populations. *For example, decide whether the words in a chapter of a seventh-grade science book are generally longer than the words in a chapter of a fourth-grade science book.*

CCSS.Math.Content.7.SP.C.5 Understand that the probability of a chance event is a number between 0 and 1 that expresses the likelihood of the event occurring. Larger numbers indicate greater likelihood. A probability near 0 indicates an unlikely event, a probability around 1/2 indicates an event that is neither unlikely nor likely, and a probability near 1 indicates a likely event.

CCSS.Math.Content.7.SP.C.6 Approximate the probability of a chance event by collecting data on the chance process that produces it and observing its long-run relative frequency, and predict the approximate relative frequency given the probability. *For example, when rolling a number cube 600 times, predict that a 3 or 6 would be rolled roughly 200 times, but probably not exactly 200 times.*

CCSS.Math.Content.7.SP.C.7 Develop a probability model and use it to find probabilities of events. Compare probabilities from a model to observed frequencies; if the agreement is not good, explain possible sources of the discrepancy.

    CCSS.Math.Content.7.SP.C.7.a Develop a uniform probability model by assigning equal probability to all outcomes, and use the model to determine probabilities of events. *For example, if a student is selected at random from a class, find the probability that Jane will be selected and the probability that a girl will be selected.*

    CCSS.Math.Content.7.SP.C.7.b Develop a probability model (which may not be uniform) by observing frequencies in data generated from a chance process. *For example, find the approximate probability that a spinning penny will land heads up or that a tossed paper cup will land open-end down. Do the outcomes for the spinning penny appear to be equally likely based on the observed frequencies?*

CCSS.Math.Content.7.SP.C.8 Find probabilities of compound events using organized lists, tables, tree diagrams, and simulation.

    CCSS.Math.Content.7.SP.C.8.a Understand that, just as with simple events, the probability of a compound event is the fraction of outcomes in the sample space for which the compound event occurs.

    CCSS.Math.Content.7.SP.C.8.b Represent sample spaces for compound events using methods such as organized lists, tables, and tree diagrams. For an event described in everyday language (e.g., "rolling double sixes"), identify the outcomes in the sample space which compose the event.

    CCSS.Math.Content.7.SP.C.8.c Design and use a simulation to generate frequencies for compound events. *For example, use random digits as a simulation tool to approximate the answer to the question: If 40% of donors have type A blood, what is the probability that it will take at least 4 donors to find one with type A blood?*